SEE
NO
EVIL

Life Inside a Hollywood Censor
by

JACK VIZZARD

SIMON AND SCHUSTER · NEW YORK

FIRST PRINTING

The "Ode to Revised Motion Picture Code" by W. A. Scharper, excerpts of which appear on page 340, originally appeared in *Daily Variety,* 34th Anniversary Edition, October 1967, and is reproduced by permission.

The quote of Bosley Crowther on page 211 originally appeared in *The Atlantic Monthly* and is reproduced by permission of the author. Copyright 1951 by The Atlantic Monthly Company.

SBN 671-20479-3
LIBRARY OF CONGRESS CATALOG CARD NUMBER: 76–101885
DESIGNED BY EVE METZ
MANUFACTURED IN THE UNITED STATES OF AMERICA
BY H. WOLFF BOOK MFG. CO., NEW YORK

To the one who said "Yes. Be!"
My wife.

CONTENTS

8 CONTENTS

1 Where Censors Come From

BEING A CENSOR is like being a whore; everyone wants to know how you got into the business.

Well, with different people it's different things.

In the case of Milt Hodenfield, for instance, it was simply a process of sliding over in his chair, as secretary to Will Hays, the movie czar, and taking up a seat on the Production Code Board. It was an easy elision. But somehow Milt never seemed to have gotten his heart into it. He was a storklike fellow, with a gawky way of going about things, and a personality that appeared, in a curious way, to resemble his name. He gave the impression that he regarded all human conduct as an idiot dance, and expressed his frustrations and defeats about life in the one word, "Balls!" It was balls on this, and balls on that, until he sounded like Captain Queeg, rattling them around in his mouth instead of in his hands. With all that, he had a strangely human heart, and one would imagine that he would be a good man to have around if one were cast on the floor with a sudden gallstone attack. And maybe his reticence to jump into the Code work with both feet was a compliment to his Nordic shrewdness after all.

With Charley Metzger, who was constructed like a lump of unleavened dough, and who was continually hawking into a wad of Kleenex he carried around in his left pocket, it was a different story altogether. They changed chairs on him, all right, but in desperation.

Charley, the rumor ran, had been the legal representative of a chain of theaters in Indiana, from which position he peppered old Will Hays with complaints, admonitions, and constant reminders of his responsibility to make pictures that would not "besmirch the unsullied minds of the youth." To get Metzger off his back, Hays finally hired him, and promptly buried him in Hollywood, where he could ply his talents on the producers. Charley did not disappoint him. He loved his work.

Typical of his approach to the job, he set up a meticulous system of jotting down every decision that had been rendered by the Code staff, on practically every subject under the sun. These he kept in a set of loose-leaf binders, which were fondly referred to in the office as the "black books." Charley used them as legal precedent. When a producer wanted to argue in favor of using the word "damn," Charley could flip open the pages of his black books and put a square finger on chapter and verse, citing how we had refused permission in the case of *this* picture for Paramount, or *that* picture for Universal, and how a special exception had been made by the Board of Directors, for Metro, in the case of *Gone with the Wind*.

After a stroke had carried Charley away, Doc Dougherty and I took the black books off his shelf and began riffling through them for funny items. I am afraid our intent was slightly prurient. We quit when we came upon one entry, "IDOLS: sex organs thereof."

Charley was not a frivolous man. He had an evangelical seriousness about keeping the world in order. He was the type who scurried off to the National Guard Armory every Wednesday night to keep up on his Manual of Arms, and the proper working condition of the Springfield rifle. When World War II began to brew, Charley began to stir around pompously, brushing off the dust on the certificate that hung on his wall, testifying to the fact that he was a captain in the Reserves. He could rattle off at a dizzying pace about the plans that had been laid to mobilize the cities and to draft the eligible young men. It was clear that he expected to be swept into the fray and elevated to a position of august authority. But the Army passed him over, and Charley had to swallow the mortal blow. It was back to censoring for ol' Chuck.

He surprised everybody at the end. He was in New Orleans attending a convention of the American Legion, which was thinking of taking a blast at the Movie Industry. Charley was there to placate them, and actually succeeded in getting them to pass a resolution commending the Industry for the high quality of its films. But that was not all. Charley, who would hardly pass for a sport, had a girl with him. It turned out he had been friendly with her for years. But to top it all, Charley asked for a priest, so he could make his last confession. When Joe Breen, the Code boss, heard this, his eyes bugged out like grapes. Charley was the most bitter critic of the Catholic Legion of Decency on the whole staff, and created the suspicion that on off-days he might be attending meetings of the Ku Klux Klan. "Jesus," Breen exclaimed, "I wouldn't've been more surprised if you'd told me that all these years . . . my wife had been a Mohammedan!"

Charley left behind a tradition of applying the Code that was not easy to overcome. The nit-picking in which he indulged became a part of the record, and it is an embarrassing record. One day, as might be expected, a prying anthropologist got loose in our files and dug out item after item that made the Code look very poor indeed. The scientist was a lady, by the way, with the crowd-stopping name of Hortense Powdermaker. There was nothing else for her to do, on the basis of all the picayunes she was able to cull together, but to draw the conclusion that the Code and its administrators were either stupid or dishonest. Among other examples on which she rested her judgment was the case of the sex organs of an elephant. It seems someone on the staff had ordered a scene out of a picture which displayed these breathtaking paraphernalia.

Geoffrey Shurlock, Joe Breen's chief assistant, got angry. He felt that the lady investigator had committed a breach of courtesy. She had been given free access to the files, which are partially private, and she had abused the privileges extended her. He sat down at his typewriter and wrote a rebuttal. "If Miss Powdermaker," he said, "should ever see the sex organs of an elephant projected on a 65 ft. outdoor drive-in screen, before a typical mixed American audience, she would understand why the request was made and acceded to."

An altogether different kind of case, and personality, was Arthur Houghton. Arthur was a dapper Bostonian with red cheeks, white hair, and blue eyes. He was born, accommodatingly, on the Fourth of July. As opposed to Metzger, Arthur hated the job.

He had been the personal manager for Will Rogers, and before that had worked for the famous entrepreneur Dillingham as manager of the Globe and New Amsterdam theaters in New York. From his conversation, it seemed as if his main duty had been to survey chorus girls and pass on the fitness of their figures for the front line. It was easy to be convinced that he was an expert in these matters from the way his eye jumped, even in the eighth decade of his life, over the contours of any female who happened to be walking toward him, or away from him.

Arthur somehow conveyed the feeling that he had been euchred into the job on the Code, kicking and screaming. He had been friendly with Joe Kennedy, the father of the President, when that financier had been putting together the package that later emerged as RKO studios. What his duties were with the senior Kennedy would be hard to define. Suffice to tell that when Kennedy left for the East, his enterprise completed, Arthur stayed behind, perpetually startled over finding himself a censor. But his surprise was the Code staff's gain. He was an ebullient and delightful man. He spent his best hours on the Code regaling us with memories of bygone days, and brought alive for us a world outside of Hollywood, from which, in many respects, the film colony had sprung. He recalled, for instance, the time he was worried about Ethel Barrymore being able to perform in a play Arthur was staging, because she was well along in pregnancy. "Don't worry about Ethel, Arthur," soothed her brother John. "She'll go on. Ethel doesn't have babies. She just retires behind the wings and steps out of them."

From Houghton to my own introduction into the Code work is a rather natural segue, to use an industry term that means a sort of musical dissolve. For I was invited to take my place around the table with the idea that Arthur would soon be "leaving." However, Arthur's exit was like a farewell by Ben Bernie. It was a full four years before he departed.

After he left, he sought out the Kennedys again and became, in the more acceptable sense of the word, a court jester in the great household. From time to time, he would burst in on us with all the animation of the American flag and give us a tongue lashing for our laxity in applying the Code.

To convey the *spirit* with which I joined the Code staff, it is necessary to conjure up in the imagination a picture of the Southern Pacific streamliner the Daylight laboriously wending its way up through the yellow rocks of the Santa Susana mountains, having just left behind the blue and foaming shoreline near Santa Barbara. On the train sat a bright-eyed young man of thirty, tall, his hair parted carefully on the left side, and looking newly minted and rather unused. He also looked like he might be swimming in the euphoria of a freshly engaged marriage; and, on top of that, looking as if he had a "purpose."

I had a purpose, all right. I was rushing down out of the theological hills to save the world from those goddamn Jews.

What I really wanted, of course, was to be part of the scene I was anxious to rescue everybody from. But I did not know this yet. It was not until later, when those I was trying to rescue everybody from redeemed me, that I was able to acknowledge my true heart. By then it was a trifle late. But it is never too late to come into the inheritance of one's humanity. Even in the simple act of dying, it is not possible to leave the human race unless first you have been in it.

What I was was a perfectly programmed mechanism. For sixteen long sequestered years, I had studied for the priesthood, three-quarters of that time as a member of the Jesuit Order—the Marine Corps of the Catholic Church. Now I was leaping, like something full-blown out of the forehead of Zeus, into the very World of the World, Hollywood, the symbol of sin and entanglement in things carnal. To me the train was not a train. It was more like a long, pliable aluminum-clad medieval charger, breathing steamy indignation, with great tossing plumes of white mane filling the wind. The noise of its rails was the clackety-clack of flying hoofs. I was St. George, with lance leveled, and down on the coastal plain below me, in the sprawling tidal basin called Los Angeles, lay the Dragon.

Now such a marvelous mentality is not easy to come by. Neither is it any accident. It is the result of master calculation, and the fruit of a Plan.

A word about the nature of this Plan is in order, even though it might be slightly diversionary, and lead us down the garden path into a Portrait-of-the-Censor-as-a-Young-Man. Because the forces which produced that anachronistic state of soul that was riding along on the train also produced the Code. The Code was more than some printed lines on a few pieces of paper. It was a value system. Whatever happened with it, over the more than third of a century of its existence, was neither casual nor random. All the episodes, all the vignettes, all the tens of thousands of letters that were written on over twenty thousand films, all the story conferences, all the editings, all the inventions, all everything was the articulation of a homogeneous set of definitions regarding Man, and Life, and Reality, and the nature of the Human Condition, and the Business of Man in Life.

Furthermore, it was a value system that was incarnated in people. I was the Code, and the Code was me. Not I alone, to be sure. But I at least.

On top of that, the Code is worth inspection. It was a small piece of Americana that was important in its own way. In miniature, it was the summation of all of the Past out of which we came, but translated into the American idiom. It has often been said that it was the capsulization of the Judaeo-Christian system of morality. No doubt it was. But stylistically it was pure U.S.A., even to the point that the method was exported back to certain parts of Europe, and even to the Orient. The Japanese system is based almost identically on the Code. Lastly, it was Americana of a certain period. It was a product of the age of Babbitt, and of the Crash. It could never happen again. Therefore, it is important that it not disappear into oblivion now that our gazes are turned toward the moon.

With me, it all started on a foggy afternoon in San Francisco in 1927. The foghorns were filling the watery distances with their mournful sounds. I remember my mother was ironing shirts, and it is the image of her arm bearing down hard on the board, like the trademark on a box of Arm & Hammer baking soda, that lingers with me. I recall murmuring, in a voice not too loud, in the hope that I might not be heard, "I think I want to be a priest." I was thirteen years old. My mother, of course, had the advantage. She was about thirty-seven.

She, dear soul, halted as though she had heard the golden notes of Gabriel's trumpet. The magic formula had just been said. Her virtue was being rewarded. Her son was being given the Gift. It was a good omen for her salvation. She would make the supreme sacrifice, she would give up her son in generous response to the Divine call, and she could look to God for reciprocal generosity when it came time to stand before Him in Judgment.

"What did you say?" she wanted to know.

Like an Islamic husband, who has to reiterate the fatal words three times if he wants to divorce his wife, I was obliged to echo my statement once again. That way, there would be proof of no mistake. Also it would be something of my own free will. That was the Game demanded by the System.

"I think . . . etc."

That was enough. The next thing I knew she was stuffing the tails of her blouse into the elastic bindings of a large pair of bloomers, and we were on our way over to see the Pastor, Monsignor Ryan, at Star of the Sea church on Ninth and Geary streets. He patted me on the head, excused me from the last half of the eighth grade, we fade out, we fade in, and I am in the seminary.

It was a lovely place, with cloisters and colonnades in the Spanish style that is typical of California, with a tall campanile crowned with glazed colored tiles. The buildings sat exactly astride the San Andreas fault, and a couple of quakes made the great tower sway like a reed bent by the wind.

The surrounding countryside was daubed like a palette in springtime, with splashes of gold and purple on the electric green hillsides, with here and there a fountain of pink bloom erupting from the trunk of a peach tree, or of white blossoms from the depths of an almond.

Thus, we were little prisoners in silken bondage. Overhead, in the middle of the blue arch of sky, burned the invisible Eye of God, like on the back of an American paper dollar. It was inflexible, and unblinking, and as impartial as the cool scanner of a computer. No one could escape. One of the faculty tried. He jumped out of the third-story window of a hospital and broke both his legs. The mortification put him under such pressure that he got pneumonia and died.

My own frantic efforts to break out of the entangling filaments of heavenly love took another turn. I leaped even deeper into the abyss. Within four years I had transferred my allegiance into an even more profound commitment, and behold, I found myself walking the grape-covered hillsides of the Sacred Heart Novitiate in Los Gatos. I was wearing the flowing black cassock without buttons down the front, which was modeled on the academic gowns of the University of Salamanca, and which is the well-known uniform of the Jesuit Order. Everybody was double-proud of me that I had had the capacity to go the whole way, and I was double-proud of myself.

The limestone hills of the region, some twenty land leagues to the south of San Francisco, were an apt setting for a cradle of spirituality, where the "new man" is formed. So beautiful were they that they seemed halfway to heaven to begin with.

In the months of March and April, the floor of the Santa Clara Valley below us was solidly carpeted in white from the profusion of fruit blossoms, pears and plums and apricots and almonds. Walking along the roads between the orchards was an illusion of otherworldliness. The air was filled with slowly swirling petals, like a soft snowstorm, and the atmosphere was perfumed with faint fragrances which crossed with the musk of new-plowed earth.

At the far side of the valley, the nether hills swelled up again like leaping phosphorescent green dolphins, smeared here and there with patches of bluish purple from the wild lupin. At sunset, the higher shoulders caught the flat rays of the sun declining into the Pacific and were laved in lavenders and roses and coppers.

Illuminated by such sights and by such surroundings, a poetic ember was inclined to take root in one's spirit and to linger beneath the ashes of any vicissitudes whatsoever. This may explain an incident that occurred many years later. Hal Wallis, the famous producer, called Joe Breen one day from Paramount and cautioned him he had better keep his eye on the members of his staff. Someone had just sent him a couple of pages of admonitions on one of his scripts which he could only describe as "lyrical."

On summer evenings, it was the custom for the novices to

wander out along a decomposed-granite path that was cut into the sides of the hill, to a far flank that had been leveled and encircled, and in the middle of which stood a giant horse-chestnut tree. It was called the Postulants' Tree. Around its trunk a bench was constructed, where we used to sit and watch the traffic pass through the canyon below us, returning from a day at the oceanside spa of Santa Cruz. The strange silence that fell on the novices was a sign of their thoughts, secretly yearning for the freedom to move at will, to have a home to return to, and to spend a day at the beach surreptitiously measuring the lithe figures of girls moving like gazelles over the sand. The tree itself seemed to conspire against us. It sent out its first leaves in a magenta hue, as soft and fleshlike as the inner lids of the eye. Gradually they turned a pale champagne green, to be followed by a hoard of prickly chestnuts, suspended from stems like Noel balls, but which emitted a suspicious sexual scent suggestive of male seed.

When the strident electric bell would sound from the walls of the Novitiate wing in the far background, we would struggle to our feet and tear ourselves away from under the provocative branches of the Tree. The bell was the obediential finger of God, crook'd and beckoning. It was the rule to break off one's conversation immediately, in the middle of a sentence, or even, if one were a very good monk, in the middle of a word. This was a chastening discipline indeed, calling for the alacrity of spirit of a neurotic angel. But it had its awkward consequences. It tended to leave one's companion standing there with an expectant smile on his face, forever unresolved, like a figure on a Grecian urn.

And so we straggled back along the granulated path, lined at intervals with gnarled, silvery old olive trees, and took great care if we had to sneak out a little wind, lest a noisy occurrence betray the fact that we had not yet achieved spirituality.

And in we went; back into the forge.

The figure is not altogether inappropriate. We were working to turn ourselves into forgeries. Nor, in saying this, is any malignancy meant. We were all products of our times, and we were all victims of our cultures. There was no ill will anywhere.

Technically, and for the record, we were entering on the first rung of the ascetical ladder, the ultimate goal of which was to "put on Christ." As a first step, which was known as the "Purgative Way," we were striving to "renounce the world" and to shed ourselves of ourselves, as a snake renounces its skin, and slithers out of it. It never occurred to us to question the possibility of such a thing. It seemed entirely feasible to step out of the world while still living in it; as though a fish could "renounce" the very ocean in which it swam.

Down below us, on the road to Santa Cruz, the "world" rolled by; while up there on the summit, a little below the edge of the clouds, we toiled to rub out the encumbrances of the flesh.

Someone might say that it was precisely by "renouncing" the ocean waters that the blue and adventurous flying fish developed wings, and eventually became a soaring eagle—or, better yet, a bird of Paradise. There might be something in this. But on the other hand there is the legend of Icarus, who tried to fly too high, too fast, and was sent to his doom by the very sun he was seeking.

For my own part, I am inclined to think that the business of man is to find his place inside reality, not out of it. I am partial to the notion of Socrates, who held that the fruit of human inquiry was to "make man feel *at home* in the universe."

We were busy trying to make ourselves feel like strangers. We were taught to think of ourselves as citizens of two worlds, *in* this world but not *of* it, as the saying went. Our gaze was fixed on the City across the River, the New Jerusalem, where true existence began, and for which this life was only a preamble.

The overriding reality in our dualistic world was the existence of the soul. The only pure tragedy that could befall a Christian man, or even any human being for that matter, was

to "gain the whole world, and suffer the loss of his own soul."
One had to go through great disciplines to subdue the body
and subjugate the round of materiality, since these were the
enemies of the soul, and encumbered it. The soul was like a
Bird of Light that wanted to aspire, but it was caught in the
throes of a sticky lake of tar. To lure the lovely winged
creature down into the mire was to wage the cruelest decep-
tion possible on the human race. Whoever did this was the
Enemy.

The movies, of course, insisted on celebrating life. Even
worse, they enlarged on it and exaggerated its romanticisms,
its sensual joys, and its carnal commitments. Thus they perpe-
trated a great evil. They intoxicated the mind of man and
filled his soul with the fumes of eroticism and locked his
attention into the here and now. Thus, it was the business of
men who had the "inside story" to bend every wit and every
wile into staving off this False Picture of things. The Code was
an instrument designed to present reality on the screen not as
it *was*, but as it *should be*. Its purpose was to protect audiences
from the reality out of which they entered the theater, and
into which they were going to return.

The insistence on distorting the Vision was, of course, hung
on the Jews. They were the Deceivers. It was their role to carry
on in the mode of the Tempter on the top of Mount Tibi
Dabo, and to present a glittering and seductive picture of the
cities of this earth, as though they were not ephemeral, as
though they would not melt away like a mirage once one
reached out to touch them. I know this all sounds pretty silly
now, but it is hard to remember that people thought like this
only one long generation ago, and to those of us who were in
this state of miasma it was all very real. One forgets that in
between then and now there were the ovens. A lot of what was
being burned was thought to be the taint of the fleshpots of
Egypt. The taint could have been washed away in the Blood of
the Lamb, but this stiff-necked race had rebuffed the Lamb.
For this their eyes were made hooded. They were cursed with

an inability to appreciate that luminous quantum in man, the soul, that was the end-all and the be-all of everything.

The strange thing is that this concept of a soul was not a Hebraic idea at all. It was Greek. In the Aramaic language spoken by Christ there is not even a word for the "soul" as we understand it today. Therefore, He was not even capable of getting the notion, since there was nothing in His vocabulary that would evoke the idea. Christ was not a dualist. He was, like all traditional Jews, a whole-ist. There is reason to suspect that He may have been a cosmic dualist, from the vivid way He speaks about the Prince of This World and his powers. But that is a question for the scientists to sort out. However, whether He was or whether He was not what the professionals call an Iranist, it is quite certain that He was not an anthropological dualist. His idea of man was whole-istic. The concept of a division between the spirit and the flesh in man is Platonic, and is a product of the early Mystery sects of Greece, such as the Orphic cults and the Dionysian cults. The definition of a soul may have seeped into Christianity through St. Paul, and it may not. There is considerable dispute on this point. But one thing, at least, is clear. When Christ was using the word "soul" He was using our equivalent of the word "selfhood"; or else, when He was using the word "spirit," He was using the equal of our words for the wind, such as the breath of God being like the wind, the source of vitality, or some other such transliteration.

Be that as it may, there we were, back in the Novitiate, struggling with a way of life that, when all was said and done, was not even Christian. The gift of the Jews to me, from having lived among them so long, and from having tried to save the world from them, was to come to a contra-understanding of certain terms that I thought to be fixed and absolute. This, in turn, led to enough scholarly inquiry on my part to find out that even among Catholic savants today all these things I have said are admitted and conceded. That is one reason there is such a ferment in the Church at this particular moment. But that is now; and I am talking about the early years of the thirties, when our textbook was a three-volume set called *A Study of Virtue and of Christian Perfection* by Alphonse Rodriguez, a Spanish Jesuit. "Rodriguez," as the work was called, was the approved primer for all religious orders throughout the world. The asceticism that sprang from these pages was purely anchoritic. All the descriptions of Virtue, and all the examples of them, were taken from the lives and writings of the Fathers of the Desert. These were idealistic men who had fled the "world," probably in disappointment over the failure of the Second Coming, and who were spending their lives in holding the human experience at bay, in the expectation of greater things to come. The ultimate expression of this school of asceticism is to be found in the figure of a Simeon Stylites, sitting atop a tall pillar (and what couldn't the psychiatrists do with a phallic symbol such as this?), alienated from the ground, already partly elevated above it, and symbolically disembodied and in the sky.

Even in those Novitiate days, one was prone to have what have been called "vague oceanic feelings" of doubt about the consistency of all this theory of life. One did not dare face the fact that a program of human conduct along the lines we were following seemed to make a bit of a dunce of the Deity. What kind of a god would God be, who would create flesh and blood and then make man spend all his energies trying to contradict them? It is not that the thought did not cross one's mind. It was simply that the temptation to court the idea had to be crushed out of existence immediately. There was that great Eye in the sky. It knew whether we were faithful or not. We lived in a closed universe that was given, and accounted for. It was a world of childhood, with apples and serpents, and angels ascending invisible ladders between heaven and earth. It encompassed fiery chariots carrying the prophet Elias off into the sun, and it postulated a brilliant image of man in the figure of Adam before the Fall. It did not occur to us that the first man might have been just barely a man, a liminal creature. Unless he were a brilliancy, he had no high estate to fall from. If he were scarcely more than a primate, he could hardly be expected to have the clarity of mind and the autonomy of will that would be needed to make a decision as great as Original Sin.

In our locked-in world of things, filled with definitions in which all the T's were crossed and all the I's were dotted, there was no room for individualism. We were taught that Faith had been bestowed upon us, and that this gift is never lost except through the culpability of the individual. God is faithful, and so long as we did not deliberately squander our birthright, He would never take it away. The one threat that hovered over our heads was the text that "He who puts his hand to the plow and looks back is not worthy of the Kingdom of God." We did not want to look back. We did not want to be left standing like saltless pillars in the midst of the terrestrial landscape.

In this encharmed state of mind, a dozen years passed since the transition from the minor seminary into the Novitiate. They were not bad years. They were just not my years. They would be more of an obscenity to others than they were to me. One lived in the company of Graceful men, and that is a great plus. One absorbed a feeling for the real meaning of elegance of personality, because one lived in an environment of unselfish human beings. That is something that is hardly to be duplicated elsewhere.

The decade of the thirties did a slow lap-dissolve into the decade of the forties. The Depression had been absorbed. World War II raged. And the date of Ordination was drawing near.

This was the noose that could never be loosened. Along with Baptism, it left an indelible mark on the soul. A man was a priest forever, according to the order of Melchisedech.

Like the poet in "The Wreck of the Deutschland" my buried selfhood began to writhe. It was a case of

The frown of his face
Before me, the hurtle of hell
Behind, where, where was a, where was a place?
I whirled out wings that spell
And fled with a fling of the heart to the heart of the Host . . .

My host was Hollywood.

Here is how the magical moment occurred.

We were in Theology by this time, in a great redwood-studded estate in the Santa Cruz mountains, just across the cleft from the famous violinist Yehudi Menuhin. It is said, incidentally, that all Jesuit houses, by tradition, are located in the hills, where the inhabitants can look down on the world—as opposed to the houses of the Franciscans, which are nestled in the valleys, where they can mix with people.

In any event, it was a Thursday, the break-day in the middle of the week, and a carful of us were coming down out of the heights and were headed in the direction of San Jose. I remember there was Walshe Murray in the back seat, bent in concentration over a novel by Dickens, and so enviously "gone" that he was oblivious of everything else. Alongside him sat Father Mike Casey, one of the faculty members, a specialist in Biblical studies who could read Sanskrit and Egyptian hieroglyphs and Babylonian cuneiform. He was considered fairly daring, because he pointed out with candor that the Babylonian symbol for woman was O-O, in obvious imitation of the breasts.

In the front seat sat Father Hilary Werts, a saturnine fellow with an underthrust jaw who spoke in a voice so soft that it was as if every opinion he gave was confidential. We considered him, too, to be a feline-footed liberal. The example that was always cited was the case of a Catholic pharmacist who would be asked to sell a customer a condom. Father Werts, in his capacity as teacher of Moral Theology, opined that this would be a permissible thing to do, since there were grounds to think that the device might be used for something else besides birth control. It seems that certain French Army officers during World War I had used the famous "rubbers" to stretch over the muzzles of their revolvers as a protection against mud and rust. Since the device, then, was capable of "various" usages, the pharmacist was allowed to distinguish in his own mind and sell it to the customer.

This is how we all thought in those days.

I was going in to the dentist's to have a tooth pulled. Already I was losing parts, and I hadn't even dipped my toe into the waters yet. I was twenty-nine.

I was watching the scenery going by when the words filtered through to my ears. "I know a man," Father Werts was saying, "who keeps the two volumes of Noldin on his desk all the time. He uses them as a reference source for his work."

My head flew around, and all my sensors clicked into focus. Noldin was the textbook for Moral Theology, just as Rodriguez had been for asceticism. One could flip his pages and find predigested answers, in Latin, for delicate questions. A girl working in an Italian factory, for example, might have asked whether it would be permissible for her to continue at her job, despite the fact that the act of pedaling her sewing machine stimulated her sexually. The answer was yes, for the same reasons that it was all right to continue horseback riding, because this was necessary.

"Where does he work?" I inquired of Father Werts, careful to feign an academic interest only. It would have been a giveaway to appear too avid.

"In the movie industry."

A strange lance of excitement came and went. "What does he do?"

"He works on the Production Code."

The constellations began to stir. "Who is he?"

"He's an old classmate of mine. Al Lynch."

I turned my head quickly to look at the fruit trees, so nobody would see the gleam of pleasure that was running over my features. Holy God! This was *it*. The thing I had been vaguely waiting for. This was my chance to have my cake and eat it too. I could stay on the side of "decency" and yet get out into the world and wallow around in it. My spirit soared above my body like Tinker Bell, with hummingbird wings on her feet. I could get out of the grip of God, and yet not leave Him. He would understand, for I would be knocking my brains out for *Him,* struggling against the thralldom of materiality, driving back the Human Experience, grappling mightily with Life to shape it as it ought to be, not as it *is.* All those years of gritting my jaw against normality suddenly made sense. *I* knew Noldin. *I* could read Latin like nobody's business. *I* knew what was expected of a Crusader. And *Hollywood.* Of all places! The Sodom of the Twentieth Century. It was like being wafted off to the threshold of heaven. I could meet Satan face to face, stare at him with a cold, flinty eye, and flick a length of cigarette ash into his face. God almighty, I could cruise right into that dentist's office and let him pull my tooth without Novocaine. I wouldn't feel a thing!

The process of signing out, after twelve very special years, is stunningly simple. A statement is read, a paper is signed, it is witnessed by dimly smiling men and handed to you. You go back to your room, take off your cassock for the last time, and hang it on the back of the door. Someone will use it for a spare. You unfold the paper, and glance at the lines: "I, Joseph J. King, Provincial . . . testify that he lived for a certain time in our society . . . legitimately released . . . in testimony of which . . . San Jose, California . . . 1943."

It was over.

The train was wending its way past the last walnut groves of the San Fernando Valley and was beginning to pick its path through the maze of tracks that litter the marshaling yards in central Los Angeles.

A year had passed. It was October 1944. I had been in correspondence with Joe Breen, maneuvering and jockeying for a place in his group, with a certainty that somehow took it for granted that there could be no other conclusion to my applications. He had nodded approval from a distance when I had married a girl whose mother's name was Breen. "You will find," he wrote, "that all of us Breens are noted for our good looks, our personalities, and particularly for our piety." He had sent Al Lynch to San Francisco to have a preliminary meeting with me in a Chinese restaurant and, I imagine, to scout the general bearing of the rookie. The fortune cookies must have come up with the right answers. It was all systems go.

The streamliner rolled carefully past stacked boxcars, and the chiaroscuro was like the flickering of a slowing movie projector. I stood up. A censor was made, and was about to begin. The object: to turn Pegasus into one of George Santayana's pack asses.

Of course, the irony of it all was that I was fleeing right into the arms of the very thing I was trying to escape.

2 Where Censorship Comes From

THE TRAIN disgorged me at Union Station like one of Aladdin's jinnis swirling up out of a great earthenware jar. So this was it! Sin Land!

I squinted around covertly at the faces of passersby, and found them to be deceptively ordinary-looking. In fact, the vast domed ceiling of the California mission style depot looked more like the nave of a cathedral.

Walking up Main Street in the evening, I had my first eyeful. An unshaved drunk slid slowly down the wall of a pawnshop and sprawled out on the pavement. A policeman sauntered over to his prone figure and kicked tentatively at the sole of his shoe.

This was more like it. I was in the right place.

In the distance, a large neon sign, red as a ruby, blinked against the darkling sky, "Jesus Saves."

I looked around and wondered why I felt so all alone. I shifted my suitcase to my other hand as a little gesture of self-assurance. The sidewalks were empty. Los Angeles is the city of no pedestrians.

The next morning I stood across the street from the Code building and surveyed it with undefined emotions. It was remarkably unpretentious-looking. It was a white four-story pile that rose straight up from the concrete, on the corner of Hollywood Boulevard and Western Avenue. It had a certain

sterilized look about it. The impression was probably fur-
thered by the fact that the ground corner of the building was
devoted to a drugstore. Was this the building within whose
walls was the whirring machinery of morality? Could so bleak-
looking an edifice contain the white-hot forces of spiritualiza-
tion? I was standing on the very edge of the Western Front,
and only a streetcar rocked by to break the silence.

I shouldered my way through a peculiar-looking crowd in
the vestibule, who seemed to stare at me with an unabashed
intensity, and melted into the elevator as quickly as I could. I
was relieved to hear the picket gate of the elevator rattle into
place. I was not familiar, at the time, with the fact that the
second floor was occupied in its entirety by Central Casting,
the organization which supplied extras for films. It was not
unusual to have to struggle across the foyer through a sullen
group of midgets, old maids, bowlegged cowboys, broken-
down boxers, seven-foot Russians with bushy beards, profes-
sorial-looking dandies with pince-nez glasses, leather-jacketed
hotshots in blue jeans, cripples, cranks, grand dames, street-
walkers with sagging arches, queers, fanatics, and saints. Once
in a while they would accost you. Joe Breen was bustling his
way through their midst one morning, when a woman with a
fright wig and carrying a religious poster blocked his access to
the elevator. "Young man," she demanded, "do you fornicate?"

He looked her up and down in a curious way and finally
snapped, "Certainly."

She was so stumped that she let him slip into the elevator
without further ado, and he vanished upstairs with her impre-
cations chasing him like a cloud of sulphur.

That night, he made the mistake of laughingly relating this
to his wife. She was listening with fascination. When he had
finished, she let out a shriek. "Since *when?*" she demanded in
chagrined double take.

The first impression of the Code offices themselves was of
worn-out carpets. The reception room was smothered in a

sickly green flooring, which looked as though a hustle and bustle of traffic had passed over it until the burlap backing was beginning to show through. Buried in one wall was an alcove with an antique switchboard. I went up to it hesitantly and asked for Mr. Lynch. I had the fleeting feeling that the oak woodwork needed to be sanded and varnished.

Al Lynch came out with his brisk, swinging stride, looking like an expensive doctor in his rimless glasses and gray pin-striped suit. He also radiated the atmosphere of having too many muscles for a desk job.

He greeted me with a guileless smile and led me by the arm down the green-carpeted corridor.

Halfway down the passage, a stocky, energetic, intensely intelligent-looking man burst around a corner. He stopped short and peered at me from head to foot, as though he were measuring me for a pole vault. "Mr. Breen," Al introduced, "this is Mr. Vizzard."

He stood back smiling, cast a glance at Lynch, and finally expressed his opinion. "Jesus, he's a big one, isn't he?"

Al smiled like an Oriental.

"Well," concluded Breen, "take him to his office. Show him the ropes."

With that, he churned past us down the corridor to wherever he was headed. I had an odd feeling like a fish that had been thrown back into the water.

Joe was like that. He had a way of leaving you with egg on your face, and yet devoid of any reasons for feeling offended. Typical was the encounter experienced by "Socker" Coe, an early-day vice president of the Motion Picture Association (who got his nickname, incidentally, from the fact that he had been heavyweight boxing champion of the Pacific fleet in the U.S. Navy). Socker relates how he had come to Joe privately and had asked him, "Joe, off the record, and for my own personal use, what kind of a guy is Joe Doakes?"

Quoting Coe: "Breen patted his paunch, licked his lips, scratched his chin, straightened in his chair and in tones indicating extreme confidence responded, 'Joe Doakes, Socker, is a bigger pain in the arse than you are!' "*

Al Lynch sat me at a plain old-fashioned oak desk from which the varnish was beginning to crack. Its only ornament was a dun-brown desktop blotter. I looked around the room. The walls were as bare as a monk's cell. There was one guest chair. That was all. My preconceptions of Hollywood were of opulence and wall bars where everybody had a drink for lunch. This was more stark than my cubiculum in religious life.

"Wait here," Lynch was saying. "We'll send in something to start you off."

I folded my hands in the midst of the engulfing silence and made my soul resolute. At any moment now the phone would ring, and I'd have a dirty producer on my hands, and my role in life would begin. Figuratively, I would leap across the intervening distance, grab his throat in both of my hands, and begin squeezing indecency out of him like juice out of an orange.

I was startled by a slight tapping on the doorframe. Quickly focusing out of the reverie, I looked up to see an unearthly creature undulating slightly in the areaway, a small smile on her lips. "May I come in?" she asked in a voice rich and melodious.

"Please do, please do," I invited hastily.

In her arms she carried a large pile of scripts, letters, and similar sundries. When she moved, it was like searchlights going off in all directions, all black diamonds and polished jasper. "I'm Emily," she announced.

I swallowed. Someone must have converted Lilith. "I'm Jack," I reciprocated.

She stretched out a hand. "Pleased t'meetcha," we both said at once.

She fished something from off the top of the pile in the

* *Never a Dull Moment,* by Charles Francis Coe. Hastings House, New York, 1944.

crook of her left arm. "They said you were to read this," she said, tossing a yellow document on the desk. It was thin, and about eight-by-ten in size. I glanced quickly. It was the Code.

"Thank you," I assured.

"It's nice to have you aboard," she complimented.

"Yeah, well . . ." I made a helpless little gesture. "I'm new yet."

"You'll learn. Toodle-oo. I have to pass out the rest of the mail."

When she was out in the hall, I heard some conspiratorial gaggling among female voices. "I'm sorry," one of them was admonishing, "He's already married."

This Code life was full of surprises.

My first duty was to start riffling pages of the famous document, and what my eyes fell on was a veritable Trimalchio's feast of prohibitions, cautions, admonitions, statements of high principle, and specifications about the treatment of certain subjects that would have done justice to Noldin in his palmiest passages.

The air had been inflamed in those days, for instance, by the practice of kidnaping. With the abolition of Prohibition, many of the darker forces in American society had turned to this terrible craft as a means of raising the money they were deprived of in bootlegging. There had been three notorious kidnapings in quick succession. About ten years before there had been the Lindbergh kidnaping, the Weyerhaeuser kidnaping in the Northwest, and finally the Alex Hart kidnaping in San Jose. This last crime had been especially cruel. The boy had been the scion of a reasonably successful merchandising family of the Jewish faith. They had taken him to the base of Dumbarton Bridge in the lower San Francisco Bay, with the intention of drowning him. They had struck him over the head and thrown him in the water, but the boy recovered. He was a strong swimmer and tried to make his way to one of the cement pylons at the foot of the bridge. The kidnapers had climbed down along the understructure. They struck the boy again when he was trying to grope for survival, and then had shot him.

The cold-bloodedness of the crime sent a great flush of rage across the nation. The criminals were captured and put in jail in San Jose. The rumors ran rampant that the respectable citizens of that city had formed into a vigilante committee and had sent secret word to their friend, the sheriff, that they were coming to lynch the kidnapers that night, and that he had better absent himself, because he couldn't shoot them, and they didn't want to hurt him.

The next morning the story was out across the nation. It had been a Walpurgis night. The vigilantes had come, the sheriff had made a token resistance, but the crowd was too great, and they broke into the jail like the mobs at the Bastille. In their excitement, they first grabbed the wrong prisoner. He was screeching his innocence, to no avail. Finally, one of the committee kept enough wits about him to recognize the error, and they returned the man to his cell. Never before had a prisoner been more delighted to be put in jail. When they found the right cell, the kidnaper was at first not to be seen. Entering through the steel door, they looked up to find that the man had somehow gotten himself up near the ceiling, where he clung spread-eagled in horror. They dragged him down kicking and fighting. To subdue him they brutalized him. The other kidnaper, the wild one's partner, came with docility.

They took them out into the public square on which the courthouse faced, called St. James Park, and they hanged them as crudely as the early California miners hanged horse thieves. They wanted to make a lesson.

The next morning, small pieces of the tree on which the criminals were lynched were passed around the Santa Clara Valley as relics.

It was then that the occurrence was compounded. Important people across the land were starting to speak up and to comment on the lynching. Some were for it, since there was a great impatience in the country at the way the law was ground to a halt by the lawyers and made a mockery of. Others tried to regret it, in the name of sobriety. In the midst of these reactions, the Governor of California, James Rolph, Jr., a polished Santa Claus-looking type of man who wore Western boots under his conventional suit, and who had been mayor of San Francisco, made a public statement to the effect that it was about time that sensible citizens had taken things into their hands. This drove the storm of controversy up to the highest government levels, and the maverick Governor of California was praised and condemned in all quarters.

The incident, however, had certain salutary effects. For one thing, it drove the mood of shilly-shallying out of the air, and produced a spirit of summary justice, which soon eventuated in the famous Lindbergh Law. This made it an offense punishable by death to transport a kidnaped person across state lines or to inflict bodily harm of any sort on a kidnap victim.

All of the elements of seething public indignation that were aroused by these events were incorporated in the Code provisions governing kidnaping in those days. A person reading the stringent restrictions now might miss the flavor with which they stood in the Code at that time. As a matter of historical fact, the kidnap clauses were not in the original document signed by the members of the Motion Picture Association in 1930. They were created later by the people on the Code staff itself, largely by Geoffrey Shurlock, and incorporated as an addendum.

They provided:

> With special reference to the crime of kidnapping—or illegal abduction—such stories are acceptable under the Code only when the kidnapping or abduction is (a) not the main theme of the story; (b) the person kidnapped is not a child; (c) there are no details of the crime of kidnapping; (d) no profit accrues to the abductors or kidnappers; and (e) where the kidnappers are punished.

In other words, there was frequently a substantial "story" behind many of the Code clauses, which was immediately recognizable in the times in which they were written, even if today some of them seem to have come out of the Land of Oz. Some of the regulations, of course, have the time-slot quaintness of expressions like "twenty-three skidoo" which was the "in" phrase in the days of *Thoroughly Modern Millie*. For example, one sees disapproval of such expressions as "hot" (applied to a woman); "tom cat" (applied to a man); "whore," "damn," and "hell" (with a long stringer of exceptions attached).

Borrowing from the future for the moment, it is interesting to note that it was David Selznick who pried loose the use of the words "damn" and "whore" from the Code custodians. The first case has already been mentioned. It was the curtain line in *Gone with the Wind*. The dialogue was "Frankly, my dear, I don't give a damn." In the second case, years later, Selznick had remade Hemingway's *Farewell to Arms* with his wife, the beautiful Jennifer Jones. In this picture, there was a scene in which she walks into a red-velvet room, with a large ornate bed, and mirrors on the ceiling. She remarks, "I feel like a whore." Selznick insisted on maintaining this word, even though it was considered a shocker for mixed audiences into the decade of the fifties. Geoff Shurlock, who was making the decisions in those days, tended to see things Selznick's way. He ended up walking around in circles muttering to himself that if the word was good enough for the Bible and good enough for Shakespeare, it was good enough for him. Ignoring the Code, he defiantly passed it. From the reaction, however, one would have thought that he had approved a public defecation on the audience itself. He came to the regretful conclusion that "We are dealing with a generation of prudes."

One Code clause was incomprehensible to me even at my first encounter with it. It was the prohibition against showing "scenes of actual childbirth, in fact or in silhouette . . ." The enigma to me was the fact that they would even bring the subject up. Surely nobody would be tempted to put a camera on this privacy. I asked Joe Breen. He turned around and peered at me as though I'd been in a long sleep. He snorted. "They'd put fucking in Macy's window, if you gave them a chance," he said, ". . . and they'd argue till they were blue in the face that it was 'art.' "

Technically speaking, the Code had been in existence for fourteen years by the time I took it into my hands for a first look. It was a powerful and efficient machine in those closing days of World War II. However, it had not come into this estate automatically or smoothly. It had gone through two turbulent phases.

The curtain raiser was the original adoption of the document in 1930. The signing was on the eve of April Fools' Day, March 31. It was accompanied by the usual hoopla and photographs of Will Hays sitting there in his high starched collar and wearing a mole-tooth grin, strangely evocative of the cartoons of Mr. Prohibition. Hays had been Postmaster General in the cabinet of Warren Harding, whom he had helped elect, and whom some would nominate as the worst we have ever had. Those who wanted to approach Hays in a friendly manner called him "General."

Prior to the Code there had been a generic list of "Don'ts and Be Carefuls" which had been adopted by the California (Producers') Association on June 8, 1927. Additionally, there was a proscribed list of literary properties which the Companies had sworn never to touch. The list included "Rain" by Somerset Maugham, and, in general, a cluster of works that are considered minor classics today. It is safe to say that all of them were made into films.

It is said that the Code was signed into existence because of the growing threat of censor boards; and that is probably true. As early as 1922 there were eight state boards in operation, including Maryland, New York, Florida, Ohio, Pennsylvania, Virginia, Kansas, and Massachusetts (with the oddity that exceptions taken in New England were applicable only on

Sunday, a blue law trick that made it impractical to reinstate the excised parts during the rest of the week; thus giving us the flip side of the popular upcoming picture *Never on Sunday*). Florida was practically inoperable, and Kansas was interested in relatively only one thing, as we shall see shortly. The bureau with the greatest reputation for severity around the movie industry was in Ohio.

Below the state level, there were at one time as many as ninety municipal censor boards of varying degrees of severity and efficiency, including the granddaddy of them all, the Chicago Municipal Board which, because of its influence throughout a populous distribution area, meant adding Illinois and a good chunk of the Midwest to the state roster. On the other side of the ledger, there were innumerable national censor boards in the foreign market, including such peculiarities as the office in Indonesia, where the official state censor had his private army to enforce his decrees. (Nor will it be forgotten that Dostoyevsky was condemned to death by the censorship in Russia, for his writings against the state, and was actually put through the cruel hoax of being marched into the square, stripped to the waist, and fired upon by an execution squad, whose guns, it turned out, were loaded with blanks. The trauma never left him.)

The mushrooming threat of the censor boards was undoubtedly provoked by the quality of the pictures in those days, but it was further irritated by outside incidents such as the well-advertised Fatty Arbuckle scandal. Stories surrounding the episode with this famous actor have become misty with age, but the talk still lingers that there was some kind of an orgy, and a girl died of hemorrhage after being attacked sexually with a Coke bottle. Arbuckle was acquitted, but the echo of scandal remained.

One thing which, I think, is generally forgotten in accounting for the inception of the Code is that the mood of the times was one of severe backlash. Psychologically, I think it is very important to recognize this. From the end of World War I until the great stock market crash of 1929, the country had embarked on a prolonged binge, which was saying, in a manner of speaking, that we did have here a lasting dwelling place. It is probably accurate to say, historically, that there were two fallout consequences of World War I that had almost endless shock waves. For one thing, it brought to an end the last crumbling remnants of the feudal system, during which kings fell like tenpins, or turned into mere figureheads. It was the end of the patriarchal and the patrimonial structure of society, which grew up out of the fact that, for centuries, man was a "landed" creature. This idea prevailed right up through the hierarchical scale through princes and popes to the abiding father figure of them all: God. This was one thing that began to come to an end with the Armistice of November 11, 1918. From that date on, there was a great turnaway from Tradition.

Concomitantly there was, as it were, a celebration of freedom over this fact. The Industrial Revolution, which was greatly accelerated by the demands of World War I, came full circle and finally into its own. It presented itself as being able to cope with and control man's environment. Instead of tossing in the sponge over unseen and unknown forces in his ambiance (which had to be neutralized and placated by forms of magic, miracles), man was now able to take his contemplation off an afterlife, and pitch into the here and now, with a feeling of responsibility for himself. This called for a party. And so there came the flapper and the jazz age and speakeasies in defiance of Prohibition and a great speculative fling on Wall Street—and there were the movies. They were impudent about life, and saucy about acclaiming it, and the devil take the hindmost.

With the crash, the party was over. In the littered debris of confetti and tickertape, an enormous sense of guilt set in. One does not turn from the past so suddenly and so unaccountably. A creeping fear that Big Daddy was striking back set in. In a mood of sobriety, a chastened citizenry reacted against those symbols of its great debauch and began to punish them. The Securities and Exchange Commission was made into a powerful bureau to control excesses in the stock market. And the F.B.I. was resurrected from the mothballs and made into a mighty arm of righteousness under the young Director J. Edgar Hoover. The imaginative system of the "ten most wanted" criminals was created, the rumrunners and racketeers were routed, and Prohibition was repealed.

The movies were more wily. They promised to control themselves. Since this solution seemed more coordinate with the American ideals of freedom and of the undesirability of censorship, the gesture of good will was accepted generally by the public.

I believe that this was pretty much the mood in which the Code first came into being.

The directors of the Motion Picture Association appointed as their first manager of the Code machinery a tall, bland, fine-looking man from Montana named Jason Joy. Whereas Hays was always called "General," Joy was called "Colonel," and early pictures show him wearing what look like cavalry boots and campaign hat. He was given the title of Director of the Studio Relations Committee. It was his job to see to it that the picture makers lived up to their pledges and conformed to their Code.

Jason, however, was quickly fleeced. Everybody in the business of making pictures was resolute in his determination that the Code should be upheld—by the other guy. The country was slowly sinking under water into the great Depression, the studios were disintegrating into bankruptcy, a buck was hard to come by, and if people wanted a speck of titillation, well, what the hell, a laugh was a laugh in a time like this, and a person needed it to keep from going crazy. If this is what people wanted—a little excitement (like Jimmy Cagney squashing a grapefruit into a girl's face) or a little raciness (like in the Jean Harlow films) —who was to say he could tell the gr-r-rea-a-at Amurican public what it could see and what it couldn't see? Fukkit!

Joy's ride was short and sweet. He was absorbed into an elegant job with a big office at Twentieth Century-Fox, and a successor was picked from the ranks of the opposition. Not being behind the door when the wits were passed out, the Industry reached into the highest levels of the enemy camp and hired the chairman of the most powerful censoring body in the world, the New York State Censorship Bureau, a Dr. James Wingate. If Hollywood's first efforts at amendment had faltered, well, human beings are allowed one slip, so long as they quickly and intelligently correct it.

Wingate took refuge in the Hollywood Athletic Club, where about all he was allowed to do was work out on the barbells. The Industry went plunging right along making the *Little Caesar*'s and the Mae West epics as if nothing had happened. Wingate wrote letter after letter admonishing this studio and that regarding properties they were preparing, but his mood of bewilderment and of inability pervades the correspondence even to this day. He was not to be faulted if he took a second cup of cheer at cocktail time.

In later years, after Joe Breen had succeeded in snapping a dog collar around the neck of the producers and they were relatively mellow about the whole thing, it became a custom among some to smile, like a company of Good Thieves, and to say, "Me. I was the one. Single-handedly I brought on the whole Code. Did you know that? Yeah. Ask Joe Breen. He'll tell you. Ask him about *Convention City*."

Of all the pictures that were occasionally cited as "having brought on the Code single-handedly," the two most frequently mentioned were *The Story of Temple Drake* and *Convention City*. They can be taken as symbols of a small hoard of other films that continued to be thrown, like pies, into the face of a public suffering in the throes of the deep Depression. A cursory exploration through the files of these pictures, in the morgue of the Production Code office, gives us a taste of the nature of the problems.

Temple Drake would probably top the list of the ten most feared pictures of 1933. It was based on what was then considered to be the scandalous novel of William Faulkner, *Sanctuary*. Even today this small masterwork is not exactly considered pabulum.

It was the story of a "wild" girl from a family of good stock, who gets involved with a group of primitive moonshiners in a backwoods hideaway. The leader, Popeye, later called Trigger in the movie, takes to this girl, and rapes her in an unnatural manner. He then brings her to Memphis and puts her in bondage, until she kills him in self-defense. She is made to pay for her great orgy by confessing her shame on a witness stand, in order to exonerate one of the moonshiners falsely accused of an earlier murder. The quality of her bloodlines comes to the surface, and the theme is that "class will out." The respectable lawyer who really loves her is proud of her.

Two things are remembered about *Temple Drake*. The most vivid is the rape, which occurs in a corncrib, with the clear inference that Trigger violates her with a cob of corn.

The second factor that still smolders in the memory is the torrid nature of the affair in Madam Reba's house. What the impact of the sequence was all about was this: A girl abandons herself to her lusts and "goes earth," in the sense that one might use the phrase "goes ape." This sequence would be the very quintessence of the point we have tried to make as being central to any understanding of the Code. Here is a girl who has temporarily turned her face away from "soul realities," and who lets herself get totally immersed in carnality. To a reviewer in those days, with any lingering convictions about religion and the nature of the human frame, this is the ultimate diabolism. The factor of abandonment to the flesh is further irritated by the sly inference that the girl is the slave of a supermagical tool owned by Trigger (thence the change of name). There is a little ambivalence here, since it seems that the act of raping her with a corncob would suggest impotence.

Be that as it may, the proof of all this pudding is the fact that the *motivation* of her repentance was a cause of some anguish to the Code people in those early days. The girl never came back to a correct set of values. She was lauded and made to seem sympathetic not because she disavowed her black experience, but because she wanted to restore what she had withdrawn from the bank of "ancestral integrity."

There are a couple of peripheral items of minor interest. For one thing, the actor with the fabled plumbing system was Jack La Rue, who, the studio argued, would give the part some sublimation, inasmuch as he had just played a Catholic priest in the original version of *A Farewell to Arms*. His sister was the Emily of the Code file room some ten years later. For another thing, a "lost" statistic of the time shows us that the two principal offenders of the Hollywood menage were Paramount Studios, with twelve entries in the bawdy race, and First National-Warners', with the same number.

This figure gives us a natural elision over into the second example of the period, *Convention City,* made by Hal Wallis, with the young Henry Blanke also listed as Producer.

The censor board of British Columbia, which at first rejected the picture outright, had this to say about it:

> Depiction of a "Convention of Lecherous Salesmen" as described by one of the actresses in dialogue, seems fitting and would make this orgy of drunkenness and sensuality unsuitable for family theaters. Sufficient eliminations would make picture useless from entertainment angle.

It is easy to imagine what this coarse romp was all about. One does not want to pander by going back and dragging out all the "dirty" lines, but it is interesting to see what was considered offensive in those days. And anyway, George Bernard Shaw observed that it is hardly possible to discuss obscenity without becoming obscene. So it's all a calculated risk.

For one thing, we find the roots of Joe Breen's latter-day eloquence in the line objected to by the Code office: "We suggest modifying the line 'stage our *honeymoon* in Macy's window' . . . perhaps replacing it with 'our wedding.' "

One line caught by practically every censor board in the world was spoken by a drunk: "I want to make a motion that we put our merchandise in slot machines and put 'em on every street corner in the world. You can never tell when an emergency may arise."

But the detail remembered by Geoff Shurlock as perhaps the most provocative was a comedy bit about a drunk who was chasing a sheep around the lobby of the hotel, trying to lure it up to his room. "That really drove the Catholics up the wall," he said.

In the midst of the reams of changes demanded by censor boards in every quarter of the country and of the globe, one wry item seeps to the surface. On January 12, 1934, a letter from a Mr. Cole of the Paramount [sic] Distributing Office in Kansas City was addressed to the Motion Picture Association, pointing out that he had prevailed on the Governor of that state to persuade his censor board to be "a little more tolerant on the question of liquor in pictures in the State of Kansas . . . Anything in a picture that will tend to ridicule prohibition or the drys will certainly be removed . . . the State of Kansas is considered extremely dry."

While all the world was agitated about sex and criminality, the central U.S.A. could see morality equated with only one thing: drinking.

3 Committing Suicide— On the Other Guy!

WHEN YOU COME right down to it, the Code, in its first whirl, was pretty much of a Protestant affair. True, the document itself had been written by two Catholics: Martin Quigley, an influential publisher of motion picture trade journals and a graduate of Niagara University and Catholic University of America; and Father Daniel Lord, a Jesuit priest from St. Louis, Missouri.

To the contributions of these two men, certain embroideries were added by Will Hays, who did not want to abandon the "Don'ts and Be Carefuls" altogether. What resulted, of course, was a mongrelization between a philosophical document and a proscription list.

The officers of the Association were too canny, however, to hand over the operation lock, stock, and barrel to the Catholics. The Romans were structured, and would have taken away the play with the ease of the Green Bay Packers. This would have been a defeat for the Protestants, who, before ecumenism, were a pretty purse-lipped community themselves.

Therefore, the management of the Code stayed with a tight little knot inside the Association composed of Will Hays, an elder in the Presbyterian Church; Francis Harmon, a vice president and what one could call, without acrimony, a "Professional Protestant"; Jason Joy, who was some kind of divine or divinity student; and Geoff Shurlock, who passed for an

Episcopalian, even though he was an eclectic, and, in the deepest currents of his soul, a theosophist.

Joe Breen: of him the character Moustache in Billy Wilder's *Irma la Douce* would say, ". . . that's another story."

Joe, in his youth, had been hither and yon. Graduated from St. Joseph's College in Philadelphia (where he would have you believe he was a basketball player to be reckoned with), he osmosed his way into the American Consular Service as a minor secretary in Jamaica. Thence, somehow, to Budapest, where he was involved in the American Aid Mission, probably under Herbert Hoover. As a bestower of largesse, he was popular and met such luminaries as the young Joe Pasternak and the young Henry Koster. He developed a peculiar love for the twin cities on the Danube, as well as for Vienna, and, in acknowledgment of his contributions in Central Europe, was awarded the Order of Knight of Saint Stephen, an honor of which, as an Irishman, he was justly proud.*

From Budapest he somehow got to Ireland, where, he claimed, he was arrested by the British for his part in fomenting sedition and condemned to death. The American Foreign Service secured his release from the Emerald Isle.

By what routes are not known, he ended up in Chicago, where he found his true center of gravity. He became a newspaper reporter in the days of the Great Chicago School, the days of Ben Hecht, Heywood Broun, and others. He counted his years in the Windy City as the best in his life.

By luck and by design he secured for himself the post of Public Relations Director of the famous Eucharistic Congress in Chicago. He made considerable personal hay for himself recounting and publishing the mysterious story of the monstrance that was used in this event. It was a fabulously jeweled and structured oriflamme designed exclusively for carrying the consecrated Host in procession during the Congress. It seemed

---

* Although his main boast was the rank of Knight Commander of the Order of St. Gregory.

doomed. Many untoward things happened to it, and, in the end, when it was being transported back to the bank vault, there was a great accident, and the monstrance was smashed beyond recognition. Joe was crafty enough to intimate the invisible Finger of God.

In any event, he concluded this undertaking in the Catholic limelight as an established figure. He was definitely Churchy.

Two more steps brought him closer to his ultimate goal. Working as director of press relations for the Chicago World's Fair, he became acquainted with and was eventually employed as personal assistant by Stuyvesant Peabody. This led him to an acquaintanceship with Martin Quigley, who induced Breen to enter his office to work on matters pertaining to the Code in New York. Breen, as usual, got the jump on Quigley by dubbing him "Pops," an annoyance, since Martin was the younger.

Thus it was that Breen came to the attention of Will Hays; and when the General saw that his little barque was beginning to spring leaks, he began looking around for someone outside the Fold on whom to lay off the action. I say this not of myself, but as passing along the opinion of Father Dan Lord, who was dying of lung cancer at the time, but who said without equivocation that Hays was looking for a patsy.

Therefore, Joe was sent out to Hollywood in the early thirties to be, technically, a publicity man for the Association, but actually to be the eyes and ears of Hays with reference to Code work. To start with he "helped people listen," as they say. But soon he sent his first estimate to Hays. The "Studio Relations Committee" would have to go. It was a Board. And, as the General knew, "all boards are long, and narrow, and wooden."

While Joe was prowling the corridors being an observer of the fraud that was being waged on a gullible public, the same sense of sedition that had gotten him in trouble before began to percolate in the back of his Hibernic mind. Something needed to be done.

It was too much to expect of human nature to think that the picture makers would lift themselves by their own bootstraps up to levels of high idealism. Even men of good will, who actually desired the Code in the way a stream wants banks, were being dragged off by the weight of common community practice into a dank and stagnant marshland.

Joe smacked one fist into the palm of his other hand and decided to take a chance. Getting on the phone, he invited Martin Quigley, who was looked on as the Wise Man from the East, to meet with him on the Coast. If memory serves right, the place of conspiracy was to be Joe's newly acquired beach home in Malibu, in the heart of the colony, where the sound of the surf would make it impossible for them to be recorded or eavesdropped. To fill out the troika, Joe then called Monsignor John Corrigan, eventually Bishop, and Rector of the Catholic University in Washington, D.C., to participate with them.

The three convened and made their schemes. Joe pointed out that the only organization with the potential for precipitating a unified public opinion was the Church. Already, certain small segments of it had taken the initiative. In Chicago, a Jesuit priest by the name of FitzGeorge Dineen had started a movement to proscribe evil movies, which he had labeled with the catchy title of the Legion of Decency. It had a ring to it, like Chesterton's poem: ". . . comes up along the winding road, the noise of the Crusade!"

At the same time, in New York, the International Federation of Catholic Alumnae were publishing reviews of "recommended" pictures, and in St. Louis, the nationally circulated periodical *Queen's Work* was beginning to list five "condemned" pictures each month.

What was needed now was a coordination of these fragmentary movements by the Episcopacy of the United States. This body was meeting in its annual Synod in November. At that time, it should be proposed that the hierarchy take over sponsorship of the Production Code of the Motion Picture

Industry, and lend its influence to the enforcement of it. This meant the boycotting of certain pictures, and even the picketing of the worst offenders. The result would be the only sanction the producers would heed: economic.

There is a cunning involution in this planning which should not be glossed over by the swift reader. The Code was touted as a *voluntary* system of self-regulation. What Joe was now proposing was that the Industry be put in a position of being *forced* to regulate itself voluntarily. It was very much like the process with which he himself, as a Catholic layman, was familiar. In Baptism, the gift of Faith is imposed on the child, as it were, in an act of custodianship; with the proviso that it be "freely" adopted by the recipient when he achieved maturity. But woe to the man who did not voluntarily take that which had been prescribed!

Joe, then, was willing to trade one hoax for another; nor is there any profit, at this late date, in weighing which was the preferred risk. The vital factor and the governing reality of his plan was this, that he was being paid by the Industry and not by the Church, so that it was up to him to play the game of being the stalwart of Hollywood against the Adversary. They would understand, those two men sitting with him. Once they parted company, it was double-agent time.

If memory does not play tricks in this fuzzy area, it was Monsignor Corrigan who undertook the responsibility of approaching Archbishop McNicholas, the Dominican Ordinary of Cincinnati, who, in turn, most likely proposed the whole idea to the assembled Synod of Bishops in November 1933. At any rate, the plan was accepted, and Archbishop McNicholas was named the first Chairman of the Bishops' Committee; which, not to get too fancy about it, eventually turned (April 1934) into the National Legion of Decency.

What ensued has been called the Bishops' Revolt.

Father Dineen secured the support of Cardinal Mundelein in Chicago. The Chicago Legion enrolled 500,000 Catholic women to campaign against theaters. The Jesuit from *America* magazine, Wilfred Parsons, S.J., obtained the endorsement of Cardinal Hayes of New York. Bishop Michael J. Gallagher of Detroit turned loose a Monsignor Hunt, pastor of the cathedral in that city, in a bitter vendetta against scandalous films. Detroit Catholics started using bumper stickers proclaiming "We Demand Clean Movies."

The part played by the various great Protestant groups in boosting this movement was neither frivolous nor sycophantic, but to unravel the entire tangled skein would be to invite the complaint that "the love song is slowing down the show." The only factor of human interest in this connection is that which is recalled by Monsignor John Devlin, the Hollywood representative of the Legion of Decency. He points out that the Protestant backing was strong until, in 1936, Pope Pius XI issued his encyclical on the movies *Vigilanti Cura*. In a nonce, Protestant interest melted away.

Now it so happened that Warner Brothers (one of the two chief culprits, remember?) had a heavily concentrated chain of theaters in Philadelphia. On top of that they were indiscreet enough to put up a large and offensive billboard opposite the residence of the fiery prelate of that city, his Eminence, Denis Cardinal Dougherty. Every morning when this man climbed into his limousine to go to his downtown office, the provocative sign caught his eye. As a man of prudence, he turned his head away as long as he thought he could. But when the display did not disappear, he one day felt he had had enough. Climbing into his pulpit, he categorically forbade all Catholics within his jurisdiction to attend *any* movies, under pain of mortal sin. There is reason to think that to this day the prohibition has never been rescinded, an interesting technicality.

The issue exploded.

Joe Breen was called back to New York, where the company presidents were in hasty and panicky conclave over the debacle. As should be obvious, the Philadelphia area was heavily

Catholic, and the effect on Warners' was immediate. I let Breen take over from here (the "caps" indicating the decibel quotient of his voice) :

> "THERE WAS HARRY WARNER, STANDING UP AT THE HEAD OF THE TABLE, SHEDDING TEARS THE SIZE OF HORSE TURDS, AND PLEADING FOR SOMEONE TO GET HIM OFF THE HOOK. AND WELL HE SHOULD, FOR YOU COULD FIRE A *CANNON* DOWN THE CENTER AISLE OF ANY THEATER IN PHILADELPHIA, WITHOUT DANGER OF HITTING ANYONE! AND THERE WAS BARNEY BALABAN, WATCHING HIM IN TERROR, WONDERING IF HE WAS GOING TO BE NEXT IN CHICAGO, AND NICK SCHENCK, WONDERING WHEN HE WAS GOING TO BE HIT BY A BUCKET OF SHIT IN NEW YORK."

While all this crying was going on, Joe, according to his own account of the occasion, was hovering effacingly in the back of the room, lost in a bevy of lesser executives. Outside of the fact that he had undoubtedly been lobbying for weeks to get the job, his "natural modesty" and "shrinking violet" tendencies forced him to obliterate his presence.

Meanwhile, up on the dais, the presidents knew that the jig was up. They would have to empower somebody properly. But who?

Imagine Joe's surprise when suddenly, contrary to his wishes and expectations, some unknown Personage pointed a long muscular finger toward the back of the room and announced, "Gentlemen! We have the very man right here in our midst."

Joe looked over his shoulder at the blank wall, to see if someone behind him was being designated. When no one appeared, he put a startled fingertip to his chest, and asked faintly, "Who, me?"

When everyone began to applaud, he allowed himself to be

reluctantly dragged forward. Protesting vociferously, he let himself be led to the dais.

He stood there a moment in stunned silence (for the last time) and then turned firm. Putting his hand to his breast, as in a salute to the flag, he announced, "Very well, gentlemen, I accept the job. But on one condition. And the condition is that you understand that I come from a race of people who have a long history of committing suicide—on the other guy!"

Joe never did disappoint them.

Breen made good his threat almost immediately.

He was accompanied to Hollywood by Francis Harmon, the chief vice president in New York who was importantly tied in with the Baptists and the Rockefellers. This was a slightly patronizing move with a suggestion of face-saving for the Protestants.

At any rate, Francis escorted Joe, early in their rounds, to Columbia Studios, the lair of the redoubtable Harry Cohn, who was not in the habit of attending Association meetings in New York. After introductions, Joe presented his portfolio of qualifications and accomplishments to Harry, who glanced at them quickly, ruffled them in his hand, and challenged, "What's all this shit?"

Joe looked off on a slant, as though his mind were registering "tilt."

In an almost ruminative manner, he replied, "Mr. Cohn—I take that as a compliment."

Startled, Harry struck back. "What does that mean?"

"My friends inform me," Joe replied, "that if there's any expert in this town on shit—it's you." He paused for the obligatory beat. "So if I have to be judged, I'm glad it's by professionals!"

Harry may have lacked polish, but he did not lack talent. From that needle-point instant on, a grudging admiration for Joe began that later ripened into a more or less warm support. In his declining years, Joe used to seize a tuft of his pure silver hair in the tips of his fingers. "You see this?" he would query. "You know how it got this way? Not from early piety. From Harry Cohn."

Not long after, one of the producers of *Convention City* flared out at Joe for a letter Breen had sent him on one of his scripts. In a sarcastic tone, the executive commented to Joe that maybe it would be better for the producers to go into the milk business, since Breen was turning the industry into such a bland operation that in a short time that's all the producers would be able to sell. Joe's eyes turned into two furious asterisks. Instantly he hit back, telling the fellow that "maybe that would be a goddam good idea. If people like you would get out of the way and sell milk, maybe it would free the screen of a lot of its whorehouse crap, and decent people could sit down and enjoy themselves in a theater without blushing."

It appears that it even got as far as fisticuffs in one instance. It involved the popular director Woody Van Dyke. We have only Joe's side of the picture, but Van Dyke, being a showman, would probably have approved anyway.

Joe had apparently finished reviewing one of Van Dyke's films in the Code projection room and had delivered an unpalatable opinion on it. The director, miffed, made an uncautious slur on Joe's honesty. Joe took a roundhouse swing at the man and hit him on the nose.

Breen used to go on at great lengths to describe how Woody was all dressed up in a tuxedo, all set to go out to some affair; something on the order of the Academy Awards. Woody ludicrously set his top hat on his bloodied cranium and marched out with dribbles of red on his white shirtfront. He perched himself at the bar, when he got to where he was going, and spent the whole evening telling everyone what a terror this new censor was.

It was fascinating to watch the way this story grew and was embellished as it was repeated over the years. By the last time it was recited, it went something like this. Joe said, "What did you say?" and Woody replied, "You heard me. I said you're crooked." Whereupon, Joe hit him such a blow that Woody went catapulting over the projection room seats, his head striking the arm of a chair as he fell to the floor. Joe gave the prone body a cursory glance, dusted off his hands, and stalked out. The man might be a corpse, for all he knew. But he had asked for it, and now he had got it. Imagine Joe's surprise, then, when he found out later that he had been the toast of the evening, thanks to the enthused recitations of Woody Van Dyke at the big function. When all the while, Joe had been sulking at home, waiting for the doorbell to ring and to be confronted by a policeman with a warrant for manslaughter!

Legend has it that there were clumsy efforts, too, to soften up Joe's tempestuous assault on Hollywood. One Christmas morning he woke up to find a shining black Cadillac, adorned with an enormous red ribbon, standing in his driveway. He studied it goggle-eyed for a moment. He put on a bathrobe, marched down to the driveway, inspected the card dangling from the ribbon, and went stomping back upstairs. He called the manager of the offending studio at his home and told him, at a pitch which made it almost unnecessary to use the phone, "to get that GODDAMN THING out of here—TODAY!"

The studio had to comb the service agencies to find a chauffeur who would come and pick up the car on Christmas Day. It is to be betted that the driver, when he finally did arrive, was so taken aback by Breen's fury that he drove off the gift without bothering to remove the ribbons.

Bryan Foy, who was such an expert at the quick low-budget film that he was dubbed the "King of the B's," had a theory about storytelling. "You always start off in a high wind," he claimed.

Breen must have learned from Foy. This is an ideal description of how his career in the movie capital got off the ground.

What ensued now was the apocryphal period that could be called "the Code."

To start with, the old Studio Relations Committee was wiped out, and the "Certificate of Approval" was invented. For what it is worth, the first "Seal" was issued on *The World Moves On* for Twentieth Century-Fox. The date was the gambling number, 7/11/34.

The system of financing the Code Administration is based on a scale of sliding fees, which has been changed upward over the course of the years. In general, one can say that the price for Code "Certification" ranges from $84 for the least expensive, to $3,000 at the other end, for work done on films with a gross negative cost in excess of $1.5 million. But traditionally the Code office has never been paid until the actual issuance of the Seal. If it had to reject a film, it did not receive a single cent, even though it might have done a considerable amount of work on it.

There has always been an "Appeal" over the heads of the Code staff to the Board of Directors of the Motion Picture Association in New York. This review group is made up of the company presidents, to which have been added in more recent years the representatives of the world of exhibition, and representatives of the independent producers. The decision of the Appeals Board is final. It is the true guts of the whole structure, for it is the way the Code decisions are made more strict or more lenient. In theory, it is a well-devised system, since it follows the American scheme of checks and balances. It is the Industry's protection against an excess of zeal on the part of its regulators; but it is also its Achilles' heel, since it created a device whereby the Industry could strike the posture of sanctimony while actually being self-serving.

To defy the Appeals Board meant to run the risk of being fined $25,000, but, for anti-trust reasons, the Industry was always very chary about trying to level this penalty. It may have been assessed against United Artists in the case of *The Moon Is Blue* and against Howard Hughes in the case of *The Outlaw* ("How would you like to tussle with Russell?"), but in neither case was the sum collected. UA left the Association, and Hughes sued it. Hughes lost; UA returned eventually; and the fine was abolished.

With the technicalities accounted for, and introductions completed, Breen was now ready to roll up his sleeves and make the thing work. His own description of the situation was that he stood like a man on the seashore, trying to hurl back the tides of the ocean with a pitchfork.

An interesting estimate of Breen during this period was afforded by a fascinated spectator, the representative of the New York *Times* in Hollywood, one Doug Churchill. Doug tended to drift into Joe's company, not only because of their similar newspaper backgrounds, but because, additionally, he felt a genuine sense of concern for the movies, which were in a syndrome of self-destruct. So familiar a fixture did Doug become around the Code office that, according to lore, he one time got mixed up in a Christmas party. Getting a trifle buzzed, he went off to take a snooze on a couch in the girls' room, and when he woke up, it was December 25th, and the place was locked. He had to spend part of the weekend in escrow.

He used to call Joe "my little Irish boy," which was permitted to him in his role as elder statesman. One day he buttonholed Joe. "I've been watching you, my little Irish boy," he said, "and I've finally come to the conclusion that you're going to make good. Yes sir, you'll make it here. You know why? I'll tell you." He waggled a finger in Joe's face. "You'll make it because you're—just—dumb—enough!"

Joe used to tell this story and then wait alertly to see from the expression on your face if you were—just—smart—enough to get the point of it. He was fully conscious of what he was saying. The story contained a deep truth about life.

Joe was the Censor *par excellence*. Not that he would accept the title, or even think of himself as one. Hardly any censor ever does. In the world of television for instance, the censors

call themselves "Editors" either in the "Department of Broadcast Standards" or in the "Continuity Acceptance Department." Even the clerical officers of the Legion of Decency took
great pains to point out that they were only a "rating" system,
and acted only in an "advisory" capacity for their constituents.
One of the few men to admit flat-out that he was a Censor was
the witty Silverthorne, Censor from Toronto, Canada. He was
in the habit of standing before an audience and saying, "Here
I am, the one you've been hearing about—that shadowy figure
who lurks behind the scenes with a scissors in his hand. I don't
duck it. I am an officially appointed officer of the Province of
Ontario. Take a look."

The Code Administrators were accustomed to use a phrase
coined by themselves, in contradistinction to a system backed
by the force of civil law. They were known as Hollywood's Self
Regulators. "I don't know about that, though," said Morris
Murphy one day, looking apprehensively into empty space, "I
don't think it's so good to be called a self regulator. It sounds
like someone who plays with himself."

4 The Monitor Ass of the Universe

ONE THING about Breen. You never did have to worry about missing vital parts of his stories.

Once he had thrust his chin in the heel of his hand and started burrowing his rump into the leather seats at the Peacock Lane restaurant, or around the corner at Dante's Italian hangout—two of our favorite lunchtime rendezvous—it would become apparent that we were about to be regaled with another of Joe's recitals about the winning of the West. He would stare around the table with his china-blue eyes, the loose rolls of flesh around his neck oozing over the edge of his palm, and begin by asking tentatively, "Say, did I ever tell you my famous story about *Scarface?*"

This was the storm warning, and all present would begin adjusting their derrières also, while Joe looked around like a little boy waiting for permission to do what he was going to do anyway.

Once in a while you'd make a feeble attempt to head him off by replying, "Oh, you mean that one about the chief of police and his captains? Yeah. That's a pretty good one."

Joe would stare at you blankly, a little runnel of unpleasant emotions would fill the air, and then he would adjust his generous hams once more. "Well, let me refresh you on it," he would rally. "It's good for you younger fellows to hear."

Undaunted by the wisp of despair that flickered from eye to eye, he would break into a rapid canter of narration, going over the same ground he had covered seven times before. If your attention began to flag, he would resort to poking you on the forearm, like a series of exclamation marks!

Scarface had been one of Joe's earliest encounters. The title, of course, was a reference to the nickname of Al Capone.

Howard Hughes had made the spectacular gangster classic at a time when sentiments were running particularly high against organized lawlessness. The censor boards, reflecting this mood, had banned the picture *in toto* in several of the Eastern states. A big investment was in danger of going down the drain.

Breen was called to New York in the hope that he could invent some device to break the logjam. The key state was New York. If the censor board in Albany would rescind its ban, the other states could be expected to follow suit.

When Joe arrived, the situation had reached a white hot pitch. A series of hearings were being conducted in the state capitol, and the papers were blazing with reports that were being submitted to the legislative body expressing the public's antagonism against crime, racketeering, and all its works and pomps. In one newspaper article was the outline of a speech delivered on the floor of the investigating committee, with the arresting title "The Menace of the Gun."

Quick as a flash, Joe seized on this catchy phrase. He retired to his hotel room, dug out his old reporter's typewriter, and rattled out the gist of a prologue that could be affixed to the picture. Using the epigrammatic title "The Menace of the Gun," he composed a condemnation of gangsterism and attacked the lawlessness and disorder embodied in the picture.

Whipping the completed paragraphs out of his machine, Joe hastened over to the phone, and put through a call to city hall. He asked for the Chief of Police, whom we will call "Chief Big" for convenience.

Joe explained the situation with *Scarface* to the Chief, and then proposed that he had an idea for salvaging it, if the Chief had a minute to listen.

The Chief accepted, and listened. What Joe had in mind was to invite the Chief to be photographed for the prologue, sitting at his desk, and delivering himself of a statement deploring the contents of the film, and pointing to it as an example of the kind of thing the enroused citizenry were combating in their drive against crime. Joe argued this would take the curse off the film, as well as give the Chief a valuable public relations opportunity. It was like putting a bow tie on a gorilla and calling it a gentleman, but what else could you do?

The Chief conjectured that the idea had some merit, so long as he could hear specifically what he would be called on to say.

"I have a draft right here in my hand," countered Joe. "Let me read some of it to you and get your reaction."

"Go ahead," said the Chief.

Joe read the first draft, and it caught the Chief's fancy. "I'll do it," he agreed.

"We'll get a camera crew down to your office first thing in the morning," assured Joe. "It ought to start the picture off on an impressive note."

Having committed the picture company to the device, Joe now had to scurry around to see if it could be done. It was no easy job. However, by dint of persuasion and swinging haymakers right and left, he got an agreement from the picture company, and at last had completed the myriad details of assembling a camera crew, with generator trucks, lighting equipment, baffle boards, sound booms, heavy-duty wires, dollies, light-duty wires, and permission from the unions. He was just set to send the whole menagerie to city hall, when he was checked by a last minute telephone call. It was Chief Big. "Hold up," he ordered Breen.

"Has anything gone wrong?" asked the stunned Breen.

"No. Not that," said the Chief. "But I was just talking to some of my boys, and they tell me it's not very wise of me to go ahead with this before I've seen the picture. I agree. Would it be too difficult to arrange a screening, so I can see what I'm getting into?"

Joe breathed a sigh of relief. He assured the official the request was not unreasonable, and promised to set up a screening in private. The Chief was pleased.

Thereupon ensued a new cycle of excitement, calling off the camera crews, getting in touch with a projection room, notifying the producer, getting a print of the film, and rechecking with police headquarters to pinpoint time and place. Out of the swirl of activity and the frantic ringing of telephones, an orderly arrangement was finally fixed on, and Joe hastened to an uptown projection room to be there ahead of time, lest any flaws develop.

On the way, he hopped out of his cab in a moment of inspiration, and bought a handful of expensive cigars, which he tucked in his vest pocket, like a row of shells for an elephant gun. He was pacing the projection room with nervous energy, when there was a knock on the door. It was three-thirty sharp, the time agreed on.

Joe, square and paunchy, stepped over to the door and swung it open. Standing in the framework, massive and muscular, was the Chief. Behind him, like three cliffs of granite, stood his assistants. Joe looked up at the assemblage of brawn and his heart quailed.

"Chief Big?" asked Joe, putting out his hand.

"Yes. You're Mr. Breen, I presume," said the Chief, taking his hand in a great iron grasp. He stepped forward in a chesty way. "I want you to meet my captains. This is Captain X—homicide." The first captain, a powerful broth of a fellow, stepped forward, shook Joe's hand, and walked to a seat.

"Captain Y—detectives."

Joe reached up like a turtle beginning to shrink into his shell.

"Captain Z—crime prevention."

The officer bowed gravely, and wrung Joe's hand for the fourth time.

"Would you gentlemen like cigars?" asked Joe, walking from one to another with the long brown pellets.

"No, thank you," they declined. "We don't smoke."

"Oh, I begyourpardon," hastened Joe, stuffing the offending things back into his pocket. "Well—! Shall we go, then?"

"Any time you're ready." The Chief waved.

Joe signaled the projectionists, and the lights went down. He took one of the lush seats, sliding down a bit on the back of his neck. He noticed that the captains still sat bolt upright. He shrugged, dug out one of the cigars, bit the end off, and lit it up optimistically.

The picture churned through melodramatic sequence after melodramatic sequence, up to a wild conclusion. At the climax, all stops were out. Bullets were flying, corpses were tumbling, and sirens were screaming, while police cars with flashing red lights were squealing around corners. At the height of it all, the fire department came boiling into the picture, with great double-jointed hook-and-ladder trucks scattering traffic to join the fray. Under cover of a hail of fire from the police, they rushed to the building under assault and threw up long ladders to the windows. Up the ladders poured the police with revolvers drawn. They overran the place and subdued the criminals.

The bash was over; the music dropped to a lull; the lights in the projection room gradually came up; there was a vacuum of silence. Joe noticed that the four captains were still sitting, strangely, bolt upright in their seats.

He bounced out of his chair. "Well, gentlemen," he ventured, "what do you think of it?"

They looked around in unison and glared at him. "Are you kidding?" one asked.

Joe's heart flipped like a fish going over on its belly.

"What kind of gall do you have," demanded another of them, "asking the New York Police Department to connect itself with this picture?"

"Is something wrong?" Joe fumbled. Realizing this sounded

a little hollow, he hastened to explain. "I mean—something you could put your finger on? Something that could be cut out of the picture? To improve it? Something you found particularly offensive?"

Two of the captains rose from their seats and hovered over him, livid with anger. Joe backed slightly away.

"We don't like to be taken for suckers," emphasized one of the captains, prodding Joe on the chest with a heavy finger. Joe felt one of the cigars crumble.

Grasping at a straw, Joe turned to Chief Big. "No chance?" he suggested desperately.

The officer rose from his seat. "I wouldn't say that," he replied. "But you wouldn't make the changes we'd want."

"What are they? What are they?" asked Joe quickly.

"What *are* they?" interrupted one of the captains. "What would you *think* they are?"

"I'm at sea, sir—I wouldn't know. Tell me."

"That part about the fire department, of course!"

"The *fire* department?"

"Yes. The FIRE department! Do you mean to suggest that we sponsor a picture which infers that the New York Fire Department has to come to the rescue of the police? That pack of bums who play checkers all day and sleep all night? Don't be *ridiculous!*"

And with that parting shot, and a scowl all around, they put on their hats and stalked out.

It is a commentary on Breen's prowess as a raconteur that, years later, one does a double take, and realizes that none of us ever did find out how *Scarface* got past the New York State censor board, which it obviously must have, some way or another. Neither did we ever learn whether Joe's prologue was used. At the moment of hearing, it never occurred to us to ask.

One of the first things Joe had to do in Hollywood was to clear the air of falsities and evasive pretensions. A classic example of this tactic occurred in the case of the well-known Central European director Jo Von Sternberg, who had come into the Code office to outline a story he proposed to make.

Von Sternberg was the kind of man who would plod through a plot with a thick accent, stopping every now and again to breathe on his glasses and polish them slowly while you waited in exasperation for the next turn of thought.

He was holding his glasses up to the light of the window for the sixth time, peering through them to look for dust specks, when he made a gesture of reasonableness. "At this point, of course," he said, "the two principals have a brief romantic interlude."

Joe's rear end was twitching with impatience. "You mean they fuck," he said, coming down icily with his voice on the word.

The director adjusted his glasses in a startled manner and looked blankly at Breen. "I beg your pardon?" he said.

"What you're trying to say," fumed Breen, "is that the two of them hopped into the hay. They fucked."

"Mr. Breen, you offend me."

"Listen friend, fucking's fucking. It's not a 'romantic interlude.' If you want to say it, why don't you say it?"

"But Mr. Breen, this is *love*."

"Oh it *is*, is it? Will you kindly tell me what's the difference?"

The director spread open his hands helplessly and looked around the room for aid. Seeing none forthcoming, he stammered an explanation. "Sex, with love, is something *beautiful*. It's not like two dogs. I think sex without love is the dirtiest thing in the world. But when two people *love* one another . . ."

"What if these two people happen to be married? As they are in your story?"

The director again spread his hands. "They cannot help it. They are overwhelmed by the mystery. It is something bigger than both of them."

Breen snorted like a sea lion. "Oh, I see," he said. "If they love one another, it's not adultery. It's love."

The director again looked appealingly for help and then shrugged, hugely and softly. What else?

Breen shook his head in despair. "The last of the romantics," he said. "The Ten Commandments go right out the window, when love flies in. Is that it?"

The director was now offended. "If you want it that way," he said, attempting sarcasm.

"Oh, for Christ's sake, will you stop the horseshit and face the issue. We can help you make a story about adultery, if you want, but not if you keep calling a good screwing match a 'romantic interlude.' Now what do these two people do? Kiss and go home?"

"No," said the director, getting the point, "they fuck."

"Good!" yelped Breen, pounding the desk, "now I can understand your story. Now, let's go on. What next?"

The director completed his outline, and Breen told him how he could handle it in such a way as to pass the Code. The picture eventually made a lot of money, and the director was grateful to Breen for life.

In his autumn years, I once asked Breen about the ease with which he reverted to sulphurous language, and he replied without ruffle that he had used polite language when he first came to Hollywood, but it was not the idiom of the time or the place, "and they thought I was a sissy. I had to show them I meant what I said."*

---

* As an aside to this issue, there is the landmark law case in which the director Charles Vidor sued Harry Cohn to break his contract with Columbia on the grounds that life was unbearable at the studio because of the barbarousness of Harry's language. At the conclusion of the trial, which was really a test as to whether outrageous language was legal in the film business, the magistrate delivered the following opinion:

> The court finds that Harry Cohn was accustomed to and in the habit of using obscene language in talking to Mr. Vidor and others.
>
> Mr. Vidor knew before he went into the contract of 1944 the

Of course, not all of Breen's ripostes were verbal in character. There were times when the Irish pixie bubbled to the surface, and words spilled over into deeds.

A case in point occurred at MGM, where he was summoned one afternoon to give his opinion on a costume for a dance number. It was for a picture by Joe Pasternak, I think.

Joe came bouncing in on the set and saw a girl standing there covered with balloons.

"Is this the costume?" he demanded incredulously.

"This is it."

He stalked over to the girl, who was beginning to feel silly.

"Hold still, darlin'," he told her.

He took the stub of a cigar out of his mouth and put it to the nearest balloon.

POP!

Then the next one.

POP!

Then right down the line.

POP! POP! POP!

He turned on his heel and strode out. That was the end of the discussion.

---

habits and characteristics of Mr. Cohn; knew the kind of language he and others in the employ of the defendant would have to encounter; knew the general environment and type of language habitually used at the defendant's studio. Mr. Vidor lived, thrived and prospered under such existing conditions and accepted them as a matter of course.

In my opinion, when Mr. Vidor realized that the present contract was no longer attractive to him, he sought an excuse to void the same, hence the present action.

It has been suggested by counsel for Mr. Vidor that a finding in favor of Columbia Pictures would place the court's approval on the promiscuous use of obscene, unoriginal epithets that are far older than the film industry itself. This court is not called upon nor is it its function in this case to act the part of a censor of the personal conduct or code of ethics of the principal actors.

• • •

Joe's personality traits ranged from brass to courage, and, since fortune favors the brave, he was kissed with more than his share of good luck. Perhaps it should be called "serendipity," since he exposed himself to the possibility by ranging the Hollywood community far and wide.

A prime example occurred late one night when he got an emergency call at his house from an eminent writer. "Joe, can I come over and see you, right away?"

Joe recognized the urgency in the voice and told him to come at once.

A half hour later, the life-and-death mystery was unraveled.

It seems that a conference had been held a few weeks prior between the writer, a big producer, and Joe at Romanoff's posh restaurant, in which a story outline had been discussed. Joe had been invited along to hear the idea and to tell whether it would pass the Code or not.

The writer had come early and had located himself at the bar, stoking himself with a few drinks to oil up his voice. But the producer had come late, so that things went a little further than had been planned. By the time the three sat down to dinner, the writer was well on the way.

He was lucid enough, however, to recite the idea, which was not yet down on paper. Joe had approved, as far as the Code was concerned; and the producer had liked the notion enough to buy it on the spot.

"The trouble is, Joe," the writer explained, "I was so enthused when I had a check for twenty-five thousand dollars in my hand that I returned to the bar after the dinner, and began celebrating. I celebrated the idea right out of my head. Now I'm in real trouble. Because I've spent the money, and I can't for the life of me remember what I sold. Then I thought of you. Do you recall what the hell I was talking about?"

He waited with bated breath while the gears whizzed around in Joe's head. "Certainly," said Joe at last.

The writer almost collapsed. "Tell it to me—tell it to me, for God's sake."

"I'll do better than that. I'll write it out. I'll dictate it to my secretary. How's that?"

The writer practically swooned around Joe's shoulders. "Listen," he added as an afterthought, "if you get any ideas of your own, throw those in too, will you? It'll probably be better than the thing I sold."

For the most part, Breen tended to reserve to himself what were called the "social problem" pictures, which meant those that attempted to be more meaningful, and in which the problem was more likely than not to be sex. Below this category there was a whole mass of "action" pictures on the bread-and-butter level. All of these lesser films, which television eventually drained away from the Industry, Joe was inclined to delegate to his henchmen, particularly to Charley Metzger. Joe gave Charley free rein in this area, and in his own circle Charley was pretty much of a kingpin.

One day, however, in a lull between squalls, Joe's invisible antennae began to oscillate, and he thought it might be a good idea to examine what was going on on the other side of the horizon. He bustled into Metzger's office, told Charley what he had in mind, and concluded by bundling a stack of scripts under his arm, to take with him to his beach home over the weekend. It is significant to note that each time this story was told, the number of scripts became larger and larger.

Joe breezed his way through the whole pile and on Monday morning came to the surface with one clear conviction. There was too much killing in pictures. Put side by side, the overall impression from the cheaper pictures was one of wholesale slaughter of human beings. And this was specifically prohibited by the Code. A regard for the sanctity of human life was being destroyed.

Joe came steaming back into Metzger's office and told him his impression. Metzger, always ready to crawfish with great rapidity, assured Joe that this item had been on his mind for a

long time, but that Joe had been inaccessible. Now he was glad
to get the boss's opinion on some remedy.

"Well, I'll tell you, Charles," said Joe, scratching his head,
"what do you say we work on the principle of cutting them in
half? Count the killings when you read the script. If there's
twenty, tell the producer he can only have ten. Is that fair
enough?"

Charles' mind figuratively clicked its heels and saluted. A
suggestion was a command to him. "And if the producer refuses to cooperate?" he dared to suggest.

Breen came to a boil immediately. "Well, then, goddamit,
throw his film out. Refuse to give it a Seal."

"I'll try it," promised Charles.

"Try it, my EYE," growled Breen. "Just *do* it!"

Ten days later, Metzger was back in Breen's office, all proud
smiles. "I rejected a picture today," he announced.

"Good!" exclaimed Breen, his mind on something else and
not caring a whit.

"The producer's sore too," said Metzger.

A warning buzzer rang in Joe's psyche. "What about?" he
asked, looking up.

"About this picture I threw out. He wants a Seal."

"What the hell'd you throw the picture out for?"

"Killings! Too many killings."

It was like throwing the main switch. All the lights went on
in Joe's interior. "Ah!" he said, "that's good, Charles. You did
very well."

"The producer's going to get his lawyer."

The Irish feelings bristled. "Well, we'll see about that. In
the meantime, you stick by your guns."

"I'm glad you approve. I wasn't certain—"

"Yes, I approve. Now get the hell out of here."

Charley scuttled.

On the following Monday, when Joe returned to his little
Western Front, Metzger was paddling up and down the corridors with a file folded securely under his arm. He inter-

cepted Breen as he stepped off the elevator. "They're here!" warned Charles.

"Who's here, for Christ's sake?"

"You know. That producer I told you about, with his lawyer. Too many killings?"

"Well what the hell're you so nervous about? Let'm speak."

"They're in your reception room. I just thought I'd warn you. And I have the file here, with all the letters I wrote to them. I *told* them they'd have to cut the killings in half."

"Let 'em sue," said Joe, stomping like a warhorse.

"They're going to," promised Charles.

When Joe reached his office, two diminutive figures popped out of the furniture and surrounded him. One was stubby and barrelly, with a fat black cigar protruding from the corner of his mouth. He gave the impression of having seen *Little Caesar* once too often. The other was less stocky and wore bottle-bottom glasses and a long alpaca frock coat. The scent of the docket was on him.

In the office, the producer whipped the cigar out of his mouth and began making circling gestures with it. "Mr. Metzger," he attacked, "tells me we cannot have a Code Seal for our picture. Tell me why! All my money is tied up in the film. If I cannot get justice here, I seek redress in court!"

The attitude was too peremptory for Joe, and he felt himself beginning to bristle. "Now just a minute, gentlemen," he composed, "suppose we keep our tempers in check."

"That's right, baby," said the lawyer, stepping quickly forward and patting the producer on the shoulder. "You sit down. Shut up. I will do the talking!"

The producer meekly did as he was bid.

Joe pointed a finger at the lawyer. "Excellent," he said. "Now let's begin all over again. What's the problem?"

"Mr. Metzger here—he refuses to give my client a Certificate. Why?"

Charles leaped forward with the file open, exposing a carbon of the letter he had sent. "It's right down here in black and white," he said. "They had twenty killings in their script, and I told them to reduce them to ten."

Joe raised his hand placatingly. "Did your client receive a copy of this letter?" asked Joe of the lawyer.

"Did you, baby?" asked the lawyer, turning to the producer.

The producer grumbled and acknowledged he did with a curt wave of the cigar.

"All right, no more," ordered the lawyer. "Shut up!"

"Did your client think we were kidding?" Joe wanted to know. His voice rose a few decibels. "Gentlemen, we have a problem on our hands. We are trying, goddamit, to reduce the amount of unnecessary slaughter on the screen. How the hell do you expect us to stop it, EXCEPT BY STOPPING IT? Now why didn't you pay attention?"

"Mr. Breen," the lawyer wheedled, "there were extenuating circumstances."

"For shooting . . . how many men, Charles?"

"Thirteen."

"Thirteen men?"

"Yes, sir—if you'd only listen."

The producer had been puffing his cigar in furious silence. "I will tell him," he announced.

The lawyer rushed over to him. "Sit down, baby," he ordered. "You will lose your temper. Keep quiet."

The producer struggled to his feet. "No," he determined. "I will tell him. *You* sit down."

The lawyer went over and sat near Metzger.

"Mr. Breen," began the producer, "I tell you the truth. I'm guilty as hell. Sure I shot thirteen. But I got an excuse."

"Tell me."

"You got a wife, Mr. Breen?"

Joe smiled knowingly. "And six children."

"Good. Then you understand. I got a wife too. You got relatives?"

"Me too. All on my wife's side."

"You have my sympathies."

"Yeah. And mainly I got three lazy bums of brothers-in-law. My wife's brothers, you know?"

Breen nodded again.

"They won't work. So what do I do? My wife keeps nagging me to give 'em a job. Me, I don't want'm on the payroll, but I gotta keep my wife quiet. So suddenly I got a great idea. I put them on the payroll, but I fool the hell out of my wife. I give 'em the parts of heavies, and I get 'em killed at the end of reel three. Blam, blam, blam. Now I'm rid of them, my wife's satisfied, but I got thirteen killings. I don't want thirteen killings, Mr. Breen. I want ten. But whatta you gonna do?"

Joe, by this time, was grinning good-naturedly. He turned to Metzger. "Better to be in trouble with us than with his wife, huh, Charles?"

"Oh, definitely," Metzger agreed.

"Issue a Seal," ordered Joe.

"And next time," assured the producer heartily, waving his cigar levelly at Joe, "I promise you. Ten killings—no more. I carry those bums to the end of the picture!"

Of course, in those abrasive days, it was only a matter of time before another incident occurred involving Harry Cohn. Although Joe was present at this encounter, it was his associate Geoff Shurlock who was the chief protagonist. It seems that the two of them had repaired to the Gower Street studio to talk over an enterprise with the ever-colorful Harry. Present also was a fourth man with an indistinct countenance, who blended politely into the background.

Cohn had been planning a big spectacular in color for his extremely popular light-opera singer Grace Moore. As Harry saw it, the climax of the picture would revolve around the fall of the Bastille in Paris. In his creative eye, Harry could envision an enormous crowd rushing the fortress and swarming over it, motivated to their bravery by the heroic figure of Grace Moore singing the thrilling strains of the "Marseillaise."

It was a good idea, until Geoffrey intervened, out of his

inexhaustible fund of erudition. "You can't do it, Harry," he said.

Harry whipped around on Geoff. This was tantamount to an invitation to go ahead, just for the devil of it. "Why the hell not?" he growled. "Who says so?"

Geoff shrugged. "The 'Marseillaise' wasn't written until three years after the fall of the Bastille."

Harry was stumped. "Well, who cares?" he wanted to know. "Who'd know a thing like that but a queer like you?"

The faceless gentleman came forward from the paneling. "I would know," he volunteered, "and so would my countrymen."

Cohn glared at this brashness. "And who the hell are you?" he demanded.

The man stood to his full height. "I am the French Consul, sir."

Harry absorbed the shock without expression. "So you are, are you?" he rallied. "And what, may I ask, are you doing here?"

"I was asked to come, sir, to give technical advice."

"Well isn't that just dandy. Suppose you keep your technical advice to yourself. When I want it, I'll ask for it."

"With pleasure, Mr. Cohn. But I am sorry you will make yourself look foolish. However, if you are determined to, you will. I only ask you to consider—how would it look to you if we sent a picture over from France of Washington crossing the Delaware, in which the soldiers were singing 'The Star Spangled Banner'?"

Harry was nonplused. It didn't sound like such a bad idea. "Listen," he struck back, "I don't have to listen to a dude."

"A dude, sir?"

"Yeah, a French dude. Wearing gloves, in an office, in the middle of the day. I suppose you have spats on, too."

The Consul looked down at his hands. "Oh, these," he said, holding out his gloved limbs. "I'm sorry, sir, if they offend you. But you see, I wear gloves because, unfortunately, I lost my arm fighting for my country. I merely keep the artificial hand covered to avoid embarrassment."

He bowed punctiliously and left, before Harry could get the egg off his face.

There is another story about Harry Cohn which is too characteristic to pass, even though it involves a slight deviation from Joe Breen and his initial adventures. It is told by William Perlberg, a producer of fame, who at the time worked at Columbia. In his capacity as producer, he was approached by Herman Mankiewicz for a job.

Herman was one of the pioneer "figures" of Hollywood. In his best days, he had given a lift-over to many a neophyte moviemaker, including Bill Perlberg. Herman was basically a writer, and a talented one; but he was always doing himself out of a job because he was his own worst enemy. He was argumentative, loud, self-opinionated, and so on. When he came to Perlberg, he was finally down, and out.

Perlberg listened to Herman sympathetically and at last agreed. "Listen, Herman," he said, "I'll hire you for my picture. But I have to talk to you like a Dutch uncle. You talk too much. You should learn to keep your mouth shut. You and Harry Cohn couldn't be in the same room together for five minutes. He'd say something, you'd contradict him, pretty soon you'd both be shouting, you'd insult him, and that afternoon you'd be out on the streets again looking for another job. Now what I want to do is make a deal with you.

"Come over to work with me, but *stay away* from Harry Cohn. You know what that means. Stay out of the dining room. *You* know the way Harry comes in and sits at the head of the table and pontificates. You couldn't stand it. So stay out. Bring your own lunch in a box, or go up to the corner drugstore and eat, or skip lunch. But no executive dining room for you. Is that a deal?"

Mankiewicz was in no position to be choosy. He agreed.

For two faithful weeks he abided by his assurance. Every day at lunchtime he padded his way up to the drugstore on the corner of Gower and Sunset and sat dolefully on a stool, while he munched on grilled cheese sandwiches.

At last, the pressure was too much. Herman had images of Harry sitting up there on his chair, and maybe passing remarks about him. It was a necessity. He had to defend himself.

Perlberg was quietly lifting a spoon of soup to his lips when Herman made his entrance. The spoon clattered into the bowl.

Ignoring him, Herman took a quiet seat at the far end of the table, at the opposite end from Harry's throne. He ate busily, not talking, only listening.

Presently Cohn appeared. He hesitated in the doorway, surveyed the table with one sweeping flick of the eyes, made a mental note, and then walked over to his chair. When he sat down, a silence fell over the dining room. Nobody wanted to make a statement, lest Harry pick it up and make an issue of it.

Harry cleared his throat, and opened the proceedings. "Saw a picture last night," he said. *"Lizzy Glutz's Wedding."*

He waited for a reaction. When none came, he added the coup de grace. "It stunk."

Everybody let this pass. Unfortunately, however, the picture had been made by a dear friend of Herman Mankiewicz, and the execution went through him like a knife. He lifted a coffee cup to his lips in the vacuum of silence, hesitated, and then decided what the hell. "You didn't like it?" he asked carefully.

A gleam of dark light went across Harry Cohn's eyes. He had a taker. "No, I didn't like it," he repeated. "It stunk."

Herman started to turn red. "What makes you say it stunk?"

Harry shifted in his chair. "Well, I'll tell you, Mankiewicz," he said, leaning forward. "I have a secret device for telling me if a picture stinks. My ass tells me."

Herman simply stared back in a hostile way.

"If my cheeks settle down comfortably into the seat," continued Cohn, "I know it's a good picture. If they start to twitch, it's a lousy picture. Does that answer your question?"

Mankiewicz put down his coffee cup. "Mr. Cohn," he

brayed in his usual tones, "what makes you think you have the *Monitor Ass* of the universe? Are you wired for sound to ten million other asses so you're somehow infallible?"

That afternoon, Herman was out on the streets again.

Getting back to Breen, it must be remembered that the mainspring of his vitality was the fact that he nurtured not the slightest seed of self-doubt regarding his mission or his rectitude. He was right, the moviemakers were wrong, and that was that.

Animated by this feeling, he simply plunged into the community with both feet, and enjoyed it to the fullest. His financial rewards were proportionate to his contributions to the Hollywood scene. He had a handsome home in Holmby Hills, across the street from the actor Frank Morgan, as well as the biggest piece of real estate in the beach colony. His descriptions of his running battle with Morgan's pet Great Dane, who insisted on relieving himself on Breen's well-manicured front lawn each morning, were epic in proportion. The dog was too big to go out and shout at, so Breen used to stand at his window in his pajamas pounding on the glass pane, while, as the story grew, the mound left behind by the animal grew bigger, and Bigger, and BIGGER!

Breen cultivated what might be called the Irish Mafia in Southern California in that day, and became one of the central characters in that influential group. The list was star-studded, from Pat O'Brien and Jack Haley to Loretta Young and Irene Dunne, and thence to directors like Leo McCarey and Jack Ford, and all the way up to the head of production at Twentieth Century-Fox, Winfield Sheehan. There was even talk of how the cowboy star Hoot Gibson pulled out his irons at a party at Breen's and did a mock shoot-up of the front parlor.

Add to this Joe's acquaintance with some of the Central European figures, such as Pasternak, Felix Jackson, and Henry Koster together with Winny Sheehan's wife, the opera singer Jeritza, and such personages as the young Sam Spiegel, and you have the definition of a man in the very thick of things. In fact, it is told that Joe put up his Malibu house as bond, in guarantee that Spiegel would not become a public charge, when that eventually eminent producer ran into some bad financial luck and was stuck across the border in Mexico.

A measure of Joe's acceptance in the film Industry can be gathered from the fact that, after seven years on the Code job, he was offered the position of head of production at RKO Studios. He resigned from the Motion Picture Association, and plunged into a whirlwind program of moviemaking, thus turning into the very image of the Man against whom he had bent his best efforts.

The honeymoon in this position was brief. Joe soon discovered that the main stockholders in RKO were more interested in this corporation as a tool of equity maneuvers than they were in the film program. After one year, Joe left RKO, and in no time at all was back at the old stand as Director of the Code.

As a result of his madcap assault on the movie capital, Joe reduced the studios to what can only be described as a state of talking to themselves. Strangely, they all sounded like echoes of Breen himself. In demonstration of this, I reproduce a memo, circulated from the files of a major studio, and so dated by now as to be beyond the statute of limitations. It was written as an "in house" commentary by a minor executive, regarding a new book which an eager producer had bought. It goes like this:

> I have read this charming piece of philosophical crap and find quite a few items that should be avoided in the script.
> To establish the pansy character will be purely a matter of casting, as he will not be allowed one line or gesture to point up his weakness. In fact, if he makes one slip he will be thrown out on his effeminate behind.
> Any inference that Victor wants to take a nigger wench on the boat for purposes of keeping his prostate in condition will be rejected. It would be wiser, in fact, to eliminate the

colored gal entirely. However, if an acceptable spot is found for her, you'll have to cover that left tit that the author seems to like to play with. And making it a white girl won't help any.

Buddy must not be characterized as a raper of little girls. Nor even of big girls. And you will please keep his hands out of his pockets.

Any lines of dialogue from the Christ-like character that seem to condone the fact that La Rue was an abortionist will cause Mr. Breen and other orthodox Catholics to throw up their hands in horror and generally kick hell out of your picture. La Rue had better be in for some other crime.

It may also hamper the adaptation of this story to know that the British censor will not allow the name of Christ, or Jesus, or any quotation from Christ, on the screen. Any use of such words will require an alternate shot for the British market, unless you want the London exchange to do their own butchering.

The words "son of a bitch," without which the author could not have written the book, are not allowed on the screen.

I'm afraid there's not much left but eleven men in a boat and a hell of a lot of wind. I hope you can get an acceptable story worked out, as I think the characters are swell.

P.S. And don't forget that snakes can empty a theater faster than stink bombs.

5 The Rookie Rises from the Bench

THIS, THEN, was the Code, when I got aboard the merry-go-round in the fall of 1944. The music of the steam calliopes was tootling loudly and uninhibitedly, the tracks were well greased, and the wooden stallions were all going up and down. After a few tentative circles, it would be time to begin reaching for the brass rings.

The routines which had been proven efficient through long usage had crystallized into veritable rubric. For instance, it was the fixed custom to start apprentices on the Code staff by assigning them to a serial with Harry Zehner. The scripts for these stylized and venerable forms were the size of Manhattan telephone books and would tend to make one blanch at the sight of them. They were sixteen or twenty-four episodes in length, each new segment beginning with the cheating premise ". . . what you really didn't know at the end of the last chapter, when the heroine was going over the cliff in a flaming automobile, was that the hero . . . etc., etc." However, the problems posed by these mild monstrosities were so kindergarten in character as to be practically immune to the clumsiness of Code beginners.

Harry, the Freshman Coach, was a suave, symmetrical man, whose simplicity was the result of experience, not of naïveté. He had regular, handsome features, a shock of wavy gray hair, and swarthy Bavarian coloring to his skin. He was perhaps an even six feet in height, chesty of build, and had a certain subdued power in his walk.

Harry tended to go plowing through the pages of these serials like there was no tomorrow. Holding a colored pencil in his hand, he would mark places where it was incumbent to extend cautions against excessive brutality, or extremes of gruesomeness. He would then dog-ear the page for the roundup, when it came time to write a letter to the producer. In rare instances, he would even score passages that seemed to call for too much decolletage.

He had a horror against missing something in a script that somebody else had marked. He was inclined to take it as a reflection on his Germanic thoroughness. It became a game to catch a spot that Harry had not marked. He would jump up and cry, "I marked it! I marked it! I just forgot to turn down the corner of the page. See!" And he would hold up the script for you to inspect, and even come across the room and thrust it under your nose to make sure you were convinced.

A few years after my blood bath with Harry, it was another novice, Morris Murphy, who was being subjected to the same routine. Big Murph had by this time chewed his way through the obligatory half-dozen or so serials and was getting fed up with them. He was also getting annoyed at the manner in which Harry was belaboring the obvious. After all, it does not take more than once to learn how to say (in the letter to the studio), "The clunk on the head on page nineteen should be completed out-of-frame."

When Harry repeated these tiresome instructions for the umpteenth time, Murph finally did a slow burn, and looked up. "Harry," he said petulantly, "for God's sake, don't be so patronizing."

Harry jumped to his feet in indignation. "What do you mean?" he demanded. "I've never kissed anybody's ass in my whole life!"

Murph spent the rest of the day leading Harry to diction-
aries and giving him a lesson in semantics.*

With all his innocence, there was a certain elegance to
Harry. He could speak flawless German, and when he died he
was studying Russian too. Harry had made a pact with life,
and to him it was a velvet rut. He kept bees, for a little side
money, and lived in a big old Spanish house that overlooked
Universal Studios, where he had been assistant to Carl Lae-
mmle, the boss, for years. He could sit back, put his feet up on
the desk, light up a meerschaum pipe, and speak, in a voice
that sounded like warm embers, of the big romance he had had
in Geyser National Park, a fling for which he threw away a
good job at the Waldorf-Astoria Hotel.

Harry sometimes tended to be prolix. He would drone on at
inordinate lengths about banalities. One morning in the daily
"huddle" he was reciting an endless story that he had read the
day before. At last, even he became aware of the growing
tedium. He checked himself, looked around at the suffering
faces of the staff, and asked politely, "Am I going on too long?
Am I boring anyone?"

Arthur Houghton, who was sitting straight up in his chair,
with eyes alert as a lynx, spoke up at once. "No, no, Harry," he
assured, "keep going. Because as long as you're talking, you're
not smoking that goddam pipe!"

When Harry got his final heart attack, it was as free of
intricacies as his very life. He was in Texas with his wife. He
felt a drastic pang. He stumbled to a couch. He looked up at
Mary. "This is it!" he said worriedly.

It was.

I marked it.

* Another classic gauche which should not be passed up here is narrated
by Monsignor Devlin, the "technical advisor" for the Los Angeles Chancery Office. Called to a studio to give his opinion on one of the early
Casanova-type films, he complained to the producer that the leading man
was a source of concern. Asked why, he said that the fellow was "quite a
libertine." A smile of relief flooded the executive's face. "Oh, sure, Monsignor," he enthused. "So are we all. We all *love* liberty!"

. . .

"Huddle" was the heart of the Code operation, as I found out the next morning. It started at ten o'clock sharp, like assembly call. It was nothing more or less than a story conference, in which the staff members reported on the scripts they had read on the previous day. It was during the huddle that decisions were made and lines of strategy were drawn up as to how this problem would be met, or that riddle dealt with. After the huddle, the staff members scattered and went their separate ways, some to studios for knock-down-drag-out fights with producers, some to the projection room to review pictures, some to write letters on scripts they had covered, and some to plunge into yet another script. Keeping up with the endless flow of scripts that poured through the office was like trying to run up a hill of sand. While the main body of the work was done on the scripts before the productions reached the sound stages, the right was always reserved to see the picture also, to check how accurately the producers had accommodated our various demands. Every letter written on a script and sent out to a studio contained the stock closing paragraph: "As you know, our final judgment will be based on the finished picture." It also contained the identical final salutation, "Cordially yours," even though we had just finished ripping the script to pieces. Every letter was also signed, no matter by whom written, by the Code Director, to give the appearance of uniformity and of monolithic power.

Not knowing all this, yet, I floated into my first huddle with my mind as uncluttered as a blank slate. I watched the quick moves made by the various staff members, under the hawklike eye of Joe Breen. Joe Breen had one good eye, and one bad eye, which drooped slightly. It was the droop of disillusionment with life.

Joe finally called out *Monster from the Deep* (a serial) from the daily script list. He then sat back, tucked his thumbs into the corners of his vest, and smiled.

"I read it," said Harry, nodding.

"Anything in it?" asked Joe.

"No. The usual," replied Harry.

Joe turned to me. "Did you read it, young man?" he wanted to know.

I had been astounded that Harry was finished with it already. I had become stupefied with reading it the day before and had stacked it to one side. That night, I had gone to the show to catch up on some of the pictures I had missed in the theologate. Foolishly, I told the truth. "No," I said, "I only read about half."

Joe Breen galvanized forward like someone had given him a goose. "You haven't *finished* it?" he yelped. "Listen, young fellow, we run a daily around here, not a weekly."

I turned scarlet.

"What the hell does he think this is—a country club?" he continued. "Anybody with an eye in his ass could read one of those things in one sitting." He gazed around at the staff for confirmation. All hands, knowing that this was coming, simply maintained their silence.

Breen turned his stare back at me. I bristled, but bit my tongue instead. Breen saw the hostility, and secretly liked it. "You get out of here after this huddle's over and finish up that script before lunch," he said.

I nodded slowly, accepting the order. The animosity and the grudging admiration between the Sorcerer and the Apprentice had begun.

Those were the days before the free-form types of movies, with fractured time sequences, came into the popularity that they enjoy today. Pictures were constructed with the rigidity of a sonnet, so they could be summarized according to formula. The heart of the story was "the Problem." The body of the story had to do with the steps taken to solve the problem. If the problem was unsolved, the story was a tragedy (in the Aristotelian sense). If the problem was solved, the story was, in the Greek usage of the word, a comedy. A comedy in the classic sense is not necessarily funny. It only means a happy ending.

From the point of view of the Code, the morality or the immorality of a story had little to do with the problem. It had to do with the quality of the steps taken to solve the problem. These were either right or wrong. If they were wrong, they should be labeled as such. It should not be left up to the discretion of an immature mind to decide for himself or herself whether the characters had acted rightly or wrongly. This was too important a consideration to leave to luck. Therefore, the *quality* of the solutions used in the plot would be spelled out in words of one syllable. This device was largely invented by Joe Breen, and was called "the Voice for Morality."

The nearest equivalent of the Voice for Morality would be the Greek chorus. If this device seems slightly awkward now, and slightly bald-faced in its lack of trust of the audience, it must be remembered that the only other medium of mass family entertainment at that time was the radio. The movie theater was not the sophisticated place it is now. It was the most influential of all the entertainment media of its time, and was frequented by audiences of every mental color in the spectrum, from sage to just plain stupid. Even the Bible, which did not stop to comment on the morality of the conduct of its cast of characters, enjoyed more relative liberty in reporting its stories. But then, the Bible was limited in its reading audience pretty much to adults.

The motto in those days was to try to make pictures "reasonably acceptable to reasonable people." That phrase had a nice round ring to it, and was almost beyond challenge, since it seemed to put the complainer in the wrong camp. As this motto wore out, another substitute grew up and took its place. It was that Hollywood would try to make films that would "neither offend the innocent, nor frustrate the intelligent." I fear that I was the sole inventor of this slogan, but when Joe Breen heard it, his ears immediately perked up, and he knew that I had arrived as a Code Man full force.

The key to all this intricate approach to story doctoring was, however, the problem. Unless the problem of a story could be stated with clarity and succinctness, there was no proper handling of the material as a whole. Therefore, Joe instituted a discipline in huddle of beginning all story recitations by first stating the problem. So thoroughly did he put trainees through this calesthenic that one eventually acquired a diamond-bright ability at telling a story in capsule.

This discipline was a stumbling block to Big Murph, when it came his turn to be indoctrinated. Doc Dougherty and I had been campaigning with him very intensely to impress him with Joe's demand that stories be synthesized correctly. But Murph had a florid streak in his soul and enjoyed giving his own rendition of things. He wanted to give the version of "the man in the street." Doc and I hammered away, insisting that this would not do. He would have to begin by rote: "This is the story of [a carpenter, a soldier, a housewife, a chorus girl, a king, or whatever] who . . ." Then you stated the protagonist's problem. After that, you sorted out the protagonist's attempts to solve the problem.

I fear we dinned this routine into Murph's head beyond the point of no return. He became frightened of it. It was too rigid, and altogether suppressive of his own individual personality. Instead of getting more familiar with it, therefore, he began to freeze on it.

Nobody on the staff will ever forget the day Murph was called on to recite his first story in huddle. Joe had given him a generous time to get ready. At last he assigned him to a script as "first reader," which meant that he would have to write the letter on it.

At huddle next morning, Murph was secretly mumbling to himself, rehearsing his condensation of the script. He kept glancing nervously at Joe, until he was in a cold sweat. At last Joe made a check on the daily work sheet and called out the title of Murph's script. Murph turned white.

He cleared his throat as though he were touching the gas

pedal a few times. Joe's thumbs by this time had found the armpits of his vest.

"This is a story," began Murph . . .

Joe did not budge.

". . . set in a little fishing village on the west coast of Oregon . . ."

Joe's thumbs flew out of his vest. "Who gives a shit where it's set?" he barked. "I don't give a goddam if it's set in Timbuctoo! What's the story *about?*"

Murph's voice hitched up a notch. "About . . . ?" he essayed.

"Yes—*about!* Tell us what the story's *about.* What's the *problem?*"

Murph cleared his throat again, and his voice slipped a hitch higher. "The problem?" he stalled.

"Yes, the *problem.* All well-constructed stories can be stated in terms of a problem. What's the *problem?*"

Murph's tongue ran nervously over his lips, his cheeks were half ashen, and his voice went into falsetto. "Well," he began, his throat getting tighter and tighter, "the problem of this story is . . ." He got stuck and looked in panic at Joe, and his eyes suddenly glazed over. "Judas, Joe," he appealed, "I've run out of gas!"

The situation dissolved like light. Everybody laughed until the tears ran out of their eyes, including Breen, while Murph looked around the room as if at a jury.

"Murph," said Joe at last, "I've been misled. They told me you were a good man on your feet."

"That's the trouble," spouted Murph with nervous laughter, "I'm sitting down."

Joe reached into his vest pocket, pulled out a cigar, and slid it down the table to Murph. "Take this," he said, "maybe it'll help you get your breath back."

Murph broke the cigar out of its cellophane wrapper, bit off the end, spit out the fleck, and Doc chivalrously struck a match and held it up for him. While Murph was puffing away, still shaky, Joe said, "All right now—if you're comfortable, let's start again."

Murph made a grand little gesture with the cigar, smiled in a self-bolstering way, and plunged in. "This is a story . . . set-in-a-little-fishing-village-on-the-west-coast-of-Oregon—"

"Good!" exclaimed Joe. "Now that we've got that out of the way, what's the problem?"

Murph considered momentarily.

"Stand up if it helps," coached Joe.

Murph came to a conclusion. "I don't think it has one."

"It doesn't have any problem?" queried Joe, unbelievingly. "Then it's a lousy story."

"That's *it!*" finished Murph. "It's just a lousy story!"

Joe's drillmaster techniques in running the Code were, of course, a natural consequence of his days in the newspaper business. In the Code office, he handled himself in the style of a hardboiled city editor whose attitude toward his minions was "Never mind the editorializing—we have a department for that—just give us the facts." It fitted the Hollywood scene admirably, since the philosophy among the production-line producers of those days was "We don't want it great. We just want it Friday."

In fact, it is undoubtedly accurate to say that Joe never did graduate into any other frame of mind except that of a news-paperman. It would not be right to say that he was a movie fan, in any meaningful sense of the word. His basic relish was not in the films themselves. He was not the type to pursue a picture for the pleasure of sharing in a small masterpiece, nor did he have any enthusiasm for the foreign film, which was then in its embryonic stages. He liked *Open City* and *Shoeshine* and *Bicycle Thief* when they came along, but he wasn't jumping out of his skin about them. In fact, he mistrusted them. He rigidly resisted the liberties these works began to take, and was adamant in refusing to approve the scene of the little boy starting to pi-pi in *Bicycle Thief*. It made no difference that the youngster's back was turned, and that he never did quite get to perform his intention. It is not that Joe was out of touch with these realities of life. He had six children of his own. It was simply that scenes like these were the thin edge of the wedge. To approve them was to establish precedent. "For Christ's sake," he would say, "you pass stuff like that and the next thing you know you have a scene of a dapper young fellow in Paris standing at a pissoir, leaking away with a smile on his face. And then, along comes Marilyn Monroe, walking like this [and he began to demonstrate] and our boy turns around, and does a big tip of his straw hat, and says 'Bon jour, mademoiselle,' and she says, 'Bon jour, mon ami. What are you doing?' "

Joe's basic interest was rather in the events that surrounded the making of films. When he went to a studio, for instance, he exuded the atmosphere of a newshound with his nose close to the ground sniffing for a story. Actually, it is more accurate to say that he was more interested in the story he might be able to report *after* he got home from the studio than he was in the central issue of the conference itself. Much of Joe's dynamism in his work came from the zest he had in covering the Scene.

I remember well a case in point. Doc Dougherty and I, both of us fairly new but both of us promising, had been assigned to an MGM script of some consequence. I believe it was the long-awaited first script for Clark Gable, "The King," after his return from duty in World War II. It was advertised as though this were something: "Gable's back—and Garson's got him!"

Doc and I had been moderately scandalized by a perusal of this script. We came into huddle next morning, and what Doc didn't remember by way of dirty lines and outrageous situations, I did. Joe kept sitting at the head of the table, taking all this in, his tail feathers beginning to stand up like a peacock's. He sensed a "situation."

After a huddle, Joe called Doc and myself into his office and put through a phone call to Eddie Mannix, the General

Manager of the mighty MGM. He told Eddie that it was imperative that we see him right away. A serious studio investment was at stake. A conference was set.

We all climbed into Joe's Cadillac, and while the chauffeur drove, Joe cross-questioned us again, in minute detail. We repeated, item by item, the problems suggested by the script, including what both Doc and I thought to be a lesbian character who seemed to have a lech for other girls. Such a characterization was unheard of in those days.

By the time we reached Metro, Joe was well briefed. He swarmed up the few steps of the Thalberg Building like he was invading the place.

Mannix was a gravel-voiced Mick, with a countenance of a Boxer hound, but with an instantaneous mind and a reputation that his word was as good as his bond. He wanted to know what the hell the fuss was about.

Joe told him, giving the impression that he had read the script line for line. He also threw in about the lesbian.

Mannix was taken aback. Either he had read the script hastily, while Joe was on his way over in the limousine, or he was relying on somebody's summary, in the same manner as Joe. At any rate, the mood of the encounter was of two poker players, who were bluffing the daylights out of each other.

Mannix said, "Wait a minute. I don't know nothing about no lesbian. Where the hell's a lesbian in that script?"

Joe turned to us in a startled manner. "Of course there's a lesbian in the script," he said, counting on us. "Wouldn't you fellows say there's a lesbian in the script?"

We solemnly assured Mannix that there was a lesbian in the script. We could hardly back out now, leaving Joe high and dry.

Mannix scratched his head in puzzlement. "Listen, Breen," he rasped, "if there's a lesbian in that script, I'll suck your ass at Seventh and Broadway."

Joe looked like somebody had turned all the lights on. He understood language like this, and liked it. "All right, Eddie," he agreed, "what do you say we both reread the script very carefully—I'll admit that with the rush of business I had to skim through it quickly—and if I'm right, I'll take you up on that!"

With that, Joe sent Doc and myself packing back to the office, while he himself went off to Malibu to scour through the pages. It is to be presumed that Mannix went into hiding to do the same thing.

The next day, when Joe sat us down to go over the script more carefully, he told Doc and myself that, in his opinion, we had been overly solicitous, and that he personally did not think there was a lesbian in the script. However, there was plenty else, and, in agreement with us, he himself sat down to compose a scorching letter to the studio. A copy of this letter is still in the Production Code morgue, and it is noteworthy not only for its meticulous detail, but also for a classic faux pas.

In dictating to his secretary, he described the character of Harry, the lead, "as a kind of a cocksman." This was a favorite word with Joe. However, the secretary was mortified; and, since it was a story about seamen and crews and the like, she automatically cleaned it up and presumed the word to be "coxman."

Al Lynch caught the error and objected strongly to Joe. Breen, he claimed, would expose himself to ridicule to sign his name to a letter like this. What if the press got hold of a copy of the letter?

Joe brushed Al's worry aside with a simple "Nonsense!" He couldn't care less. It was the "situation" which had interested Joe, and not these peripheral small points. "Coxman," "cocksman"—what was the difference? The incident was over, and it was all yesterday's newspaper to him.

Joe's high roll, in going out to accost the studio without having read the script, was not a totally new experience for him. In going back through the records, one discovers that he employed practically the same methods from the very outset. It seems that he jumped on the bandwagon, praising Dr.

Wingate and his office for managing to get *any* kind of story from that notorious novel *Sanctuary*. Later, in the same memorandum, he admitted hastily, out of the side of his mouth, that he had, unfortunately, not read the original, but was relying on hearsay. Just as Joe was not a natural movie-goer, so also he was not a natural reader. He had the style and attitude of a man of the classics, but actually I think the classics bored him.

It might also seem that he placed extravagant reliance on the judgment of two youngish members of his staff in committing himself to this adventure. He did not think so. It was in harmony with his theory of executive comportment, for which, as usual, he had a favorite story to tell. This one involved the famous George Eastman, founder of the Eastman Kodak Company.

Eastman himself, it seems, was an enthusiastic movie buff. One of his chief hobbies was to travel to far places and to bring home pictures of his private adventures.

One evening he had gathered together a group of friends to view the films of a safari in Africa. In the audience was Will Hays, high-button shoes and all.

When the showing was over, Hays cornered Eastman. Still vibrant with excitement, Hays asked, "What about those shots of the lions leaping right into the camera? How did you get those? With a long-range lens?"

"No," replied Eastman. "I was right there."

"Did a lion ever maul you?"

"Oh, no. Nothing like that. I took precautions. You see, I had an expert rifleman in my retinue. His position was directly behind me. Just as the lion reached the top of his spring, the rifleman fired, and the beast dropped dead at my feet."

Hays, dumfounded, finally found the words for the next, inevitable question. "What if . . . the rifleman missed?" he wanted to know.

Eastman harrumphed. "Oh, well, you can't think about that," he said. "After all, you have to trust your organization."

Breen took the lesson of this story to heart and, as a result, never overturned a member of his staff publicly. The consequence was a body of men who did not fear making a decision.

If this was his strong point, however, there was a compensating human weakness within the confines of the Code family itself. It was noticeable that the recitations of Joe's adventures almost always had to do with those experiences in which he was the sole participant. If there was a witness from the Code staff, Joe had a tendency to clam up. If one of us who had accompanied Breen on a studio visit thought to make mileage with the old boy by giving the rest of the staff some of the highlights of the meeting, it was a matter of basic survival to feature Joe's performance, and his alone. While you were talking, he would sit back, twirling a ringful of keys around his finger, and would grin modestly at a recitation of how smartly he had maneuvered. But the minute the conversation switched off the central actor, Breen would more than likely roll over onto one of his generous cheeks, and expel gas. Then he would look off vacantly into the middle distance and, still twirling the keys, would start whistling tunelessly, "Button up your overcoat, you belong to me." That was the signal for the perceptive man to sign off.

If someone were dense enough to push on anyway, Breen would start whistling impatiently, ". . . be careful crossing streets, o-oooh, o-oooh . . ." until you were finished. He would then glare flatly, hunch forward, lift one finger into the air, and say, "Very interesting, but not true." The phrase became a kind of bitter joke around the Code office, which we always mimicked behind his back. He would then launch into a tangent. "Now I'll tell you the *real* story *behind* the story you just told," he would say. He had an unbearable urge to give you the facts behind the facts. It was all part of the newspaper syndrome.

6 From Offstage We Hear the Scream of a Naked Woman

By THE END of the first year, I came to the realization that I had not yet saved anybody from anything. In fact, it was beginning to look like the shoe might be on the other foot.

However, I was observing what the Irish called "a power of wonders." From these, too, one learned.

Here is an example.

Geoffrey Shurlock had reviewed a film from Warner Brothers which contained a semi-nude bathtub scene. The studio was balking over making any cuts. Geoff reported to Joe, who listened to Geoff's description of the scene with great intentness, his fingers drumming on his desktop while he absorbed the issue. "That's it?" he asked, when Geoff had finished. "Yes," agreed Geoff.

"Miss Taylore," he bellowed to his secretary, "get me Hal McChord at Warner Brothers!" Hal was the Chief Editor, and a high-caliber man. While he was waiting, Joe's fingers kept up the filigree work. He was thinking.

"Here's your call, Mr. Breen."

Joe flipped a button, grabbed up the receiver, and stiffened in his chair as though he'd been electrocuted. "Hello—HAL?" he roared.

"Yeah, Joe?" hesitated the voice at the other end.

"How's the old sonofabitch?" Joe assaulted him. "How's that ticker of yours?"

"Fine, Joe, fine. What's up?"

"Well, boy—listen." Joe's voice suddenly dropped into a tone of deep conspiracy. "I got something to tell you. I just came in from the East. Some of my friends've been talking to me about a great idea. We're going to pool our finances and open up a chain of small theaters, you know, specialty stuff, and we want to let you in."

"Sounds swell," said Hal.

"It won't cost much," continued Joe. "By comparison, I mean. We're each putting in about a hundred thousand bucks, but you can have in for about twenty-five thousand. You see, what we really want is a small, classy whorehouse circuit. No worry about a Code seal on the pictures, or anything like that. Adults only."

"Terrific!" chuckled Hal wickedly.

"It *is* terrific. We'll make a ton of dough. Now, my part of the deal was to call you the minute I arrived in Hollywood, and get the inside track on pictures from your studio. Everyone agrees, they're just the kind of pictures we want!"

Hal had that strange feeling that his glass eye had just been stolen. "Somebody's gotten to you," he sputtered.

"What d'ya mean, pal?" Joe wanted to know.

"That bastard Geoffrey's been talking to you." Hal was laughing by this time.

"I don't know what you're talking about, baby. Did Geoff throw one of your pictures in the shithouse?"

By now, Hal wasn't quite that sure. "Oh, hell no. It's nothing. He's just bellyaching about a bathing sequence in a picture we showed him yesterday. He says he can see all the way down to this dame's ass. He's crazy."

Joe's eyes shone diabolically. "Well, this *is* coincidence," he marveled. "You see, I *told* the boys back East I was right. It's the hand of God. That's exactly what we're looking for. Something with a *lift* to it. Nothing pornographic, you know—we'd be arrested. But a nude woman, just quickly, in passing. Perfect! That's *punch!*"

"Listen, Joe—" Hal started to interject.

"Hold on, Hal, let me finish. Now *you'll* be our pipeline. With you there, we'll get first crack at your regular product. How about it?"

"You . . . you . . ." Hal began to stammer. "Look, Joe, the scene's all right. I'm telling you. Geoff's off his rocker. He's the only one who's objecting to it."

Joe spanked the desk with his hand, and half leaped off his chair. "That's *it*, then," he enthused at the top of his lungs. "If Geoff doesn't like it, it's *in!*"

"Joe. Joe, baby? JOE! Cut it out. You win. I'll take the goddamn scene out of the picture!"

"Good!" agreed Joe. "But look, Hal. Give my offer some thought. I'm serious."

As part of my indoctrination, Joe once took me to lunch at a fine restaurant, where he was to meet with a banker. "This'll be good for you to hear," he assured.

It must be remembered that when the Code first started, many of the studios were in harsh financial straits. "Paramount's in 77-B" was the shorthand way of referring to it.

To protect their investments, the banks insisted that the various picture makers get a letter of clearance from the Code office, stating that the script was at least *basically* acceptable, before they would release funds to finance production. This backing, which was ultimate in a free enterprise system, was Joe's secret weapon, and was one of the most powerful factors in making the Code a vital part of the Hollywood scene.

But now it was a dozen years or more since the inception of the system, and the early enthusiasm for virtue was beginning to wane. It came to Joe's attention that this particular bank was going to put up the money for the making of a film from a notorious novel of the day. This rankled Joe, and so he had called up the Vice President in Charge of Film Investments and invited him to a powwow over a bowl of soup. Seated in a leather-lined booth when we came into the restaurant was a

suave, obsidian-eyed Italian, his thoughts totally hidden behind a noncommittal face.

Joe lost no time in completing the amenities, and the soup.
Then he asked, "Don't you feel any responsibility for putting
up depositors' money to support so filthy an enterprise?"

The dark-eyed fellow looked through him like he didn't
exist. "Not especially," he replied.

"Without you, it would not be possible to make this picture.
You know that, don't you?" pressed Breen.

The banker folded his interlocked fingers before his mouth.
"I suppose that could be said," he agreed, and waited for
Breen to make his main point.

"Isn't this attitude a little bland?" Breen wanted to know.
"You're washing your hands of responsibility like Pontius
Pilate."

This nicked the composure of the banker. "It is not considered to be the business of the bank to inquire into the
purposes for which borrowed money is used," he said. "We are
up against the same dilemma if a person qualifies for a loan,
and we find out later he wanted to use the money to start a
war. What are we going to do? Withdraw the money? It puts
us in the odious position of making a judgment on the quality
of the war. Who are we to say the war is a correct war or an
incorrect war? It does not seem to me to be the business of
bankers to make such qualitative judgments. We are not
moralists. Banks have no special knowledge or talent to take
such a position as moral arbiters. We just lend the money, and
let others decide on the rightness or wrongness of its uses."

Joe began to emit a kind of steam of anger that came when
he was frustrated or appalled by a point of view. He looked off
into space, as if he were sorting nervously for a counterillustra-
tion. "Well," he said, still staring into the air, "the best
business I know of is the whorehouse trade. Suppose I came to
you and said I wanted to open a string of cathouses. I offer you
the best references, and back my request with gilt-edge col-

lateral. Do you mean to tell me you wouldn't be concerned?"

The banker squirmed a bit. "Ye-e-s," he said hesitantly.

"You're goddamn right you would be!" snapped Breen, looking down now into the middle of the impenetrable eyes. "You know you'd get your ass torn off by little old Irish Grandmothers who deposit in your bank, if they found out you were putting their funds into a chain of whorehouses. Am I right?"

The banker laughed a little sickly and spread his hands reasonably. "Of course," he admitted.

"Well, where do you draw the line?"

"I really don't know," confessed the banker. "I'll have to take this question under consideration, but I can't answer you now."

Breen, seeing that he wasn't going to get any further, let the matter go with a long exasperated sigh. His attack had dropped into a dark, bottomless sinkhole.

Julian Blaustein tells a story on himself that occurred somewhere in this period of time. He was connected with the film *Portrait of Jenny* for the Selznick Releasing Organization, in the capacity of editorial supervisor. He had gotten a letter on the script for this production, and had come over to the Code office to discuss certain points.

The letter had objected to a sexual encounter, enjoyed by Jenny on, let us say, page 60. Julian, thinking to get away with a little larceny, raised a protest over this point in the letter. "You're imagining things," he told Joe. "How could this girl have sex? She isn't even real. She's a phantom—a figment of the mind."

Joe puckered up his lips in thought and weighed this. Then he addressed himself to the script and began flipping pages backwards. "Julie," he invited, "please turn back to page twenty."

Julie obliged.

Joe put a finger on a line in the middle of the page. "What does it say there, in the stage directions?" he asked.

Julie peered. "It says she's drinking tea," he accommodated. "Good!" said Joe. "If she can drink tea, she can fuck."*

In the same vein, an independent producer came into the Code offices one afternoon with a countenance full of innocence and a tone of earnestness in his voice. He had an idea. He wanted to do something worthwhile in life, something that would be a contribution to society. What he would like to do is make a picture on the subject of venereal disease. He knew this was specifically forbidden by the Code, but perhaps this prohibition ought to be reconsidered. He granted it was a delicate subject to put on before mixed family audiences, but, with Joe's help, perhaps a way could be found.

Joe listened to his impassioned argument with a straight and serious mien. For once, he did not interrupt him but kept nodding agreeingly, encouraging the fellow to say more. The poor man swallowed Joe's approving attitude hook, line, and sinker, thinking he was making a breakthrough, and would be the first producer of an exploitation picture on VD carrying a Code Seal. He was counting his millions between words.

When he had talked himself out, Joe raised his finger in an episcopal way. "You impress me," he said. "You have done something I never would have thought possible. You have convinced me of the decency of your intentions."

The man nodded brightly, waiting for Joe to come to the golden words "I approve."

Joe's finger remained in the air, however. "You know how these fellows around here are," he continued confidentially. "They tell you one thing, and they mean another. They say they want to do society a service by making a picture that will

* In a fascinating completion of the historical cycle, it would appear that the same point cropped up again in the case of a recent television program *The Ghost and Mrs. Muir*. Stanley Rubin, the producer, is quoted as having said that he had to take pains to establish that the Ghost had departed each time Mrs. Muir went to bed, lest the suspicion be left lingering that she and the phantom were shacking up together.

enlighten the public, when all they really want to do is get a dirty exploitation picture. But not you. No, I do not feel that about you. I feel you are sincere."

The fellow was nodding his head yes and no vigorously at all the proper places. But when would the sonofabitch get to the point?

"*Therefore*," continued Joe, "I am going to propose an idea to you. Since the only thing you want is to do some good, and you aren't interested in the money—not *just* the money—I have a better suggestion for you. You say that VD is a national scourge that afflicts three million people. But there is an-other—*worse*. You talk about a big audience? This touches the lives of *twenty* million people. *This* is the one you should make!"

"What is that? What is that?" the man blurted out, completely carried away.

"*Heart* disease!" shrilled Breen, his voice soaring with enthusiasm.

The fellow stood there, looking like he'd been shot. "Yeah," he said at last.

"What's the *matter?*" demanded Joe, still keeping his face filled with altruism.

"Well—you know—it's not very dramatic."

"Not DRAMATIC?" cried Breen, scandalized. "My God, man, have you ever had a heart attack?"

"Not . . . exactly. I'd have to think about it."

Joe poked a finger in his direction. "You do that," he said. "It's the most dramatic subject there is."

The fellow was scuffing the floor with the tip of his shoe. He looked up. "In the meantime," he said in a small, hesitant voice, "how about the other?"

"*What* other?"

"You know. VD?"

"Oh no, you can't make a picture about VD." He laughed, as though the whole idea were beyond the taste of idealistic men like themselves. "That's against the Code."

• • •

Of course, it is not to be supposed that the picture makers were without wiles of their own in retaliating. A classic example occurred to Joe's legalistic old familiar, Charley Metzger.

Charley had by some accident been assigned to a sophisticated script. He attacked it with the same zeal as he would have shown in any hack crime picture. In the course of his peregrinations through the script, he came upon a passage in which the writer described a girl as clothed in a "filmy negligee." Quick as a flash, Charley marked the spot and in his letter inserted a warning that no such suggestive garment would be approved in the final picture. The letter also contained many other such cautions.

All in due course the script was resubmitted to the Code office for a second examination, with all the offending items corrected. Charley checked through them very carefully, and when he came to the part about the negligee, found, to his frustration, that the writer had simply scratched out the word "filmy." Forced to push on, Charley did, until he came to the climax of the story. At that point, the settlement of the issue called for a big fight, into which the writer threw everything but the kitchen sink. He described chairs breaking, and mirrors being smashed, and glasses falling off shelves, while the two antagonists were knocking each other from pillar to post (the hero never losing his hat in the melee, of course). Right in the midst of all this gory description, the writer paused for an aside. "From offstage," he penned, "we hear the scream of a naked woman!"

Several years later, when this story had hardened into historical acceptance, the producer of the picture began to add a frill, and to claim that Charley wrote back and demanded that the word "naked" be struck from the script. However, this may have just been an effort to gild the lily.

Strange that Charley should have died of a stroke. One remembers fondly an evening in Hollywood with him, when we were still new and green at the Code work, in which Charley was the host in his lady friend's apartment. It was a good enough time, too. We had a few drinks, exchanged a few laughs, watched him work a few tricks of magic, and even got down to a few rounds of canasta. But, at ten o'clock sharp, Charley reached into his vest pocket and pulled out a watch that looked like a large, gold turnip. He snapped open the lid, said "Yep" to himself, and then turned his watery blue eyes sincerely on me. "Ten o'clock, Jack," he announced. "I always make it a practice to break things up at ten exactly. Because when you come right down to it, the one and only thing we have to sell in our work is—fresh brains."

R.I.P., old strawberry.

A decade or two later, when nostalgia had begun to creep into recollections about the Code operation, a relaxed, twinkling little man, his hands jingling change in his pockets, recounted the efforts of himself and some companions to outmaneuver the Code office.

"We used to burn the midnight oil," he said, "to find ways. So, anyway, this time we were making a comedy, and we remembered a gag from our Catskill Mountain days that we thought was pretty funny. This guy, our comic, is telling his end man that he had just caught a mouse. The end man says, 'Was it hard?' The comic says, 'No, it was easy. I set out two traps. I baited one with apples, and one with nuts.' The end man asks, dripping with innocence, 'Did you catch him by the apples?' To which the comic replies, 'No, I caught him by the nuts!' "

The twinkling fellow jingled the change a bit in his pockets and continued. "We didn't figure we'd get through you Code fellows, but we thought we'd give it a try. We waited till we got your letter throwing the gag out, then came over here full of indignation and argued up a storm. We accused you guys of having dirty minds, and insisted that we were using the term literally. All to no avail, of course. Everybody just smiled in a superior manner and told us to away and try again.

"So what did we do? We went back to the studio and prepared a revised page and sent it back to you. This time the joke was just the same up to the point where the comic says, 'I set out two traps. I baited one with apples, and the other with nuts.' Then the end man asks, 'Did you catch him by the apples?' At which, the comic just looks him in the eye for a long moment, rounds his lips, and says slowly, 'No-o-o-o.' "

The twinkly fellow ran his hands across his lips, straightened out his dimunitive mustache, and grinned. "We didn't get away with that one either," he said.

One distinguished individual, in a moment of artlessness, tried the headlong style of counterattack on Breen. The man was Seymour Nebenzal, who had acquired a prestigious reputation in Europe for his part in the making of the classic entitled, simply, *M*. (The *M* stood for murderer, just as the *A* stood for adultress in Hawthorne's *Scarlet Letter*.) Nebenzal's picture was the vehicle which provided the screen introduction of the ghoulish actor Peter Lorre.

He was in the U.S.A. now, and had submitted an adapted version of his *pièce de résistance* to Breen. Unfortunately, the story contained some inferences of sexual perversion, such as shoe fetishism. The fetish also involved little girls. This was all calculated to make Breen skittish. Three of his children were daughters.

Nebenzal, on the other hand, clung tenaciously to his original material. He was following the rigid axiom of the entertainment world, which said, "Never monkey with a hit." His stubbornness and inflexibility began to aggravate Breen, who began to berate him as only Joe could. The verbal assault was causing Nebenzal pain. Finally, he could stand it no longer. He took the cigarette out of his mouth and held it between two fingers in midair, while he bent over Breen in his swivel chair. "Listen, Mr. Breen," he demanded, "do you *have* to shout? I find it vulgar. Can't we discuss this in a gentlemanly tone of voice?"

Joe flushed. His voice turned suddenly cold. "Very well, Mr. Nebenzal," he said, "I'm vulgar. Get out. You go tell the Board of Directors in New York that you can't do business with me because I'm loud. Tell them it offends your sensibilities. But at the same time, tell them THAT YOU OFFEND *MY* SENSIBILITIES WITH WHAT YOU'RE TRYING TO PUT INTO YOUR GODDAMN PICTURE! Be sure to tell them that, too!"

Nebenzal swallowed his Adam's apple in a gulp of darkening anger, picked up his script, and left the room. But by the time he got back to his office, pragmatism had prevailed, and he returned to the drawing boards and found compromises that were satisfactory all around. The picture was made, with what success it is hard to tell, but certainly not with the reputation of the original.

Joe was arbitrary; there is no doubt about it. He did not feel himself limited to what was down in black and white in the Code. There were even occasions when we knew him to "quote" a Code clause he had invented on the spot. The conspicuous example was, with that Old Testament finger up in the air again, "Remember, the Code forbids nudity, or the suggestion of nudity—*in fact or in silhouette!*" Of course, the Code did nothing of the sort. The italicized words, which Joe would make ring with the rectitude in his voice, were only a bit of hangnail phraseology left over from the initial list of "Do's and Don'ts." But who ever examined the document that exactly? And if, by some accident, a rare legal eagle challenged Joe with the claim that there was no Code clause to cover his objection, Joe would fire back, "I don't give a fiddler's fuck [a favorite] whether it's in the Code or not. I won't pass your scene. Is that clear? I won't pass it. If you want it approved, take it back to the Board of Directors and ask them, because I'm not accepting the responsibility!"

Illustrative of this state of mind was a little incident that took place between Breen and Morris Murphy. Big Murph, all two hundred and forty pounds of him, had just joined the Code staff. Motivated by early fervor, Murph was sitting at his desk, running his hands through his black shock of wavy hair, agonizing over the dry canons of the Code, just as all the rest of us had done in our day.

Joe, having nothing better to do at the moment, began pacing the corridors, jingling his keys, and whistling softly and off tune, "Button up your overcoat . . ." Seeing Murph lost in study, he stopped abruptly and sallied into his office, a quizzical smile on his face. "What're *you* doing, my friend?" he wanted to know.

Murph looked up with the open, warm St. Bernard look that was his characteristic, and smiled slowly. "I'm studying this," he announced, holding up a lemon-yellow copy of the Code.

Joe's eyes roved over Murph, while a dim grin played around his lips. He saw that Murph was proud over being caught doing his homework. Finally he tossed his head in his leprechaun way. "Oh, for crying out loud, put that thing away and come to lunch with me," he said. "You're wasting your time."

"Wasting my time?" echoed Murph, nonplused.

"Certainly. Don't pay any attention to that thing. Just you listen to *me. I* am the Code!"

Actually, and even technically, Joe was not exaggerating with this statement. There is a curious and interesting root of such a claim in the Code itself. Joe grasped it, and I think I too grasped it, perhaps more than any other on the staff, and this bridged many gaps between us. A consideration of this factor will take us on a brief philosophical riff, but it is probably worth it.

In the third of the General Principles, which were in reality *the* Code, it was set down that "Law—divine, natural, or human—shall not be ridiculed, nor shall sympathy be created for its violation."

That statement is full of catches and tricks.

What "divine law" is, or is purported to be, everyone knows. This is the law that comes directly from God, in the only manner that it can, namely through revelation. It is of this body of law that religion is the custodian.

What "human law" is, is obvious. It is the law brought into being by man, with a view to attaining an orderly society. It is usually called "positive law." Since it is made by man, it can also be abolished by man.

But what of the third type of law in this triumvirate, that which is called "natural law"? How is that defined?

Turning to the back of the document, we will find a statement regarding the famous natural law. It is taken from the classic definition of the Scholastic philosophers. "By natural law is understood the law that is written in the hearts of all mankind, the great underlying principles of right and justice dictated by conscience."

This is a beautiful round bit of rhapsodizing, of course. The only trouble with it is that it is not a definition. It is merely a poetic description. It does not tell what the natural law *is*. It only says that it is a series of principles "inscribed on the fleshy tablets of the heart," under the dictation of conscience. What these principles are, in the concrete, is left unsaid. By inference, then, the Code (along with the Scholastic philosophers) says that if you want to know what these principles of "right and justice" are, find them in a "man of conscience." In him, they will be found incarnated. The natural law will be found as a living thing in a living man, a Man of Conscience.

Sam Goldwyn may never have studied medieval philosophy, but in the recesses of his soul he had the correct intuitions; for when it came time for him to laud Breen, he characterized him with the phrase that Breen would have considered perfect. He called Joe "Hollywood's benevolent conscience."

7 The Infinite Kiss and the Hollywood Bed

BY THE END of the second year, a personal experience was, little by little, beginning to emerge. The change was taking place in concurrence with other changes that were under way. Will Hays, whom *Time* magazine described as a bump on a log, finally retired, and his place was taken by suave and dapper Eric Johnston, President of the United States Chamber of Commerce. The old order had shown its first signs of weakening.

Johnston made the mistake of coming out to Hollywood at an early date with the thought that he could charm some of the local mavericks into harmony with the Industry as a whole. Ignoring seasoned advice, he tried the first dance with Harry Cohn. The ogre of Gower Street was no fool. He plied Johnston with honeyed words and perfumed phrases. Johnston came out of the introductory luncheon reeling. He looked around at the people in the Code office with dewy eyes and asked, "What's all this I hear about Harry Cohn? I've been told he's a roughneck. As far as I'm concerned, he's a nice man."

When Harry decided to turn on Johnston, and have *him* for lunch instead of pumpernickel, Johnston had to resort to vulgarities, and reported that he had told Cohn to "take the job [as President of the Association] and stick it up his ass, and break it off." Johnston was an ex-Marine, but he seldom felt the need to employ trench talk.

Eric also had the misfortune of tangling with Sam Goldwyn, who ended their acrimonious public debate with the declaration that "the Industry has survived many vicissitudes, and will probably be able to survive even Eric Johnston."

So stung was the poor man by these affronts to his sense of good manners that he virtually abandoned Hollywood and turned his attention to the foreign market, which was starting to awaken, and where he did a creditable job. But I narrate these facts, which might have a taint of commonness to them, because they shed some light, by indirection, on the character of Joe Breen. He wasn't to be put off by the roughhouse antics of anybody, be he hoodlum, harridan, hustler, or Oscar recipient.

It was Joe who lashed me out into the open and encouraged me to begin finding my own tempos and my own cadences. One of the earliest examples came about as a result of a studio visit in the company of Geoff Shurlock. He and I had been called out to MGM to attend a rehearsal of a song to be performed by Ricardo Montalban and the brilliantly beautiful Esther Williams. The song was slightly suggestive. Later on, actually, it became a "standard." It was called "Baby, It's Cold Outside."

We made a few comments directed toward toning down some of the more pointed lines, to which Montalban did not object, but which did not please Esther Williams. Cornering Geoff and me, she asked in a brittle manner, "Say, do you guys know how babies are made?"

We pretty much ignored her, crediting her pique to an understandable resentment against being "censored."

When I mentioned the episode to Joe, he burned. "What did you say to her in return?" he demanded.

"Nothing, particularly," I replied. "I just kept my dignity."

"Dignity!" he scoffed. "I'd have quickly enough boxed her ears. If she'd said that to me, I'd have said, 'No, madam, I *don't* know. Would you like to show me?' And, by God, if she took me up on it, I'd have insisted that she do it right on the spot."

My very first brush with a producer had been with Andrew Stone. It was in the company of Al Lynch.

Over the years, Andy has been one of the most durable independent producers, and he has done some things memorable for their showmanship. Among others, he bought the great antiquated luxury liner *Ile de France* and sank it deliberately in deep water in an effort to achieve authenticity in one of his pictures. For another, he started a forest fire in Oregon, under controlled conditions, of course, for the same purpose.

His name is a symbol around the Code office for one of the most remarkable arguments urged against Joe Breen in the early days. Joe had objected to something or other in one of Andy's scripts, on the grounds that it was in bad taste. Andy drew himself up and took exception. His family, he wanted Joe to know, was listed in the Blue Book. Therefore, his taste was guaranteed impeccable, and Joe had no right to set himself up as arbiter on what Andy had selected.

What retort the feisty Irishman used is not recorded, possibly because it was unprintable. In any event, by the time I met Andy he was well trained, and the dialogue between himself and Lynch went off with the automatic smoothness of an auction. Mostly I was a spectator. I noticed that Lynch got the bulk of what he wanted, but he made a few compromises and a few concessions. When Andy was gone, I intimated to Lynch with secret satisfaction that we had put the check to "one of those Jewish fellows." Al looked at me in an arch way. "Jewish?" he exclaimed. "Andy's High Episcopalian." He had an afterthought. "What's more, he comes from that citadel of respectability of yours—San Francisco!"

This second information was a greater blow than learning he was a gentile.

There was one fallout of this conference that stuck with me even more deeply. Some of Al's giveaways seemed to me borderline. As such, his performance was an exercise in Situation Ethics; whereas I was still full of the Casuistry of the Jesuits. In other words, each concession became a precedent for the next case. This bothered me, and I was talking about it to Geoff.

"What's wrong with Situation Ethics?" he wanted to know.

"As an approach," I replied, "it lacks consistency. I thought we were here to insure a *uniform* interpretation of the Code."

Geoff gave a little sniff of derision. "You're going to have a difficult time," he said. "You want life to be symmetrical. You should listen to Napoleon. He said, 'Consistency's the virtue of fools.'"

At the time, I thought this was cynical. To me, right was right and wrong was wrong, and there were few grays between the blacks and the whites. It took a long time to savor the true wisdom of that axiom.

In an effort to develop a dialogue of my own, I had a tendency to reach deeply into the academic background which I brought as my sole asset to Hollywood, and to fly occasionally into Latin phrases or the terminology of the classics. Thus it was that one day I urged a producer to introduce more Catharsis into his script. This would have been fine, except that the producer turned out to be a Runyonesque sort of character, whom we will call "Sam Pushkin." Sam had only one thing on his mind. He wanted that letter stating that his script had basic approval under the Code, so he could get his money from the bank.

He resorted to theatrics. He came into Doc Dougherty's office, where we had scheduled a meeting, and threw himself on his knees in the center of the carpet. He spread out his arms so wide that his wallet jiggled out of his coat pocket and fell to the floor. "I'm at your mercy," he wailed with beautiful fakery. "Kill me. You're like a sword hanging over my head." Then, noticing his wallet on the floor, he reached down, seized it, and cast it at our feet. "Take it," he said. "You might as well. You're taking everything else from me. What'm I trying to hang on to my last few dollars for? Take them too."

Doc pointed to the Code letter, which Sam held crumpled up in one of his outstretched hands. "Sam," he insisted, "listen for a minute. All we're asking is for you to put a little more catharsis in your script."

"Catharsis?" echoed Sam, his ears pricking up, "Where? Where? What's that?"

I opened my mouth like a large black bass and was about to launch into an explanation. Sam sensed danger.

"Never mind, never mind," he said, erasing the air with his hand. "I'll put some in. I don't know what it is, but if that's what you want, just tell me. I'll put all of it in you want."

He jumped to his feet. "Now can I have the letter?" he asked eagerly.

Fortunately Doc was there to say yes, or I might still be trying to get through to Sam.

For Sam, such a display of histrionics was not unusual. He was three-quarters bald, with eyes like beads, and a nose curved like the prow of a ship. He had a strident voice which he projected through his nasal passages, and which bored through walls and people's heads like a dentist's drill. "Holy smoke, whatta job!" he once enthused to Doc over the Code work. "Why you guys aren't all driving Rolls-Royces, *I'll* never know. Any guy in this office who's poor is just a goddam fool."

Sam got his, though. It seems that the old rascal had a ritual of attending the boxing matches on Friday nights at the Hollywood Legion Stadium. Preceding World War II, this was the favorite pastime for the great and the near-great, the main attraction being the opportunity to do a little betting on the side. Among other famous fans who used to yell and scream at ringside was the actress Lupe Velez, who later, unhappily, killed herself.

Sam, however, had another weakness. Having convinced his

wife that it was *de rigueur* for him to make an appearance at ringside with other celebrities, he enjoyed a perfect excuse to be away from home. Of course, what Sam had in mind had nothing to do with a box seat in full view of the public. Therefore, he concocted a scheme which, in retrospect, sounds like he took one of his own movie plots too seriously.

He took the radio announcer aside, slipped him a nice little piece of cash, and arranged for him to broadcast Sam's presence at ringside when he was naming the glamour personalities present. At home, with the radio going full blast, the whole family had a positive verification of Sam's whereabouts. Meanwhile, Sam was liberated to cut a few capers at the local motel.

Everything went along fine, until one Friday night Sam was home sick with a cold. Unthinkingly, he turned on the radio to listen to the bouts, with his wife nestled comfortably alongside him. Not knowing Sam's whereabouts, the announcer went through with his part of the deal and loudly proclaimed our friend's presence at ringside "as usual." He even went so far as to call out a greeting to Sam, and to tell the audience that the man was waving back at him in friendly fashion and looked fit as a fig. Meanwhile, back in the bedroom, Sam was shrinking guiltily under the sheets, while the great dawn was breaking on his wife. It is hardly stretching things to say that he knew what "catharsis" was after she finished with him.

Doc Dougherty, whose career was going along step by step with mine, was developing a voice of his own, too. In huddle he reported on a picture titled *This Woman Is Dangerous.* This was a film being prepared by Warner Brothers as a comeback vehicle for the actress Joan Crawford. The producer was a Bob Sisk, and the director was a Felix Feist. Doc had been assigned to the script in the company of Geoff.

They had gone out to the studio, and had fallen into an impasse with the director. Feist was being either unsympathetic or uncomprehending over a request for a more vivid "voice for morality."

"I usually go right along with you guys," said Feist, "but right now you've got me stumped. What do you mean about developing a voice for morality in this case? Tell me more."

Doc charged into the breach. "Okay, Felix," he volunteered, "let's sum up. Here you've got a story of a woman who is little more than a cheap gun moll. So what happens? She falls in love with a nice doctor, who decides that the reason she is so aggressive and antisocial is that she has a pressure on the brain. He operates on her, removes a tumor, and puts her back into society as a whole person. Now she is supposed to be welcomed back with open arms, as though she has no past, as though there is no wake of wrong trailing behind her whatsoever. You wave a wand, and a whole string of criminal deeds are supposed to be wiped out. What we want to get into the script is some *recognition* of her previous lawlessness."

"But this is a *sick woman*," protested Felix, scratching his head in desperation. "What do you want me to do? Punish her for things she couldn't help?"

"No," countered Doc. "Not that. But the whole trouble is that the doctor goes on rationalizing that every criminal is only a sick person—that he's the victim of a tumorous pressure, either on his brain or on his soul. He's not to blame for the pressures on his personality. Society is."

"Well, what's wrong with *that?*" Feist wanted to know. "This is what psychiatry is teaching us. There's no such thing as a basically malicious personality. There are only damaged psyches. Science comes along and removes the source of the aggravation, and the person adjusts."

"Great!" exclaimed Doc. "That's just peachy, isn't it? Now nobody's responsible for their hostilities or their aggressions. Everybody's let off the hook. What you're doing, Felix, is carrying your thesis too far. Sure there's a core of truth to what you're talking about. But you're running it into a wild exaggeration. You're trying to replace morality with science."

Felix sucked on the end of his pencil. "I think I get your point," he said thoughtfully. "It's a question of degree. All right, I'll make some changes and take out the exaggeration."

"*That's* the idea, Felix," agreed Doc. "But, now look. There's just one more thing. Among the details of this story, there's a very brutal killing of a state trooper. You ought to take a look at that, and soften it up a bit."

"Is that a *Code* problem?" demanded Felix, slightly nettled. "I mean, you're not just tossing this in as a *suggestion,* or something, are you?"

"No, I'm afraid not," answered Doc. "The Code is pretty solicitous to protect the inviolability of the law. It doesn't want to give currency to the idea that it's pretty easy to bump off a cop."

"Aw, nuts!" exploded Felix, jumping to his feet. "This is carrying things too far! What's the idea throwing a mantle of protection over *policemen,* for crying out loud? Listen. Two of those bums beat me up right outside my own house not more than two months ago. And to make it worse, one of them came back and tried to rape my thirteen-year-old daughter. They're a pack of no-goods, and you know it!"

All this time, Geoffrey had been sitting back with his implacable blue eyes, following the dialogue like a witness at a tennis match. Now he darted into the conversation like a lizard. "Oh, but Felix," he interrupted, eyes wide with mock astonishment, "where does all this bitterness come from? This is incompatible with the 'scientific' approach. Remember? They're not to blame. They're just sick!"

Truth to tell, these days were for the younger members of the staff the days of wine and roses. We lived in the company of a man who was, in the Greek sense of the word, mad; not insane, but mad, like an Oedipus, or a Hector, or even the lone soldier who defended the pass at Thermopylae. Along with that, we were having our first heady grapplings with reality—the reality of a storytelling business that intrigued the whole world. It was the best of times, and the worst of times. It was a time not only of legend, but of myth as well. The air was filled with false conceptions about the Code and its work. It had been in existence long enough now that weird notions of its rules were beginning to crystallize into a body of mythology that simply would not be contradicted.

For instance, the idea was cemented into the public mind that the Code required a transgressor to be punished in direct proportion to the sin or crime. Thus, if a woman were an adulteress, she should be shot in the belly; and, I guess, if she were a liar, she should lose her tongue. For shorthand, this was called the "Gilbert and Sullivan rule." It was, of course, a total confection. What the Code did insist on was the dramatic demonstration of the wrongness of a misdeed. If this could be accomplished by punishment, the moral would speak for itself. Joe Breen was convinced that wrongdoing would not be too "catching" if the more impressionable minds in the audience saw it constantly coming to a painful end.

Other myths were no less whimsical. The notion persisted, for example, that the Code set a hard and fast time limit on the length of a kiss. A kiss was allowed to last ten seconds, not a fraction more. Thus, it was imagined that the Code administrators stood around the movie sets with big black cigars jutting out of their jaws, and with stopwatches in their hands, yelling "Cease!" once the fatal moment had passed. It was considered the bounden duty of the resourceful director to eke all the lustfulness out of every kiss within the time limit. We called this the "rail bird myth," for it evoked the image of clockers at the racetrack.

Another of the myths had it that the Code under no circumstances permitted a couple to be together in a double bed. This myth had origins of some peculiar interest. It was traceable back to a picture called *Mad Miss Manton,* made by RKO in 1938. The film contained a sequence in which an elderly couple were together in a double bed in a garret or attic. The old man was a caretaker, and hearing some noise, he lit a lamp and got up to investigate. It turned out that the disturbance was coming from a loose shutter that was being rattled by the wind of an upcoming storm. The old caretaker set the latch on the shutter, came back to his bedroom, blew out the lamp, and climbed back into bed.

The scene was approved by the Production Code.

When the picture came to England, however, it ran into an anachronistic mentality that requires a word of explanation. In the British Isles at that time there was undoubtedly a hangover of Puritanism still in existence. The British attitude toward the movie house was one of aloof toleration, because the theater was regarded as a worldly place, a place of frivolity, and, therefore, as a slightly profane setting. Much the same attitude had been exhibited (historically) toward the legitimate stage and later was extended to the novel, which had to be read under the sheets by giddy girls, because the form was "easy" and, therefore, not acceptable in serious society. So far did this attitude extend in relationship to the movie house, that the British censor once flatly refused to allow a recitation of the Lord's Prayer in a picture titled *The Little Shepherd of Kingdom Come*. The objection was based on the impropriety of the setting for such hallowed words. He later tried to attack the American film industry for importing a wave of "paganism" into England. Joe Breen demanded of him how it could be otherwise, when the man would not allow any quotations from the New Testament to act as a leaven in films.

Thus it was that the British, at that time, regarded any invasion of the "sacred intimacies of married life" as being a profanation. This included such privacies as sleeping together, which was so closely connected with love-making. It made little difference that the couple might be elderly, or that the scene was not even remotely prurient in intent. The law was clear, and exceptions had a way of turning into precedent. They presented a stony countenance to the distributors of *Mad Miss Manton*.

In vain did Joe Breen, representing the American interests,

plead with the censor that the costs of bringing the picture back to the United States and redoing it were prohibitive. At last he reached for a desperate compromise. Taking the offending scene down to the laboratories in London, he ordered the technicians to reprint it, but so darkly as to be almost indistinguishable. The device was not altogether out of line, since the picture was a mystery story, and the eerie effect might appear calculated in the first place. When he brought the sequence back for re-examination to the censor, all that could be discerned was the outline of shadowy figures flitting across the screen and delivering dialogue that must have left British audiences—well—in the dark. At any rate, the picture was finally passed.

However, a severe lesson had been learned. Henceforth, each time a bedroom scene appeared in a script submitted to the Production Code office, a note of warning was inserted in the letter, letting the production manager know that twin beds would be needed for England. Since England was a good market, the production manager usually complied, and ordered twin beds for his set. And since it was too much trouble to dress two sets in two different ways, one with a double bed for the U.S.A., and another with a pair of twin beds for the British Isles, it became commonly supposed that the Code forbade the double beds, and the myth was born.

The myth took on an added twist when some inventive soul began to spread the word that it was all right with the Code to show a couple in a double bed, so long as the man kept one foot on the floor. When somebody put this absurdity to Doc Dougherty once over the telephone, he answered with some of the salt of Joe Breen, "Oh, hell, you've got the wrong number. What you want is the corner poolroom."

Bending back, parenthetically, to the British Board of Film Censors, it is interesting to note that the chief censor was a blind man; not metaphorically, but literally. He was either a political figure or a personage of Class, who had been given the job in his latter years as a sinecure, and who, of course, relied on the day-to-day custodianship of his secretary. It seems superfluous to say that the antique, stuffy mentality of the B.B.F.C. has virtually disappeared under the secretariat of the current arbiter, John Trevelyan. However, his superior, Lord Morrison, has the misfortune of enjoying the use of only one eye. This, of course, is a step forward. On the legitimate stage, the Lord Chamberlain has abolished censorship altogether. His last memorable regulation made it permissible to have nudity in plays, so long as the characters stood still and did not cavort about. And, for a final oddity in connection with the British, it is recorded that a member of the House of Lords rose on the floor to denounce the American Code for ordering the deletion of a "questionable" word from an English picture seeking playing time in the U.S.A. The inference was, of course, that the Code was being used as a tool of American monopolistic interests to block the invasion of competitive entertainment from a more talented source. At last, one of the members of the august House, curious beyond bearing, requested to know the word that had been ordered deleted. The speaker demurred. "I cannot tell you," he informed the questioner. "It is not a fit word to be uttered within the confines of these walls."

For the sake of the inquisitive, the word was "bastard."

Some of the mythology descended into the near comical. As late as the first half of the fifties, a large photograph of the actress Joanne Dru appeared in the Los Angeles *Times*. It showed her perched on the top of a stepladder, holding her skirt as high as was acceptable in those days, with generous expanses of shapely legs showing. The caption underneath the picture states primly that poses of this type were approved by the Breen office because the girl really looks too well bred, in the opinion of the censors, to be an "obviously sexy type." She was classed as more of a "charming actress and mother."

In the body of the article, accompanying the publicity picture, the girl is quoted as saying, ". . . the studio still department recently submitted some photos to the Breen office for approval. I was posed in a super-sexy swim suit, and would have bet they wouldn't be accepted. They came back stamped O.K. An attached note said: 'These are approved because Miss Dru isn't the obvious sexy type; she looks well bred.' I suppose I should have considered it a compliment, but I was livid."

Going on to another case, I think the bottom was touched when the popular actor Jeff Chandler announced that he was tired of shaving his chest for movie roles, and everyone in the film community presumed that this was because of some arcane canon of the Code, which forbade males with heavily matted chests to appear in public.

Even so, this business of actors having to shave their chests is not unimportant. It is whispered around among distant members of the family that pioneer actor Elmo Lincoln, the first Tarzan, who had his share of hairiness, was enormously distressed by the need to appear as a smooth-chested hero in his jungle films. It seems that Elmo got bristly chested after a while, and this became no mean impediment to his bed life. This may have accounted for the multiple marriages in which the unlucky fellow got involved.

The film community, of course, struck back at what its members thought were petty restraints on its "creativity." A particularly ingenious invention was used by a director to defeat the supposed ten-second limit on kisses.

What this craftsman did was to train the camera on his two lovers, and let them go the route for the full ten seconds. It was a nice warm open-mouth kiss. When the "time limit" had expired, the director let the camera travel slowly away from the blissful pair, and, in what is called a "continuing pan," passed a pool of water in which it picked up their reflections kissing upside down. Now we had the equivalent of a new time span in which to survey them topsy-turvy, still locked in their rapturous embrace. When the ten seconds or so were up, the director allowed the camera to drift past the pool, and to catch their reflection in a conveniently placed mirror. This time, of course, they were right side up again. The audience was allowed to feast its eyes on the two for another time count. Then came the *pièce de résistance*. On the shelf above the mirror was a long row of blue bottles, over which the camera wandered, picking up in each the diminutive image of the romantic pair, on into a dissolve that created the effect of infinity.

It was all very nice; but the imaginative man need not have gone to all the trouble—not for the Code, at any rate.

A more good-natured incident in the game of give and take occurred between Geoff Shurlock and his friend the deceased director Preston Sturges.

"Geoff," said Sturges over the phone, "I've got a problem. I've got a scene with my leading lady sitting at a dressing table making up for the evening. She's dressed in a half-slip and a brassiere. You think that'd be all right?"

At that time, we were trying to hold the line on costumes, and had established a rule of thumb that the least we would settle for in the line of intimate garments was a full slip. Sturges knew this, and that was the reason he was calling for help.

"Is there some special reason you can't use a full slip?" Geoff wanted to know.

"Yes," explained Preston. "You see, Geoff, the girl's preparing to put on a midriff formal. My costume designer tells me that every woman in the audience would know that you don't wear a full slip under a midriff formal. They'd laugh. You know?"

"Then have her sitting at the dressing table in a negligee," suggested Geoff.

"I *can*, Geoff, if it's really necessary. But, for goodness' sake, is a half-slip and brassiere really so exposing as all that? It's certainly more covering than you'd see at the beach. And how about the costumes of the girls in a chorus line, which you approve every day? They're certainly scantier than what I'm asking for."

Geoff rose to the bait. "I think you have something there,

Preston," he said. "But it's breaking precedent. So let me take it up with the rest of the boys and see what they think."

"Please call back in a hurry, Geoff. I'm holding things up in the costume department until I can hear from you."

Geoff scurried around among the staff members, soliciting an opinion on so weighty an issue. Milt Hodenfield was the one who came up with the answer that killed Sturges' request. "A bathing suit at the beach is a *costume*," he carefully pointed out. "Tell Sturges his wife could walk down Wilshire Boulevard in a bathing suit without being arrested. But let her try it in a half-slip and brassiere."

We were all as impressed as hell by this nicety of distinction and echoed Milt's sentiments to a man.

Defeated, Geoff hastened back to the phone, and, in a state of high animation, said, "Preston—I'm sorry! The boys all say it's a full slip, or nothing!"

Quick as a wink, Sturges seized the alternative. "It's a deal!" he said enthusiastically. "I'll take *nothing!*"

Occasionally, of course, the carefully calculated stratagems of the picture makers to outwit the Code would blow up in their faces. A case in point was the skittishly titled Columbia picture *Her Husband's Affairs,* starring Lucille Ball and Franchot Tone.

Somebody connected with the picture got a sudden inspiration as to how to circumvent the clumsy double-bed regulation. Rubbing his hands with glee, he ordered the set designer to construct what at that time was called a "Hollywood bed." This was nothing more or less than twin beds shoved together and joined by a common headboard. He sent the scene to the Code office, where, to his surprise, it was passed without a murmur.

The situation was reversed, however, when the picture went off to England and confronted the British Board of Film Censors. They turned thumbs down on the whole contraption, declaring that it was no more than a thinly disguised double bed. In the end, the entire can of film had to be shipped back to the United States, where a new set had to be built and the scene reconstructed with the offending beds spread exactly eighteen inches apart. The adventure cost the studio $30,000. Some portion of this sum must have been returned to the picture in the form of publicity, since the press thought it was a jolly good story, and printed pictures of the principals kneeling on the floor and measuring the magical span between the pads, wearing large guilty smiles on their faces.

Tactics like these, of course, tend to recall the statement of William Fadiman, longtime producer and story editor in Hollywood, and the distinguished recipient of Phi Beta Kappa honors. At least part of what he has to say would probably be applicable here. "Just as an onerous taxation program has forced otherwise honest businessmen into a sort of self-corruption in trying to find tax loopholes, so the need to try to get around the Code has forced many in the movie industry to invent evasions that make a mockery of their own movies and of the Code as well."* The sorry and amusing fact is, however, that a good portion of the ingenuity was squandered on triumphs over nonexistent shadow canons.

* As quoted in *The Face on the Cutting Room Floor,* by Murray Schumach. William Morrow, New York, 1964.

8 Who Knows About Calcutta in 1750 Any Better Than Me?

AMONG THE OTHER MEN who worked in our office was Addison Durland. Addison was a Cuban-American who had gold-flecked brown eyes, which were somehow filled with the faraway hint of ineffable sufferings. But he was too brave and too fastidious to let them show through. He walked the corridors with the air of a man who carried an invisible Damascus sword by his side. One had the feeling that at any moment he might thrust his left hand into a cocked position and that he would cry, *"En garde!"*

Addison's job was the interpretation and enforcement of Article X in the Code. This was the provision that called for the fair presentation of the nationals of other countries.

In the days of our fathers, the atmosphere was filled with grotesque simplicities. Every Russian was a bristly bearded Bolshevik carrying a round spluttering bomb in his hand; all Chinamen looked alike; and all Irishmen (prior to Grace Kelly, princess of Monaco) were great pug-faced louts who clenched clay pipes in their teeth. All Italians were gangsters; all Negroes emitted a fume in the boxing ring, and *that* (you were informed from the back of the hand) was the reason Jack Dempsey drew the color line; and all Mexicans curled up alongside adobe walls wrapped in a serape and snoozed under tilted sombreros. When they were summoned by a haughty snap of the fingers on the part of a loud-mouthed American, they scrambled to their feet, whipped off their straw hats, held them in front of them with a stance of servility, and said, "I the-e-nk!"

In the midst of World War II, when the United States was trying to cultivate the good will and the understanding of the peoples of the Americas, it was decided to try to expunge some of these caricatures from the screen. At the urging of officials in high estate in Washington, Addison was hired to try to introduce a little civilization into Hollywood. The ban did not, at the time, apply to the Nazis, who could be portrayed as sartorial monsters who walked as though they had to be wound up with a key each morning; or to the Japanese, all of whom wore huge horn-rimmed glasses and flashed buck teeth. Nowadays, of course, it is open season on the Viet Cong. Tomorrow—who knows?

Addison's was a thankless job, as ceaseless as the task of Sisyphus. But he did it so well that he worked himself out of business.

Typical of Durland's work was a dialogue that occurred between him and the marvelous, primitive Sam "Jungle Jim" Katzman. Sam was a plump apple-cheeked fellow, with a little mustache that seemed to bristle out in all directions. He would sit in his great leather swivel chair like an imperturbable Buddha, his hands crossed over the top of an ivory-headed cane from his ample collection, and announce with a creamy smile, "I don't *get* ulcers . . . I *give* them."

Addison got into a tangle with Sam one day regarding a script of an unremembered title. It was the familiar Oriental version of a Western, sometimes called "Easterns," but more often called, in the vulgar parlance, a "tits and sand." It was set in Calcutta in 1750, and was loaded with prejudices which, Durland saw, would be more inflammatory than a forest fire to the peoples of the other half of our rapidly shrinking globe.

Sam watched Durland with a calm painted smile, while the scrupulous Cuban made his presentation of the difficulties. "You are running around with the recklessness of a bull in a china shop," Durland told Katzman. "Line after line in your script tramples on the sensitivities of the Indian people. You have gross distortions of history, you are untactful, you maul traditional customs, and, in a word, you leave much to be desired. Don't you realize your picture will be banned everywhere throughout the Far East?"

"So what if it is?" asked Sam, without taking his hands from the top of his Tamil cane (he had one to fit every occasion). "You don't think I've had pictures banned before?"

"I imagine you have," conceded Durland, "but India is a tinderbox at the present moment. The Russians are trying to woo it, and the American government is trying to get it over on our side. So why do you aggravate it?"

"So what do I do then?" asked Sam, somehow impressed that the fate of the world was tied up with his small epic.

"Hire a technical adviser," said Durland without hesitation.

"A *technical* adviser?" howled Sam. "What for? Those guys cost money. It may not mean anything to you, but I'm trying to bring in my picture for a *price!*"

Addison was used to this plaint. "A technical adviser," he assured Sam, "who knew his subject, would repay you double his cost."

"Listen." Sam waved. "Cut out the malarkey. Who knows about Calcutta in 1750 any better than me?"

"Your good friend Harry Cohn just made a film about the Orient. *Salome!* It was set back in history a good deal more remotely than your story. And yet *he* found a technical adviser."

This piqued Sam's vanity. Cohn was the big squeeze at Columbia, while Sam only made "B" pictures for him. And yet the impression existed that Sam could buy and sell Harry any time he chose. To cover his weakness, he scoffed at Durland and said, "Sure, but he's got all the money of the studio backing him. He can afford it."

Addison looked sideways and slyly at Sam. "Why, Sam," he chided, "we've got the impression that *you've* got all the money in town."

"You want to know why?" snapped Sam, stamping his cane on the floor. "Because I don't go around wasting my money on silly things like technical advisers!"

Durland knew when he was defeated. He got out his encyclopedias and acted as technical adviser himself. For no pay.

I tended to drift into the close company of Addison during these years, because I felt that he had been very much in the world, and that some of his sophistication would rub off on me. It was like a man in the desert who attempts to slake his thirst by listening to another man tell how he once drank water. Addison had a bohemian dwelling in the Hollywood hills, constructed of weathered wood siding, with semitropical foliage to add a note of vitality against the gray rough-hewn boards. In the center of the entry courtyard was a small fishpond, where he used to sit in contemplation and watch the frogs copulate. He was never out of wonder at the intensity of their black rapture. Indoors, Addison took pleasure in serving casual dinners of broiled chicken, with secret wines, by candlelight, to the muted music of Johann Sebastian Bach. It was in this setting that he used to narrate some of his background.

He had been a young revolutionary in Cuba in the upheaval that unseated the tyrant Machado and opened the way for the dictator Batista. For all his pains, he was presented with Machado's white typewriter, after the palace was sacked by his cronies. He himself had been exiled to New York City.

He told hair-raising incidents about the effort to eliminate Machado, short of open rebellion. At one time, the fomenters made an arrangement with Machado's barber to slit his throat while he was shaving him in the morning. The barber's family had already been sent to safety in Miami. But, face to face with the moment of truth, the poor barber started trembling so violently that he had to excuse himself and get sick, and the opportunity vanished into oblivion. The family had to be recalled from their "vacation." At another time, a fiendish plot was hatched to drop a bomb down a chimney into Machado's bedroom. Everything went fine, and the bomb exploded perfectly. The only trouble was that the palace had been altered, so that the chimney was sealed off, and the bomb only blew a hole in the ceiling, showering Machado with plaster.

It was in New York that Addison engaged in the greatest piece of windmill tilting of the century. He had contracted for an apartment and went over to the utilities company to get gas or electricity or water or telephone services—I can't remember exactly which. When he filled out the proper forms, the company tried to exact a deposit of five dollars. Fresh from his success in dislodging a head of state, Durland decided to balk. He demanded to know *why* he had to put up the money, when he hadn't received any services yet. He had just the proper amount of accent to make the manager think that this was some simple-minded immigrant, so the poor fellow tried to explain. Addison listened courteously.

The manager gave Durland such good reasons that he even convinced himself.

"I realize you do not know me," Durland conceded, "and I realize that this is no small matter to you. After all, you are obliged to deal with occasional riffraff who skip out on their bills—*and* I understand that you must protect yourself. But, you must excuse me. I am only an ignorant foreigner. I do not know you either. How do I know, after I deliver to you my money, that you will give me the services I need? Forgive me for putting it this way, but it is also possible that you could skip out on me. No?"

The manager did not know whether to laugh or to cry. He decided to compromise. He would try just one more ounce of patience. "Mr. Durland," he said, shuffling his hands to establish a mood of reasonableness, "we are a very big company. Surely you are joking?"

"Oh, I am certain you are *big*," Addison hastened to assure him. "All things American seem to be. Also, I am sure you are very well known and most trustworthy and would not deliberately run out on me. On the other hand, you must understand that I, too, in my own way, am equally well known in *my* country, and am considered as a person to be trusted. So we are *both* trustworthy. And yet *I* am the one who is asked to give you the guarantees, and you are not asked to give any to me. This hurts me—as I'm sure you can appreciate."

The manager could tolerate this barrage of Latin logic no longer. He put his hands on the edge of the desk, as though the conversation were finished, and shook his head firmly. "Mr. Durland," he announced, "I have no choice. It is company policy. If you do not leave a deposit, I cannot give you our services. It's as simple as that."

Durland put up his hand placatingly, as if to warn the man not to slam the door on himself. "Just one moment," he begged, "perhaps we can keep it from being so simple. I will offer you an alternative. I will give you my five dollars, reluctantly, on the condition that you will deposit another five dollars in escrow, in the bank across the street, which will be payable to me in the event that you should, let us say, go out of business."

"Go out of *business!*" exclaimed the manager, aghast.

"It *is* the Depression," reminded Durland. "Many great corporations have failed."

The manager, outraged, finally pushed back his chair and stood up. "No," he said. "No. We will do no such thing. This is ridiculous."

Durland spread his hands helplessly. "Very well," he agreed. "I have no choice. You are a monopoly. There is no competitor of yours to whom I can go. I need your services. So I will have to pay. Under protest. It's as simple as that."

The manager was delighted to be relieved of this eccentric, and breathed a sigh when Addison wrote out his check and left.

At the end of the month, when Durland's first bill came due, he deliberately wrote out a check for one penny less than the amount. Warily, the company wrote him a letter, calling the mistake to his attention. Durland noticed with satisfaction that it had cost them two cents to mail the letter.

Licking his chops, Addison took his Machado typewriter off the shelf and typed out a petulant reply, complaining that the company was trying to persecute him, that it was customary for Cubans to be very exact about paying their bills, and that the company was clearly trying to extort more out of him, under threat of canceling its services, in order to punish him for the little misunderstanding that existed between them.

In this manner, he managed to keep the item open during the better part of the month.

When the next bill arrived, Durland deliberately wrote out his check for one penny extra. The company tried to return it. Addison refused to accept it, saying that the executives had guilty consciences, and were trying to reimburse him for his five dollars at the rate of one cent a month. This was an offense against his dignity.

Meanwhile, Addison had been reciting his adventures to his friends at the Latin American consulates, and they responded with glee, sending complaints to the company on their official letterheads—"the smaller the country, the bigger the crest," as Addison told it. They assumed tones of indignation, reminding the company of the rights of the individual in the face of the great corporate giants of the nation.

After a suitable time, when the harassment of the company had caused sufficient confusion, Durland wrote out two checks —one for his rent and one for his utilities—and carefully inserted them into the wrong envelopes. At the utility company, some clerk, recognizing the name of the crank, simply slapped the rubber endorsement of the company on the wrong check and mailed Addison the change. Addison had now filled his inside royal flush.

He went to the office of the manager and presented him with the evidence. "I am only an ignorant peasant," he said to the executive, figuratively standing there as though he held a sombrero in his hands, "and I do not know much about these things" (neglecting to tell about his degree in international law). "But, I the-e-nk I am going to have recourse to the courts in this case. Is it not a Federal crime to falsely endorse a check?"

The manager turned white. The utilities companies were under pressure from public opinion. The manager could see nothing but a holocaust resulting from a trial. Gathering together the best sick laugh he could summon, he tried to bluff Addison along. "Anybody can make a mistake," he argued. "The courts will understand this."

"Oh. Then you do admit that you made a mistake?"

The manager shuffled his hand again. "Yes."

"The courts might not be so kind," Addison pointed out. "I have the whole record of your persecutions of me."

The manager swallowed back the lump in his throat, and began to wheedle. "Mr. Durland," he begged, "is there something we could do to discourage you from going to court? You will only lose, but it will cost money. What is it you want?"

Addison looked at him almost pensively, and delivered the point of the sword exactly between the horns. "Mr. Manager," he said, "you know what I want. I—want—my—five—dollars—back!"

(P.S. He got it.)

Before Addison slid off, as silently as a fish, into the unfathomable waters of his own existence, he left behind a frail tale that contains a moral, and which somehow always clung to me as being illustrative of a small glinting point about life. It has to do with the distinction between a "truth" and a "fact."

Once upon a time, the parable goes, there was a stern sea captain who was utterly opposed to drinking. One day, his first mate was taken sick and retired to his cabin, where he poured himself a dram of brandy to settle his stomach. Just as the mate was raising the drink to his lips, the captain walked into the room. He glared at the mate in anger and stalked out without a word. That night when the captain was making up the log, he inserted the remark, "Today I discovered the first mate drinking in his quarters."

When called upon to approve the log, the first mate objected to the entry. "You will ruin my reputation," he complained to the captain.

"Was it not a fact that you were taking a drink?" the captain wanted to know.

"It was a fact," conceded the mate, "but it conveys an untruth. It gives the impression that I am a secret drinker. You are being unjust to me."

"This is a risk you take when you indulge in alcoholic beverages aboard my ship," the captain retorted. "Let it be a lesson to you. The log will stand as written."

The next day, however, the captain himself was stricken, and the running of the ship was turned over to the first mate. That night, the mate visited the captain's quarters to get his approval of the log. To the captain's chagrin, he read the mate's sly revenge. "Today," he had written, "I did not discover the captain drinking in his cabin."

I have always considered that this little narrative contained something for those engaged in the queasy craft of censorship, whose duty it is to see evil, but not where it does not exist.

The close scrutiny given by Durland to such niceties as Indian history in the 1700s will give some idea of the penetration of the Code work into the movie community, and some clue as to its width and breadth. Hardly any detail escaped its attention. The main concern, of course, continued to be sex. In second position of importance would be the question of crime and criminality. That was much more of an item all through the decade of the forties and up to the edge of the fifties than the question of violence and brutality, which so concerns people now. The reason for this is an interesting one. It is traceable, in large measure, to the fact that the moral tone of the times was created by the Irish, who were in dominant ecclesiastical positions in the opinion-making centers of our country.

To the Irish, violence was not necessarily connected with the debasing of human nature. It was frequently a sign of manliness. The tavern brawl was considered to be an indulgence of "the boys," and was looked on with amused tolerance. In fact, when John Ford, who was Irish of the Irish, returned to Erin to direct a film in tribute to the old sod, he ironically called it *The Quiet Man*. As *the* highlight of the film, he featured an orgiastic brawl between John Wayne and Ward Bond (over red-headed and blue-eyed Maureen O'Hara) that lasted throughout the day, and ranged from tavern to countryside, with pit stops at the bar to renew energies. It was all put forward in a good-natured spirit, and was not meant to be taken as a grand opera, but the underlying premise was, nevertheless, enforced. The Irish had learned bitter violence in the "Troubles," and cruelty was more frequently connected with lack of cowardice, and even sometimes with the virtue of patriotism. Perhaps more importantly still, the Irish culture was infected with Jansenism, which dreaded sex as being identified with the darker forces, but which did not so fear brutality, since this was not as "catching." It contained its own remedy in that it hurt.

Thus, when the historically savage brawl in *The Spoilers* hit the screen, it was advertised as something to see, something to titillate the morbid curiosity, something to be entertained by. It revolted some people because of its extravagance and because of its gruesomeness. But it was not considered "immoral" in the formal sense, on the grounds that it might be setting man back to the level of the beast.

Strangely enough, just exactly this same consideration prevailed, however, in entirely another field. This had to do with the touchy subject of the treatment of animals in pictures.

The theory was that animals could not speak for themselves. They trusted man and could be taken advantage of. Therefore, it behooved man, acting as human, not to degrade himself by mistreating them. Thus, the society that took the responsibility for overseeing the treatment of animals in pictures wisely took the title of the "American Humane Association." It had to do with Man, as much as with animals.

It had been the habit, in the roughshod pioneering days of the movies, to maltreat animals in a callous manner. A device of wires, called the "running W," was rigged around a horse's legs, with the trigger in the hands of the wrangler. The horse would be set into a full gallop, his front legs would be yanked out from under him, and he would fall headlong, frequently with drastic consequences.

The whole question came to a crisis in 1939, when Darryl Zanuck made *Jesse James* for Fox. According to eyewitness reports, a blindfolded horse was placed in a greased rocker-roller chute constructed on the edge of a cliff. It was prodded forward by the rider and the members of the cast. As the animal got past the fulcrum point, the chute tilted, and the horse catapulted into space, hindmost first, with its front feet in the air. It fell some sixty or seventy feet into a stream, came to the surface twice, and drowned. In spite of this fact, a second horse was then put into the chute and sent over the cliff. This animal was not drowned. Those who saw the film will remember the scene as one of the breathtaking highlights.

The uproar that followed was backed by the powerful Hearst organization, and evoked 50,000 signatures of protest, according to the A.H.A. representative in Hollywood. In vain did Zanuck protest that the killing was "accidental," arguing that he himself was a polo player and loved horses. The operation of the A.H.A. was incorporated into the Code, and made one of its subsidiary functions.

Henceforth, horses were taught to fall on command; but since they were prepared for the moment of impact, they were able to protect themselves. Great trouble was taken to prepare the ground at the spot of the tumble. A shallow pit was dug, and the floor was lined with empty cardboard ice-cream cartons. These were then covered over with loose dirt. When the horse hit the area, the cartons caved in but acted as a cushion. The criterion of whether a horse might have been injured had a lot to do with whether he was able to hold his head up at the moment of thudding into the ground. If he was made to tumble so that his neck curled under him, the weight of his body would break it and kill him. As might be expected, horses who were bright enough to learn these tricks became very valuable and represented a big investment. Therefore, the owners were glad to cooperate with the harsh regulations.

Success gave false encouragement to the extremists, and they began making demands that earned them the label of "humaniacs." An example from a film by the famous archer Howard Hill will illustrate the point. This entrepreneur was attempting to popularize the sport of hunting with a bow and arrow. Toward this end, he made a documentary of his exploits in Africa.

In the film, he featured his attempts to kill a lion with a hunting arrow. He carefully explained the power of the bow, which had so many pounds of pull that the average man could not even string it, let alone draw back the cord. The arrow was a broad-bladed steelhead, honed on a soapstone until it was as sharp as a scalpel.

The animal he had been stalking made its appearance from the brush, and it was a great shaggy-maned brute. It was perhaps fifty yards distant. If Hill missed, he would hardly have time to renotch an arrow.

He drew back the arrow the entire length of the shaft, aimed carefully, and let it fly. It could be seen arcing through the air like a dark shadow. It struck the lion full force. Unfortunately, however, it did not hit him in the heart, but instead lodged in the upper, bony bridge of the nose. The frantic animal leaped, and then began to paw at the offending arrow with both feet. It could not knock it out. Quickly the hunter notched a second arrow, aimed, and shot. This time he found a vital part, and the lion was killed instantly.

Encouraged by this success, Hill later tried, successfully, to kill an elephant with bow and arrow. So immense was the power of the bow that one of the arrows drove clear into the elephant's body up to the feathers. In demonstrating this fact, there was a great amount of blood and gore.

Finally, going to another extreme, the archer demonstrated his virtuosity by shooting a boa constrictor out of a tree with a single arrow behind its skull.

Although Hill fought vigorously for all of this footage, the Production Code office made him trim the frames of the arrow striking the lion's nose. In the film that was released, only one arrow was seen. However, that did not satisfy the humaniacs. They also wanted the deletion of all the gore in connection with the death of the elephant, and the killing of the boa constrictor. They claimed that no animal should be sacrificed in the making of a picture for the mere entertainment of an audience. This applied to bullfights as well as to safari pictures, and for years they resisted scenes of the pic-ing of bulls, the setting of the banderillas, and the actual "moment of truth" on the sands of the arena. Since popular sentiment was pretty much on the side of the animal lovers, the Code backed their objections, and enforced them.

A fairly ludicrous situation arose when, years later, a representative of the A.H.A. made a formal objection to a scene in a picture of a dancing duck. When asked what the trouble was, since the duck was more than likely trained, he replied that he suspected that the duck had been stood on a hotplate, and that this was the reason it was shifting from foot to foot. Geoffrey Shurlock wanted to know how he came to the conclusion that the plate was hot. "Did it ever occur to you it might have been cold?" he asked. "Is that inhuman too? The duck might have liked it. He may've been dancing for joy." The scene remained intact.

The classical revelation of the mentality of the humaniacs occurred, however, as late as 1963 (if one be permitted to borrow from the future, for the moment). The picture was the very popular *Hud,* starring Paul Newman.

The high point of the film had to do with the slaughter of a herd of cattle that were infected with the hoof-and-mouth disease. Hud, who was unprincipled, wanted to pawn off the diseased animals on some buyers "up north" (Montana). The father, who realized that he was being asked to wipe out the entire assets of a lifetime, decided that the animals had to be destroyed.

In preparation for the movie scenes, some 400 cattle were used. A large pit was dug by tractors. The beasts were sprayed with a mixture of water, sodium silicate, and mineral oil to simulate the effects of hoof-and-mouth disease. While they were milling around in the pit, a fleet of automobiles carrying men with rifles drove up to the edge of the pit. They aimed their guns at the animals. At this point, the cameras were stopped, and the animals were removed from the pit. Then the action was resumed, with the guns discharging into the now empty pit. Dummy cattle were then strewn about, simulating dead animals. The bodies were drenched with lime, and the trench filled.

As a further nicety, a trough was installed in the bottom of the pit, and filled with water every thirty minutes because of the temperature in the hole. Finally, three separate pastures were secured for the cattle.

These painstaking details will give some idea of the power exerted by public opinion on the picture makers. Everybody connected with *Hud,* however, had reason to feel virtuous, and was in an excellent position to defend practically any point that might come up.

The payoff came when the film arrived in England. The Secretary of the Royal Society for the Prevention of Cruelty to Animals wrote to his American counterpart in Denver, Colorado, complaining as follows:

> Once again I must write to you concerning a film that has reached London and that has caused a certain amount of criticism over the treatment of animals. I refer to the film "Hud."
>
> In this film there is a sequence showing a competition in which some half dozen men have to catch greased pigs. Amongst the scenes shewn [sic] were men leading in the pigs by their hind legs and pushing them forward in the manner

of a wheelbarrow. There was also one scene where one pig was pulled into position by its hind legs. Finally, there was a scene where "Hud" drags a pig over the ground to the winning square. These shots, together with a number of others shewing pigs running in all directions with men diving after them, have been the cause of adverse comment.

And so it goes.

It is no wonder that back in the period we are talking about, which would be the end of the forties, a certain unvarnished producer by the name of Bennie Stoloff rejected a suggestion by a studio representative that his script be sent to the offices of the American Humane Association for counsel and advice. "No, I don't want to have anything to do with those guys," he said unflatteringly. "You give them any encouragement, and the next thing you know, they'll be wanting me to put a jock-strap on the Red Stallion!"

As time went on and the commercial value of an animal began to increase, it was thought that this happy result could be enhanced by beginning the equivalent of an Academy Awards ceremony for the best animal actor of the year. It was called the Patsy Awards, and the winning of the trophy lifted the status of an animal from ham to that of a Star.

In one of the early Awards' ceremonies, the master of ceremonies was the present Governor of California, Ronald Reagan. At this same affair, in the Pantages Theater on Hollywood Boulevard, I was asked to represent the Motion Picture Association in bestowing the Patsy on the winning animal.

Ronald Reagan gave a nice introductory speech, in which he pointed out that all smart actors tried to avoid scenes in which there were either animals or little children. He explained that no actor could compete with these professional scene stealers, and would always come off second best.

All in due course, the time came for announcing the winner. I was at the microphone, and I tore open the envelope. "The winner," I announced in a loud voice, "is . . . Tony, the horse!" I made a great sweeping gesture to the wings at my right to welcome the animal on stage. There was a moment of dead silence, and no horse appeared. I was left there with my arm outstretched in frozen expectation. Then suddenly, over my opposite shoulder, there came the heavy thump, thump of a horse's hoofs, and whirling around, I saw the horse clopping on stage from the wrong wings. I was in the midst of trying to change my gesture, with the audience starting to laugh, when Ron Reagan, showing the wits that carried him to the top in politics, darted out ahead of the horse, grabbed the microphone and with a great grin said, "You see what I mean, Jack?"

9 The Judge, the Coffee Cup, the Brassiere, and the Letter

JOE BREEN, who had won not only the war, but even most of the battles, was beginning to get good-natured. Characteristic would be the way he entered, or rather "made an entrance" into, a producer's office at elegant Twentieth Century-Fox one afternoon. Hesitating in the corridor outside the reception room, he adjusted his tie, took off his hat, which as an old-school newspaperman he always wore, and said, "Watch this." With that, he sailed the chapeau into the room ahead of him. He waited an instant, there was a feminine squeal of delight, and he plowed into the outer office with his arms outspread like Casanova himself. "How's the most beautiful secretary in Hollywood?" he demanded of the woman who was coming from behind her desk to meet him. They embraced with mock passion. "I thought I'd send an emissary ahead of me," he explained. "If it came sailing out, I'd know I wasn't wanted. But now I know you still love me. Is that crazy boss of yours in?"

"No," she answered. "It's supposed to be a secret, but he'd want *you* to know." Her voice dropped conspiratorially. "He's over at Hillcrest playing golf."

Joe used this routine on some battleaxes that would leave a witness aghast at his doughtiness; but it earned him access to inside confidences that were poured into his ear by the bucketful.

His geniality, however, was beginning to rub off on the

pictures he was ordering approved. This was starting to cause some anguish in Legion quarters. The instrumentality which Joe had helped invent in order to validate his job was now beginning to assume a proprietorship over it, and the "child" was clearly beginning to talk like the father of the man. Publicly the Legion began questioning the Code's new-found "liberality."

Joe began submitting his resignations to Eric Johnston.

At first, of course, Johnston rejected them out of hand. He was not obtuse, and he knew in the back of his mind that if it came to a showdown, he himself was possibly more expendable than Breen. Johnston was in the position of a new bishop in a diocese who is confronted by an established monsignor whom he would like to put out to pasture but whom he does not dare touch because his parish is the richest in the roster.

Little by little, however, the submittals began to be more serious. Eventually the process came full circle, so that it would now be impolite for Johnston to ignore them. He began to search for a replacement for Joe.

My first impression of Steve Jackson was of a tall man, standing alone in the middle of the avocado-colored carpet in the Code waiting room. He was holding the rim of a fedora with the fingertips of both hands at just about waist level, as though he were trying to conceal the bullseye in the ventral quarters.

He emitted the air of an alert falcon that had been unhooded but not yet released from its ankle thongs; he seemed to sit on an invisible wrist, waiting for the command to hurtle into the blue with a battering of wings.

Steve turned his small intense features this way and that, with the slow imperiousness of a bird who knew he had impeccable bloodlines. But, as he surveyed those who crisscrossed in front of him in the routines of everyday business, there seeped through another quality that could not be altogether veiled. There escaped the feeling of a deep longing to be liked.

My second impression of Steve is of a bacchanalian figure in the living room of a Spanish-style house in Sierra Madre, kicking up a pair of acrobatic heels and swinging unencumbered arms in a joyous rendition of the Charleston. On top of the rollicking piano sat a well-dented martini.

In between these two impressions existed the man who had been sent out to the Coast to replace Joe Breen.

Eric Johnston had, on the advice of Martin Quigley, dipped into the Court of Domestic Relations in New York City, the largest such court in the world, and had engaged the interest of the Chief Magistrate, Judge Steven Jackson, who apportioned cases among the seventeen other judges in his jurisdiction.

Quigley loved Joe Breen, but he feared he had fallen victim to the fate described by Alexander Pope, in a quatrain that Joe himself was fond of quoting:

> *Vice is a monster of so frightful mien,*
> *As to be hated needs but to be seen;*
> *Yet seen too oft, familiar with her face,*
> *We first endure, then pity, then embrace.*

To reverse this trend of getting overly affectionate with the Adversaries, Quigley advised Jackson to separate himself from the film community and not steep himself in its social life. Therefore, when it came time to look for a place to live, Steve turned his sights in the opposite direction from Malibu and Bel Air, and sought out a traditional California residence well to the east of Hollywood, at the foot of the Angeles Crest mountains. Of course, the decision was made easier by the fact that Sierra Madre, with its palm trees and the "biggest wisteria vine in the world" was also in immediate proximity to Santa Anita racetrack.

The thoroughbreds were Steve's Saturday joy; nor is it to be denied that I was to be caught many a time leaning over the rail beside him, a scotch in hand, waiting for the first animal to lift its tail and deposit a banquet of steaming nuggets on the track. This would be our betting choice, on the grounds that this was the horse that felt good.

Well it was that I came close to Steve, because he later admitted that he had been advised by Francis Harmon, the Protestant, to chop off the heads of both myself and Doc. Too much Catholicity in that Code group?

In order to make it possible for Steve to function, Joe Breen arranged to make a prolonged visit to his original haunt, Jamaica, where, among other things, he could recount his "famous stories" to his old Jesuit friends, as well as to any unsuspecting tourists who might be sitting on the porch of an evening. Nobody had any illusions, however. Joe had not yet relinquished the post in any formal sense, so that far or near, he was still just as much the emperor as Tiberius on Capri. Steve's tenure as Acting Director of the Code was as insubstantial as the term implied.

As it was, he lasted a year and a half, and his term of office is characterized, in the minds of the Code staff, by three symbols: a coffee cup, a brassiere, and a letter.

The coffee cup belongs to the Walter Wanger film *Tap Roots*. Those who recall this epic will remember that it was a Civil War film, sort of a poor man's *Gone with the Wind*.

A dispute arose over a scene in which Susan Hayward spent the night in the headquarters of her erstwhile lover, a Captain Clay MacIvor, with the idea of stalling an attack he had planned on her beloved Lebanon Valley. Needless to say, her new suitor, Van Heflin, was slogging his way industriously through the mud with a hundred mules and three hundred men to come to the rescue.

The question became: "What did Susan do to keep Clay occupied the long night through, *after* the fade-out?"

The studio said, "Nothing. Clay fell asleep."

The Code staff said, "Haha—what do you take us for? She acts like she is going to make the big sacrifice when she draws up her skirts and heads for Clay's camp. And she acts as if she has thoroughly enjoyed the immolation the next morning. And lastly, the dialogue 'philosophizes' about it. Everything points to only one conclusion."

The studio countered, "You mean to say that Clay struggled out of those *cavalry* boots, did his little business in bed, and then *came back* to the living room, *put on* those boots again, as well as all those Sam Browne belts, and then fell asleep on the sofa, *sitting up?*"

We said, "You don't know those Southern men—especially one with a name like Clay."

The studio representative studied us with dumfoundment, and exclaimed, "Well, all I can say is, I congratulate you fellows, individually and as a group!"

Nothing daunted, we continued to insist on an *affirmative proof* that nothing had happened while we were not looking. It was at this point that someone suggested that we discover Clay still clutching the coffee cup we had last seen in his hands the night before.

Steve hemmed and hawed about so thin a device, and finally decided to take a chance that it would convey the impression of an unbroken occupation: sleep. But he waited in terror to see if the Legion of Decency would read it so kindly. Steve was in a state of probation, and a condemnation by the Legion could be fatal.

When the word finally leaked through that the Legion had taken the scene at its face value, Steve breathed a huge sigh of relief. It was his first Code triumph.

So tensely did he wait for the verdict, that the coffee cup became a byword around the Code corridors. Even years later, if a situation should arise in which a woman was tempted to barter her virtue for some goods ("screwing for the jewels" as it was called) someone on the staff would be apt to say, "Put in a coffee cup."

The brassiere belonged to the film *Johnny Belinda,* a beautiful story about a doctor who woos out into the open the buried soul of a deaf-mute girl.

In the picture was a scene of a legless manikin, set in a store window, dressed only in a girdle and brassiere. The sight of the strange and lacy harness intrigues the mute girl, and she goes into the store and buys one.

Steve apparently took this innovation as being a harbinger, which would lead to the exploitation of further intimacies. It was also another test of his mettle, for the studio had been warned that the prop would not be acceptable. Therefore, he dug his feet into the ground, and stood against the item with the intransigence of Martin Luther when the famous protestor declared, "Here I stand. I can do no other."

Steve finally yielded, reluctantly, to the tantrums of the studio; but not before he had badly blurred his image with Warner Brothers, a very powerful company.

The key to the failure of Steve Jackson to make the scene in Hollywood was, however, *Letter from an Unknown Woman.*

This fairly well-known play by Stefan Zweig dealt with the "romantic interlude" between a young woman, Lisa, and a rising young concert pianist, another Stefan, out of which a son is born. The pianist goes on from conquest to conquest, both on the keyboard and in the bedroom, never knowing about his child nor the enduring love of Lisa. He learns about them from a letter she sends, after both she and the boy are dead.

In remorse, Stefan accepts a challenge to a duel and goes out to be killed.

Joe Breen had set the point of view toward this story. It was one of hostility. In a remarkable letter, he had informed the executive-producer, William Dozier (whose wife at that time, Joan Fontaine, was the star of the picture) , that "we would like to have you 'punch up' the compensating moral values" and to *"punch up* the flavor of condemnation" so as to "slap Stefan down." Lisa's husband should "slap her for her stupidity, and her sin." He should also "more definitely slap Stefan." The obvious comment about all these pugilistic terms is, of course, too clear to belabor.

Steve studied the file, familiarized himself with the issues, and hitched up his belt. He recognized the party line and was not going to let Breen down.

When Breen returned from the Caribbean some months later, he found Universal Studios in an uproar. Jackson had categorically rejected the finished picture.

Steve, in an effort to counterbalance what he considered a "romanticization" of the affair, had offered Dozier a "voice for morality" which, in retrospect, sounded like a homily from Saint John Chrysostom. The studio had impolitely ground it under foot.

Joe examined the film and broke the impasse by *ordering* Steve to issue the Certificate on it.

Steve had reason to feel offended. Not only was he contravened, as the presumed director of the Code, but there was the slight flavor that Breen was doubling back on him. Joe had set the rigid tone, and Steve was only backing his action.

But Jackson had little choice. His alternative was to climb on a train and return to the Bench.

With wounded dignity, therefore, Steve sat down, and sent the following letter to Universal:

> I have just talked with Mr. Breen about LETTER FROM AN UNKNOWN WOMAN. He has advised me that it is his opinion that we should not further persist in our objection to the picture. While this is not in accordance with my view, I, of course, yield to Mr. Breen's decision.

After all the fuss and furor, the Legion of Decency put the film in the "B" category, or "morally objectionable in part for all."

When asked to explain what was meant by their statement that ". . . this film tends to justify immoral action," the

Legion responded that the leading man's regeneration "was dramatically symbolized by his departing to participate in an immoral affair, namely, *the duel!*"

"The mountains are in labor, and out scurries a ridiculous mouse!"

As a man of honor, Steve now knew that he would have to seize the nettle of this inhuman situation in both hands.

He turned to Eric Johnston and demanded that the issue be resolved one way or the other. Johnston swung to Jackson, who was, after all, his nominee. The Board of Directors in New York tended to concur. They would need only the cooperation of the studio heads in Hollywood.

A hurried night conference was convened in the house of one of the moguls, someone on the order of Louis B. Mayer, or Jack Warner. The next day, the copy of a telegram was delivered to Steve. It was addressed to the presidents, and it stated, in terms that were remarkable for their clarity and directness, that they would not do business with Jackson.

The ax had fallen.

All in all, the saga of Steve Jackson was a simple story of miscasting. By training and disposition, he was not suited to act out the necessary charades of the job. He tended to be too legal and mechanical about matters that required the ability to swallow fraud, intellectual insults, the challenge to the infallibility of one's judgment, the dissatisfaction of never being able to achieve perfection and, not the least, the frustration of living in a world of creativity without ever having artistic children of one's own.

Steve had been given his romantic interlude, all right; and we all know how Joe Breen defined that.

10 The Ingrid Bergman Affair and *The Moon Is Blue*

ALTHOUGH BREEN's life style was beginning to run low, he was not above an occasional daring sortie, which sometimes flared into a lick of luck. An example occurred in the case of the internationally liked actress Ingrid Bergman.

Joe returned from another of his multiplying absences to be confronted by an air of bitter scandal over her conduct with the Italian director Roberto Rossellini. This grieved Joe in a particular way, since Ingrid was his ideal as an actress and a lady. She was bringing dignity to the business as a whole, when she acted in desperation to shake off the image of Joan of Arc that was being impinged upon her in real life in carryover of her portrayal of the role on the screen. All she wanted was to re-find her right to be a woman.

Joe sought out my opinion in this matter, since I had been assigned to the Wanger film, and had gotten passing acquainted with Ingrid. "I'd like to write her a letter," he told me.

"Why not?" I asked.

He jiggled his ever-present keys in his pocket. "It's not my business. I feel like a buttinsky."

"You know you want to. And you know you're going to."

"I guess you're right." He left, his chin set. In a little while, he came back with a rough draft of a letter in his hand. "How's this?" he asked, thrusting it at me. I read:

April 22, 1949

Miss Ingrid Bergman
c/o R.K.O. Radio Films, S.A.I.
5 Via Romagna
Rome, Italy

Dear Miss Bergman:

In recent days, the American newspapers have carried, rather widely, a story to the effect that you are about to divorce your husband, forsake your child, and marry Roberto Rossellini.

It goes without saying that these reports are the cause of great consternation among large numbers of our people who have come to look upon you as the *first lady* of the screen—both individually and artistically.

On all hands, I hear nothing but expressions of the most profound shock that you have any such plans.

My purpose in presuming to write to you in the matter, is to call your attention to the situation. I feel that these reports are untrue and that they are, possibly, the result of some over-zealousness on the part of a press agent, who mistakenly believes these kinds of stories to be helpful from a publicity standpoint.

Anyone who has any such thought is, of course, tragically in error. Such stories, will not only *not* react favorably to your picture, but may, very well *destroy your career as a motion picture artist.* They may result in the American public becoming so thoroughly outraged that your pictures will be ignored, and your box-office value ruined.

This condition has become so serious that I am constrained to suggest that you find occasion, *at the earliest possible moment,* to issue a denial of these rumors—to state, quite frankly, that they are not true, that you have no intention to desert your child or to divorce your husband, and that you have no plans to marry anyone.

I make this suggestion to you in the utmost sincerity and solely with a view to stamping out these reports that constitute a major scandal, and may well result in *complete disaster to you personally.*

I hope you won't mind my writing to you so frankly. This is all so important, however, that I cannot resist conveying to you my considered thought in the matter.

With assurances of my esteem, I am

Very cordially,
Joseph I. Breen

Surely no one can miss the immensity of character in these lines. What might be consummate arrogance for someone else was saved by its flavor of fraternal anguish. I urged Joe to stick it in the mailbox as quickly as possible, before he got second thoughts. He did, with a strange docility of which he was sometimes capable.

The letter was received in the spirit in which it was sent by Ingrid, who, unfortunately, had very few options by way of answers. It would seem that she was already bearing the child of Rossellini. In lovely manner, she replied:

Stromboli, Mai 8—49

Dear Mr. Breen,

Since the arrival of your very kind letter I have made a statement. But so much harm is already made I believe no statement can cure it. I am deeply sorry to have hurt my friends involved in the pictures I have already made. I hope with all my heart they will not have to pay for my fault.

My sincere thanks for your concern and kindness.

Yours,
Ingrid Bergman

With Ingrid's reply, the case was closed. The letters were consigned to the files, in mute testimony of two exceptional people. The encounter began to wane into oblivion.

Not so, however, in the chambers of an august and powerful lawmaker. Senator Edwin Johnson of Colorado, who was a leader in the Swedish-American community, was mortally chagrined by the conduct of Ingrid, to whom he had pointed with pride as a model of Nordic womanhood. In indignation, he tried to punish the Hollywood movie community. He drew up a bill, which he presented to the Senate, which would make it mandatory for all people in the entertainment industry to be licensed. The bill would give responsible people an iron control over actors and actresses who were public symbols, by the simple device of making it possible to cancel their licenses for such causes as public infamy. The bill, if passed, would have dealt a serious blow to the motion picture business.

In distress, Eric Johnston, who had a peculiar rapport with Senator Johnson because of his similarly Swedish background, called to Joe Breen in Hollywood and told him to come to Washington. Joe, as a stalwart representative of the moral qualities which Senator Johnson said were deplorably lacking in Hollywood, would be an excellent adornment at a meeting in which Johnston hoped to dissuade Johnson from pressing for passage of his bill.

With the wits of a burglar, Joe Breen tucked photostats of the correspondence between himself and Ingrid into his pocket before boarding the plane.

We have Joe's rendition of what occurred at the meeting. Senator Johnson was a strong, fine-countenanced, and angry man. His attitude toward Johnston was aggressive and somewhat belittling. He held the Hollywood community in scorn because of its proclivity to foul up the lives of decent people. He was determined to press with all his might for the passage of his bill, and when Eric Johnston suggested that the licensing of movie actors and actresses was unsupportable by tradition and an affront to the American idea, the lawmaker brushed the objection aside curtly. "Where do you people think you get off?" Joe reported the Senator as saying. "Everybody has to get licensed in this country. Taxi drivers, bartenders, plumbers, anybody who can become a public menace. People who want to safeguard their level of living make sure that these people come up to certain standards. What makes actors and actresses exempt? They have a very deep influence on the lives of their fans. Why shouldn't they be made to come up to certain standards?"

Johnston then protested that Hollywood was not standard-less, that, in fact, it operated at a very high moral level and by very idealistic norms, in the form of the Production Code, and in the person of the Code Administrator, Joe Breen, here present.

The Senator then turned to Breen and said, "Oh, yes, I've heard of you, and I'm told you're quite a guy. But if everything Eric says is so, why didn't anybody speak up when the Ingrid atrocity was going on? Everybody stood by in silence and didn't lift a finger. Did *you*, Eric?"

Johnston had to say he didn't think it was his place to intrude into the intimate private lives of people in his business.

"There you go," said the Senator. "That's why we need a law. If one single voice had been raised, if one single objection had been interposed, I'd have more respect for the movie business, and would drop passage of my bill."

At this point, Joe Breen was beginning to swell with antici-pation. Reaching into his coat pocket, he withdrew the photo-stats, and said, "Just a minute, Mr. Senator. There was one voice. There was a protest made."

"Whose voice?" demanded the Senator. "I heard none."

"Mine!"

"Yours?"

"Yes sir."

"In what manner?"

"In this manner, sir. I invite you to read these." And he held forward the documents for the lawmaker's inspection.

Senator Johnson scanned the correspondence closely, and looked up at Breen in a new light. "Had I known these letters existed," he said, "I would not have initiated my bill. Now I will kill it."

It is to be surmised that the letters took Eric Johnston as much by surprise as they did Senator Johnson. This is not so extraordinary, since they were a private venture of Breen's, and Joe knew how to conceal a hole card. Neither is it to be doubted that the new "czar" began to regard his "employee" with different and respectful eyes.

Joe had that quality which Napoleon demanded of his military leaders, when he said, "Yes, I know Marshal So-and-So is a great tactician, and a marvelous disciplinarian, or whatever. But tell me. Is he lucky?"

It is no wonder that Eric Johnston called on Breen again when Howard Hughes was acting difficult over one of his pictures and was threatening to release it without a Code Seal. This forced on Johnston the ugly question of whether he should expel Hughes and RKO from the Association. It was particularly painful, because it meant a loss in revenue for the Association's coffers. But Johnston faced up to the inevitable and asked Joe in a telephone conversation whether he was entitled to throw Hughes out.

In typical fashion, Breen replied, "Can you throw him out? Well, let me answer your question *with* a question. If I am a member of a country club and I pay my dues faithfully, but I insist on pissing on the piano, do you think you can get rid of me?"

Johnston did not need an interpretation of Breen's opinion.

Neither had Joe's proclivity for sowing the seeds of sedition disappeared. He was concerned that the producers were stirring and beginning to show streaks of boldness. He knew how to cope with this, but he no longer had quite the fiery energy to launch the remedy. Therefore, he buttonholed me in private and detailed a plan he had been nurturing in secret for many years.

"What I thought to do at one time," he said, "was to start a Legion of Scriveners. This is a cash business, you know. That means that every day lost is money at the box office that is gone forever. That's why producers are so sensitive to complaints. They see a silver stream of dollars flowing under the bridge that are completely unrecoverable.

"You know the power of one good letter? I don't mean a ream of signatures on a roll of Waldorf that've been cooked up by an Irish nun in the Midwest. They just go into the waste-basket. No. I mean a thoughtful letter from the president of a bank. Or the head of an insurance company. A dozen of those'd make more of an impression than a bushel of postcards.

"All you have to do is organize. They shouldn't all come in at once. And, for Christ's sake, whoever was writing should see the picture. That's a courtesy a lot of people don't seem to think they're obliged by. And they should be regional—not twelve from Los Angeles, you know.

"It'd be easy—there's a lot of existing organizations. There's the Knights of Columbus, the Holy Name Society, you name them. They have the highest type men." He paused, cocked his head to see if I was getting the picture, and then pushed home the obvious question. "Why wouldn't that be a good undertaking for a young man like you?"

I was giddy with visions of power. This was the type thing I was programmed to do, and to do well. But there had been, perhaps, a Freudian slip in the use of one certain word. This was the term "undertaking." I somehow vaguely felt that this was more a description of what would happen to me should I take Joe up on his proposition. Without making an issue of it, I passed.

But Joe was revealed as that marvelous combination of a pyromaniac who owned the fire department.

At this point arose the case that has become a minor house-hold word in the lore of modern censorship. I refer to *The Moon Is Blue*.

This was a picture made by Otto Preminger from a popular stage play by F. Hugh Herbert. It was refused a certificate by the Code, and condemned by the Legion of Decency. On appeal, it was turned down by the Board of Directors of the Motion Picture Association. To release the film, United Artists had to resign from the Association. This they did, and, despite a storm of controversy and a mass of pressures, they succeeded in achieving a smash hit. It was a bellwether of things to come.

Most people thought that the issue with *The Moon* was one of "blue" language. Even the usually careful New York *Times* stated that one of the reasons this film fell into disfavor with the custodians of the Code "obviously" was the absolute lack of inhibition with which sex was discussed. It cited such "taboo" words as "virgin," "seduce," and "pregnant," which, said the paper, were used "with bland insouciance and cool forthrightness."

Such was not the problem. Even while the picture was still in the early stages of preparation, Joe Breen wrote to Martin Quigley, who was negotiating behind the scenes with Arthur Krim, the President of United Artists. Joe declared that Krim was definitely misled if he believed that "if questionable language was properly treated in production, the picture would probably prove acceptable."

Within the hard little knot of the film makers themselves, there was a consciousness of being daring in taking this enterprise in hand. The star, William Holden, was quoted in an interview as saying that Preminger, Herbert, and himself entered into an agreement before the picture went into production that the screenplay would not be submitted to the Breen office for approval. "I didn't see anything unmoral about the picture," the actor said. But the pact, by such sophisticated people, made later protestations of surprised innocence at the reaction to the picture sound suspiciously hollow indeed. At any rate, somebody must have slipped up, for the script was, in fact, sent in to the Code office in the waning days of 1952, and, after much soul-searching, a letter was returned to the studio by way of a New Year's present.

True, the letter contained such minuscule prohibitions as "The broken expression 'son of a . . .' is unacceptable"; and "The reference to marijuana should be omitted." But other lines got closer to the heart of the matter. There was dialogue like "Men are usually bored with virgins," and ". . . godliness does not appeal to me," followed by "steaks—liquor—and sex. In that order." Elsewhere there was the line "I always feel uncomfortable on a high moral plane." It was the flavor of talk such as this that created the question.

More specifically, the problem arose from the plot. The premise of the story was this. Maggie McNamara, a talkative aspiring television actress has allowed herself to be picked up by a successful architect, William Holden. He has just had a spat with the girl upstairs, Dawn Addams, daughter of the charming scamp David Niven. It seems that Dawn had come home the night before, only to find her father under the influence of alcohol and preparing to bed down with his current lady friend. Coming downstairs, she had appealed to Holden for a place to sleep. He surrendered his bed in a chivalrous manner and slept on a couch in the living room. In the great spate of misunderstandings that followed this arrangement, Holden categorically denied that nobility or moral principle had anything to do with his decency. He had drawn back because the girl had forced the issue on his malehood, taking away from him the right to choose the time, the place, and the circumstances. To prove his point, he had gone out and found Maggie McNamara.

Right here lay the first root problem. Inferentially, the story was saying that "free love" was something outside the scope of morality altogether, was a matter of moral indifference. Had the architect chosen to pursue the opportunity on his own terms, that was his business. Later, a lady viewer of the film wrote in without solicitation to splutter that this premise was so alien to our moral concepts that she intended to call the picture to the attention of the "UnAmerican Activities Committee of the United States."

What came into contention was the Code clause that stated, "Pictures shall not infer that low forms of sex relationship are the accepted or common thing." Philosophically this was one of the most important provisions in the entire Code document.

If "free love" were a commonplace, and were something widely accept*ed,* it was only a small elision over into the conclusion that it was accept*able.* This then became a matter of condoning evil in principle, which in turn became a question of embracing corrupt standards.

The plot went on to take another twist. David Niven, our swinger, came storming downstairs in the role of outraged father to horsewhip Holden when he heard that his daughter had slept in an alien bed. However, as he discovers that nothing happened, he is at first nonplused and then chagrined that the girl's vanity has been so sorely wounded. He decides that he ought to horsewhip the architect for compromising the girl by *not* making a pass at her.

Naturally, this element in the plot did nothing but bruise an already sore point. But the main item was yet to come. Circulating like a vestal virgin in the midst of all these complications was the aggressively chaste figure of Maggie McNamara. So emphatic does she become about her virtue that William Holden eventually accuses her of being a "professional virgin." When she asks him what that means, he tells her that she is always advertising her virginity. She wants to know, indignantly, what is wrong with that. He says that those who advertise usually have something to sell. This, incidentally, is probably the most remembered dialogue in the piece. It is a big laugh on Maggie McNamara, putting her in her place.

The only trouble was that, to the devotees of sexual continence, the figure of Maggie McNamara is the main rooting interest. The architect is someone to be looked at with envy, but not cheered on. He has to be overcome. But (and this was the key to the entire controversy) when he so patently tops Maggie, he is made to seem to win. She, on the other hand, is made to seem eccentric for being "clean," an oddball for clinging to her virtue in the midst of this "characteristically" loose way of life.

It was the recognition of this factor that made the hackles rise on the back of Joe Breen's neck and prompted him to make of this picture his last great orchestral flourish. To Joe, this was an issue involving the original set of values on which the Code was founded. To support his point of view, he called in the friendly opinion of the man who was, at that time, his favorite spokesman of the old-fashioned verities, the Hearst newspaper columnist, George Sokolsky. "Sound as a nut," Joe used to dub him, and he repeated the accolade so often that we never referred to the man except as "sound-as-a-nut-Sokolsky." To back Joe, Sokolsky wrote a column blasting the film.

The one individual close to the scene who was not in accord with this assessment of the play was Geoff Shurlock. From the very outset, he could not see what all the fuss was about. But inasmuch as he was, like the Centurion, "a man subject to orders," he did what he was told, and wrote letters on terms dictated by the man who was still Boss. But in conferring with Preminger, Geoff did not discuss any of the details of the letter which he had dumbly written, but simply encouraged the entrepreneur to make the picture according to the dictates of his "integrity" and "taste." There are those who will argue that Geoff was drawing a long bow by putting it on this basis, but Preminger loved it, and ultimately made Geoff his pet.

Actually, those who could not understand the objections raised against this film were looking at the story from the opposite end of the telescope. They believed the character portrayed by Maggie McNamara. They were not overpowered by the character of William Holden. They realized that the girl was being a bit extravagant and a bit too aggressive about her virtue, but on the whole they knew she was right, and Holden wrong. Such was the way Preminger argued. He pointed out, in an impassioned argument with Breen, that it was Maggie, the virtuous girl, who wins, in the sense that she gets her man because she is decent, and without giving the precious commodity in her loins away. Thus, virtue triumphs.

Furthermore, she was a person who worked for a living, who neither drank nor smoked, and who was completely honest and outspoken.

Even the Legion of Decency was tempted to look on the picture in this manner. After the furor had died down and the picture had gone into limbo, an influential party in this organization confessed that they had acted to condemn the film, not out of intrinsic reasons, but for extrinsic considerations—namely to support the Code and prevent the seamless garment from being rent.

It is not, however, as though Joe Breen were naïve by the standards of that particular moment in history, or that people did not agree with him in formidable array. Even the secular press, which was clearly more sensitive in the early fifties than it is in the late sixties, was aghast at the brassiness of the film. A trade magazine like the *Showmen's Trade Review* (nothing prim here) said that to hear for the first time from the motion picture screen such words as "virgin" and "seduce" "is a shock even for the most sophisticated." We have come a long way since then. Amusingly, *Variety*'s London correspondent indicated that it all got veddy, veddy boring to the English, because "British audiences don't take to unrelieved sex with the same enthusiasm as their counterparts in America." On the local scene, the *Motion Picture Daily* warned exhibitors: "If your audiences are prepared to take . . . outspokenness [they] will be amused. If your audiences are of a different stripe, you'd better see this before your house falls in on you."

The Catholic Hierarchy did not see the situation as good-naturedly as some of the journeymen in the Legion of Decency. The Cardinal's Residence in New York issued a proclamation against the picture, saying that it openly spurned the Code and was an attempt to ignore and override the moral law and to challenge the ideals of morally wholesome standards in public entertainment. It was labeled as "an occasion of sin," and Catholics were not only reminded of their obligation to avoid it, but of their pledge to refrain from attendance at theaters that flout decency by exhibiting such a picture. The Archbishop of Philadelphia, John F. O'Hara, issued a similar edict and strove strongly to keep the film out of that city. And the President of the Archdiocesan Council of San Francisco wrote to say that "Whoever was brazen enough and had the temerity to proceed lacking approval of the established standards of the Code reviewers is a direct challenge to the public."

Finally, the picture was refused acceptance by the Maryland Board of Censors, and the case was brought into the courts. On December 7, 1953, the answer was returned by Judge Herman Moser, upsetting the Board of Censors, and ordering them to license the film. In his memorandum opinion, Judge Moser said, among other things, that the film "is a light comedy telling a tale of wide-eyed, brash, puppy-like innocence routing or converting to its side the forces of evil it encounters." Preminger was vindicated.

So, incidentally, was Geoff Shurlock. All during the heated discussions involving the rejection of the picture, he kept echoing like a stuck needle that *The Moon Is Blue* was a story of the triumph of goodness. Several times he was verbally overrun by Joe Breen for clinging stubbornly to this point of view. But Geoff did not waver. He kept his secret locked in his heart and, when he finally got the chance, took it on himself personally to issue the Certificate of Approval on *The Moon* as a private accommodation to Otto Preminger. On June 28, 1961, a full eight years later, Geoff sent Certificate No. 20017 to United Artists, who came back into the fold.

The support afforded the film by the public made Joe realize that the jig was truly up.

In recognition of his feats, the Academy of Motion Picture Arts and Sciences bestowed on him one of its special Golden Oscars, largely through the good offices of Walter Wanger, a member of the Board of Governors.

Joe threw a party, and the Oscar cost him plenty. An Oscar for the Censor was surely never dreamed of when the Code was signed in 1930.

Before drawing the curtain on Joe, then, it is interesting to try to form an estimate of him. It is said that power corrupts, and absolute power corrupts absolutely. Joe, who in his heyday let the functions of the Code proliferate out in all directions, almost without let, cannot plead sanctuary from the inevitable question. Did he indulge in more wrong than he set out to correct?

He did his part in pulling an important industry out of the doldrums. That was not easy, nor should it be disposed of too lightly. The tricks he used could be described as no more than "love talk in disguise." Was he, then, as Sam Goldwyn described him, only "Hollywood's benevolent conscience"? Or was he, like his friend Harry Cohn, the "monitor ass of the universe"?

Probably a dash of each; with a small twist of Shamrock.

One thing is certain, however. Joe Breen could never have been what he was, nor would all his personality have prevailed, had not the times demanded him. He was as much a creature of the moment as a shaper of it. He had come to lead a recalcitrant and chastened people back into Traditional Morality, in order to change the frown of the Great Father in the skies into a smile. In this sense, the Code was a throwback. In the sense that tradition represented much that is sound and everlasting in human nature, it was an advance from a retrogression.

One way or the other, Breen finally reached out with his Sistine finger, and touched the fingertips of his alter ego and successor, Geoffrey Shurlock. A new director had been created. The date was October 15, 1954.

11 | A Study in Reverse English

GEOFF SHURLOCK's relationship to Joe Breen is best typified by a conversation that took place at a luncheon with the Director of the Screen Producers Guild, Mr. Lou Greenspan. Breen was complaining of an uncompleted dream he had had the previous night that had left him frustrated. He wanted to go back to bed to finish the broken fragment so he could be awake in peace.

"What was the dream about?" he was asked.

"It was about this Liverpool wharf rat," he said, poking his thumb in the direction of Geoff, and falling back on his term of endearment for his English-born confrere. "I was trying to tell him to do something, and he was standing there with a loud voice saying 'No!' I kept saying 'Yes!' but he kept repeating 'No!' I was so stumped it woke me up."

Geoff had been listening with eyes full of astonishment. "I said 'No!' to you in your dream?" he queried. "Impossible! I wouldn't even say 'No!' to you in *my* dream!"

Geoff assumed the Director's mantle with nervousness. He was a small, stocky man with even, slightly rounded features, who tended to think faster than his voice would work. In consequence, he would progress through a pressurized conversation as though he had a clogged carburetor. To accentuate the tempo, he had a habit of taking off and putting on his horn-rimmed glasses in the manner that another man might scratch his head. In the beginning, he proclaimed to all within earshot that he was not a one-man band, and that henceforth the Code would be run primarily by Junta. He wanted to lay off his opinion on the rest of the staff, for he had no desire to impose his mind on anyone, least of all the moviemakers.

His psychological center of gravity was to be found in a small story which he adopted from Joe Breen, and which he used to repeat with frequency. It had to do with a young Irishman who brought his bride to Niagara Falls on their honeymoon. Standing on the brink, the two newlyweds were awestruck. "Glory be to God," breathed the bride. "Would you look at all that water goin' over that there cliff!" The groom looked at her with lofted brows. "An' what's to hinder it?" he wanted to know.

With a consistency that was close to infernal, Geoff struck, and kept, this attitude toward producers. If they desired to make exploratory sallies out into new fields, Geoff would look at them flatly and ask, "What's to hinder you?" The look of happy befuddlement that came over the faces of the interrogators was worth the price of admission. They did not want to say, "You," since that might start a new, negative train of thought in Geoff's mind. In consequence, Geoff was free to work his ploy like a practiced larcenist. If any man had the urge to pour over any cliffs whatsoever, Geoff would not try to inhibit him. Just the opposite; Geoff would offer to push. "Then we'll both know what it's like." In this manner, he made screaming conservatives out of many a flirtatious liberal. But he knew that taste and restraint are learned more convincingly from sorry experience than from wise counsel. He could easily have assumed as his own the pungent comment of Gene Fowler: "I am glad that I paid so little attention to good advice; had I abided by it, I might have been saved some of my most valuable mistakes."

Geoff was English. And having "English" on a billiard ball means to be going forward with a reverse spin. This was Geoff. He was skidding across the slate of life, all right, but in a state of constant backspin.

Characteristic was Geoff's reaction to Breen's pending retirement. Right out of the box, he proposed to Joe that the Code should be put out of existence. Would Joe mind if he tried?

When the startled Breen regained his aplomb, he courted the tantalizing idea for a while. After all, it was terribly complimentary to think, like Louis XV, "After me, the deluge!" Even when more sober reflections set in, it still sounded good. It was a contradiction in terms to protract a compulsory system of self-control. And so he waved Geoff off on an unsuspecting industry, which Geoff promptly flew into like a visitation of gadflies from the Lord of these creatures.

We have an example.

He and I were protectively entrenched one afternoon in a booth at Lucy's, the then popular restaurant across from Paramount and RKO studios, and we were in the interesting company of Eddie Dmytryk, the director, and John Paxton, the writer. We were discussing the anti-anti-Semitic picture titled *Crossfire*. The original novel from which it had been derived, *The Brick Foxhole,* had been written by the talented writer-director Richard Brooks.

The lunch was good, and we ironed out what few problems we had on the script in short order. When it was over, Geoff, who had been itching for the business to be disposed of so he could get to his project, turned to Dmytryk and blurted out, "Eddie, you're something of a liberal. I'd like to try out an idea on you and see what you think."

Dmytryk nodded wisely and indicated for Geoff to go ahead.

"I am trying to organize a movement," said Geoff, "to abolish the Production Code. I think we ought to be wiped out. Now, what do you think of that?"

Eddie looked at Geoff in confoundment. He flicked the ashes off his cigarette. "What do you mean?" he asked, waving vaguely. He wanted Geoff to elucidate further.

"Just what I said!" pressed Geoff, beginning to remove and replace his glasses in irrational sequence. "I am trying to get a quorum of movie people to vote us out of business. What I want to know is would you give your vote to a movement of this sort—if we could get up a motion to abolish us, would you cast your vote in favor of it?"

This was like the captain of a ship calling together his passengers on the high seas and saying, "All right! I agree with you. The accommodations are no good. And it's a lousy ship anyway. Let's sink the silly thing!"

"Well," said Eddie, bewildered, "I don't know! I don't know what you have in mind!"

Geoff was equal to the occasion.

"What I mean, Eddie," he plunged on, "is that I don't think we're a good thing. I don't think the Code is good. I think it's conducive to irresponsibility among the producers. We make the decisions, we carry the load, and I don't think that's a good thing. How can we ever expect the producers to begin thinking morally unless they are forced to? And we'll never have really moral pictures until producers think in terms of morals *themselves*. We're tired of playing nursemaid to the Industry. It's keeping pictures perpetually adolescent."

By this time, John Paxton, the writer, was sitting on the edge of his seat. "But what would you do with the Code?" he asked. "Just . . . throw it away?"

"No-o-o!" exclaimed Geoff. "Give it back to the producers! Let them administer it themselves!"

Eddie Dmytryk shook his head disparagingly. "It can't be done, Geoff," he said. "It's a good idea, but it wouldn't work!"

"Why not?" yipped Geoff. "Aren't the producers capable?"

This touched Eddie where he lived. "No," he said, with an annoyed shake of his head. "It's not that!" The writer was nodding in agreement. "It's something larger than that. It's just that I don't think any form of civilized society can get along without its equivalent of a police force. It's in the cards—"

"The British seem to do it," quickly retorted Geoff. "They have no Code, and yet they seem to get along. That's why we get such fine, mature pictures from England. Look at *Brief Encounter*."

Eddie and the writer looked at each other, their eyes beginning to glint with a faint hope.

"What's the matter, Eddie?" pressed Geoff. "Don't you think *you* could handle it? Don't *you* think you could interpret the Code properly if it were put in your hands? Don't you trust your taste?"

Eddie shifted uneasily. "Oh no!" he protested, "I think *I* could handle it all right! It's not that. I have confidence in my own taste. But how about all the rest? Do you think you could just pass this Code out indiscriminately to everybody and expect them to keep it?"

Geoff was relentless. "Everyone I go to says the same thing," he protested. "*I* can do it, but how about the *others?* We'll never get anywhere with that sort of argument! Are we going to work on the presumption that *we're* going to be in business *forever?* The Code was a good temporary expedient to meet an emergency. But the emergency has passed. And are you guys going to be hobbled with us perpetually, just out of your own cowardice?"

John Paxton was making marks on the tablecloth with a fork. "You couldn't do a thing like this without preparation," he said. "The producers would have to be prepared. They're not ready at a moment's notice to take such a responsibility in their hands."

Geoff sniffed. "Prepared," he said. "They're as prepared now as they'll ever be. The Code's been in existence for—how long?—seventeen years now? During that time we've worked on every conceivable sort of problem. We're given twelve thousand Seals, and written maybe fifty thousand letters, possibly more. We've had conferences and arguments and telephone calls and everything else. It seems to me they should be through their apprenticeship by now. If they're not prepared by this time, they'll never be!"

The writer looked at the director and the director looked at the writer. They each shrugged at the other. They had no ready answer to Geoff's own rapid crossfire.

"Well," said Eddie reluctantly, "maybe you're right. Maybe you have something there. But I'm still dubious. I'm still not convinced it would work. I'd have to think more about it."

"Would you give your vote to abolish us?" insisted Geoff.

"Well," yielded Eddie with great hesitation, "maybe it might be worth a try. Yes. Possibly I would!"

"That's all I wanted to know," said Geoff triumphantly, standing up. He spanked the table with the flat of his hand. "I've tried to preach this doctrine in every producer's office in Hollywood. And you are the *first* one from whom I got an affirmative answer! I'm a success!" And with that we shook hands all around and got up and left.

When Geoff tried this routine on the famous Hunt Stromberg, the producer-director called up Joe Breen, greatly worried, and asked him if he knew he had a crazy man on his staff.

"What do you mean?" asked Joe in feigned surprise.

"Why—Geoff," replied Hunt in great indignation.

"What's he done now?" asked Joe.

"He's trying to abolish the Code," answered Hunt. "Do you know about this?"

"Oh, that!" said Joe laughing. "What did you think of it?"

"What did I think of it?" protested Hunt. "You say you know about it and you laugh? What's the matter with you? Are *you* crazy *too?*"

"Wait a minute, Hunt," said Joe soothingly. "Do you realize what Geoff's been doing? How long was he arguing with you?"

"Forty-five minutes," spluttered Hunt. "The damnedest line of palaver you ever heard—"

"Do you realize," continued Joe, "that for forty-five minutes Geoff had you defending the Code? Do you think he's crazy now?"

There was a great pause at the other end of the line. "All he was doing," assured Joe, "was pulling the old confidence trick. He was putting two 'p's' in piss to make it harder to pronounce."

Stromberg lifted his voice grudgingly. "I guess maybe he was pulling my leg at that," he admitted.

Geoff's gamesmanship was not altogether fraudulent. The streak of British in him would not let him go through the empty motions of a lost cause. If the Code was not wanted by the film world, then an effort to sustain it in existence was futile. To waste one's time on a doomed project, whose conclusion was foregone, was "worse than a crime—it was a blunder." He was skeptical of vainglorious heroics, for, to him, if you were not alive, you were nothing. He was the incarnation of the axiom *"Primum est esse."** This probably explains why he was fond of referring to the story of the French aristocrat who, when asked by his grandchildren what he did during the soul-stirring days of the Revolution, replied, "I survived."

His inclination to yield to the force of events without making an issue was at times exasperating. He did not seem to grasp that there were times when the fulfillment of one's individuality requires a gamble with life, and even a squandering of it. Without the theatrics of a Patrick Henry, and the risk, the freedom that Geoff himself enjoyed might never have come into being. Geoff was inclined to look on self-immolation cynically, the final question being, "Yes, but where did it get *him?*" However, when confronted with the charge that his permissiveness was contrary to the masculine impulse, he had an answer. He would start by taking off and putting on his glasses, while admitting that you were probably right—a disarming opening gambit in itself. "However," he would continue, "would you consider the Chinese—how would you put it?—effeminate?"

"No. Certainly not."

"Well, if you would take the trouble to study their history, you'd find that they always won by passivity. They simply

* "The first thing is 'to be.' "

endured. They welcomed their conquerors into their embrace, and absorbed them. The invaders ended up being Chinese. Who was the smartest?"

Geoff's passion for keeping himself in existence was waged in the same backwards manner as he used to keep the Code alive. He kept trying to wipe himself out, nominally, at least. In this fashion, he managed to jump over into the other fellow's shoes and to assume the position that was the opposite of the one he was supposed to be maintaining; and his potential adversaries were arguing to sustain him. He used to declaim that the entertainment business was a young man's business, "so, what the hell am I doing here?" (He was only in his shady fifties.) He used to refer to Lloyd Binford, the octogenarian censor of Memphis, Tennessee, who clung to his post like a starfish to a rock, as "that old fart." And he merrily assaulted the geriatrics club of company presidents in New York by echoing the stale old whiz, that what this business needed more than anything else was a few funerals. The consequence of all this campaigning was to turn his detractors around and make them nervous that Geoff would quit. "This job doesn't call for a boy wonder, Geoff. It calls for some sobriety of judgment. Anyway, you're much younger than the calendar says you are." He had succeeded in laying off the responsibility for his continuance on others.

Following the tactics of his upside down universe, Geoff began exploding paper tigers such as temperance societies, political censor boards, the American Humane Association, the Legion of Decency, and all other public pressure groups that made great growling noises and threatened to hinder the film makers from flowing over the cliffs. Geoff claimed that their bark was worse than their bite and exposed them by defying them. The only trouble was that these were the groups that were supposed to be Geoff's final support and strength in shoring up the Code. But Geoff felt that in dispelling the mirages, he was stronger, not weaker. He had the producers right where they wanted him. They were down to the bedrock of themselves. They could find a sense of their own integrity, or they could make spectacles of themselves for the whole world to see. Geoff would not try to stop them.

In this manner, Geoff, like Tennyson's brook, went bubbling on forever.

His adroitness at getting over on the other fellow's side of the chalk line, rather than standing fast and defending himself, was nicely illustrated by a telephone call that came in one afternoon from the redoubtable David Selznick. D.O.S. had seen a picture the night before that had been approved by Geoff. He wanted to know how the producers got away with it. "You lean on me for the completely inoffensive stuff I put in my pictures," he complained, "and then I go and see this thing, and I'm shocked."

"The reason I had to approve it," Geoff countered, "was that the producer saw *your* last picture. He used it to beat me into submission."

Selznick scrambled on a mental treadmill for a moment. "*You* can't compare my work with that piece of blankety-blank," he spluttered.

"Tell me, David," Geoff quickly parried, "how would you sum up what was wrong with that picture last night?"

"Well," speculated Selznick, picking his words, "I'd say it teetered along the brink of suggestiveness—from beginning to end."

Geoff half rose out of his chair in reply. "Well, wouldn't you say that's our job, David? To *keep* it teetering, but never falling in?"

There was a silence. David knew when he was had. "Well, do the same for me the next time I come in," he groused.

Geoff, too, was not without his experiences with that fountain of perpetual story material, Harry Cohn. One such is a classic.

It seems that good old Harry was having some trouble with one of his better-known directors. A certain Vic Schertzinger was paddling around the studio with a script under his arm, trying to convince Cohn to turn him loose on the stages so he could make a smash hit. Harry did not like the script.

In desperation, Harry at last made a pact with Vic. He told him to pass the script out among the various top executives at Columbia, and that if Vic could get just one of these important men to say he favored the property, Harry would give him permission to make the picture. Harry was going to Europe, anyway, and would not have to linger to absorb Vic's reproachful stares.

And so Vic, like Lot, went about the lot distributing his story, seeking out a responsive man.

On the morning of Harry's departure for the Continent, he called his final production meeting. Avoiding the most unpleasant item on the agenda, he placed the matter of Vic Schertzinger's script at the bottom of the list. Vic squirmed uneasily while Harry droned on, settling other matters of state. So occupied was Vic that he did not notice the figure of a young stranger who slipped into the room during the proceedings. The young man, a new writer at the studio, realizing that he had accidentally gotten into the wrong room, stood up to leave as surreptitiously as he had come. Cohn noticed him out of the corner of his eye, and took it that one of his upper echelon was walking out on him. "Sit down," he commanded, "I'm not finished yet. You leave here when I tell you." The writer promptly sat down.

Finally Harry came to the only question that interested the nervous Schertzinger. "Now about this script, which I presume everybody here's read," he said, looking up from underneath his Olympian brows. "Does anybody like it?"

Silence.

"If anybody likes it, raise his hand."

There was a motionless moment, and then one shy hand was raised in the back of the room. It was the newly joined writer.

Harry was surprised—and stuck. He shrugged and turned to Vic. "Okay," he said. "It looks like you make it."

Overjoyed, Vic grabbed the young writer in the hall as soon

as the meeting broke up, and invited him down to his office. "You're my writer," he told him.

The writer, too, was pleased. However, as the conversation began to develop in Vic's office, a peculiar chill ran through the director. He realized that the writer was talking about a script of his own, and that he had no knowledge of the Schertzinger script at all. The writer was full of congratulations with himself for his good fortune in finding a director and a production schedule for his first effort.

Calculating with the fury of the Lost, Vic went along with the misconception. He encouraged the writer to talk his head off, while he, Vic, was running through his mind the itinerary of Harry Cohn. This was a Friday. By Monday, Harry would be in New York. By Tuesday, he would be on the high seas and out of touch.

He walked over to the writer, put his caressing hand on the young man's shoulder, and assured him his material was great. "I'll tell you what," he said. "This is the weekend. We can't get anything accomplished now, anyway. Why don't you run out to Palm Springs, where you'll have some privacy, and think it out thoroughly? Don't worry about expenses. It's on me. In fact, I won't be able to see you on Monday, I've got some other business, so why don't you take your typewriter with you and *don't come back before Tuesday at the earliest,* you hear?"

The writer had no argument with this. He did as he was told.

We now fade out, and fade in a few months later. The picture is made, and Harry Cohn has come back from Europe.

One dismal afternoon, the picture was booked for showing at the Code projection room. Not knowing what was coming up, Geoffrey volunteered to review it, in company with Joe Breen, who was still in his prime.

During the course of the film, neither Joe nor Geoff noticed a furtive figure who sneaked into the last seat in the back of the room, and sat effacingly against the wall. When the lights went up, Geoff began bouncing about like Jiminy Cricket in a Walt Disney cartoon. "Holy smokes, what a film," he was emoting.

The figure with a long doleful face rose up from the seat alongside the wall. "Did you really like it?" he asked.

"Like it?" enthused Geoff. "It's great, it's wonderful, it's beautiful . . . !"

A soft glow began to appear on the unknown individual's face. "Thank you," he said. "I'm the director."

Geoff rushed over and shook his hands, both of them at the same time. He effused over the man some more.

"Let me introduce myself," said the director. "I am Vic Schertzinger. And I'd like to relate to you a rather remarkable story about this film. Harry Cohn won't look at it. He refuses to see it."

"With his own money in it?" asked Geoff. "Why?"

Vic told.

When Harry got back from abroad, the way he had found out about the "error" was when the young writer came to him and asked when Harry was going to make that picture of his— the one for which he had given permission before leaving for Europe.

When the vapors of Harry's wrath had finally settled, he informed his secretary not to let Schertzinger through his office door, and sat pouting like Achilles in black refusal of the whole project. Schertzinger could make out any way he could. Harry would not inspect what he had.

"Therefore," concluded Schertzinger, "I wonder if I could call on you for a favor. Would you just tell Harry you like my film?

"I'll do better than that," promised Geoff. "Come with me."

The two of them hopped into Geoff's car, a little old Toonerville trolley in those days, and chugged off to Gower Gulch. Instead of going to Cohn's office, Geoff took Vic to the office of Ben Kahane, Harry's chief associate, and a sobering influence on his primitive genius. Geoff began the enthusing act all over again. "Is it as good as all that?" Kahane wanted to know, surprised. "I'll tell you how good it is," said Geoff. "You can tell Harry that he never has to pay me for Code work again. I'll take two per cent, just two per cent of what this picture's going to make. I'll be on easy street the rest of my life!"

Impressed, Kahane passed the word to Cohn, who now got so curious that he had to take a private peek. Harry was no boob. What he saw kept his monitor cheeks entranced.

The picture, as it turned out, was one of the greatest smash hits in the history of Columbia.

12 Cannon to Right of Them . . . Cannon to Left of Them

HARD ON THE HEELS of Preminger's assault on the Code, the venerable apparatus was subjected to a second battering by an even more powerful and headstrong individualist, the wealthy Howard Hughes. The picture involved was the last in his career. It starred Jane Russell, and was called *French Line*.

The script arrived when Joe Breen was phasing out. Geoff Shurlock was the de facto head of the Code, but not yet the Director de jure. The letter setting forth the Code objections to this script was long and bristling, citing item after item which would be a great bore to revive at this late date. In sum, however, their general tenor was equal to the phrasing of the Legion of Decency in condemning *French Line*. The Catholic estimate stated, "This film contains grossly obscene, suggestive, and indecent action, costuming, and dialogue." Even the less partisan trade journal *Harrison's Reports* found it necessary to comment that Jane Russell's "violent wiggling and movements are indeed scandalizing."

Upon review, the picture had been rejected by the Code office, but Hughes went right ahead with plans to distribute it through RKO anyway. But since this corporation was a signatory to the agreement not to distribute a motion picture without a Code Certificate, it was laying itself open to the $25,000 fine for "liquidated damages," should it effect the release. The meaning of the phrase "liquidated damages" is a noteworthy aside. It was a penalty for the disruption of "the stability of the industry" and for causing "serious damage to all members" of the Motion Picture Association. Money collected from the fine was to be used for the expenses incurred in the administration of the Production Code. Joe Breen used to say jocosely, "If we ever collect one of those, we'll all be wearing beaver hats."

Plans had been made to release the controversial film in the city of St. Louis, Missouri. Geographically, this was almost dead center on the map, the very heartland of the United States. But before a formal citation of RKO could be made, clear evidence was needed that the editors had not secretly trimmed the picture without informing the Code office. The film exhibited would have to be the exact copy of the one which had been refused the Seal. Since I was acquainted with all the trouble spots, reel by reel, right down to the last wiggle, Joe booked me into the Chase Hotel, bought me a plane ticket, and directed me to scrutinize the premiere, making notes if necessary. It is interesting that we took care to shun passage on TWA, since this airline was owned by Hughes, and we feared the possibility that a name on the passenger list might somehow leak upstairs to the invisible Man at the Top.

The film was shown in the palatial Fox Theater in downtown St. Louis, and it was the version everyone feared, with no sign of a frame changed. Breen accepted my report and promptly fired off a letter to James R. Grainger, President of the corporation, suing him for the fine. The letter was ignored. It was at this point that Eric Johnston wanted to know whether the Association could dismiss RKO, and Breen gave his answer about membership in the country club.

The money, however, was the least consequential of all the considerations. What was at stake was the survival of the whole system, and even of the whole concept, of achieving decency in the movies. A successful breakthrough by Hughes, exploiting the bulge created by Preminger, would spell eventual doom for the entire experiment, unique in the annals of literary history.

The body that grasped this notion best was the Catholic Church. It concurred in the thought of Lenin, that the film was the most influential tool in existence for the forming and fixing of ideas. Lenin had claimed that he could convert the world to Communism in brief order if he possessed the movie industry. The Church was committed to a stern program in the area of screen morality, and it was under no illusions that its first line of defense was the Industry's own Code. If that were to be destroyed, the Church would be driven back on itself, in a naked confrontation with great economic entities that had no god but Mammon.

These various considerations did not escape the attention of the prelate of St. Louis, the estimable Archbishop (eventually Cardinal) Ritter. This churchman was a soft-spoken but fearless German, who later came to national attention by excommunicating a woman in his diocese for impeding race integration in Missouri. For this he was acclaimed by all who were anxious to see the South move out of the mentality of the middle ages.

Joe Breen had suggested that I should get in touch with this prelate and let him know I was in the city. He welcomed me in a warm manner and invited me to meet with him in his great stone chancery office. The first thing that was talked about was the possibility of a press statement, deploring the fact that Hughes was selecting St. Louis for his adventure, and implying that the industrialist was insulting the citizenry by leading them across the *pons asinorum*. This was discussed in the company of the Auxiliary Bishop. When the words were all worked out, the Archbishop, who had been pondering by himself, finally spoke up. "I've been thinking," he said, "of forbidding all Catholics under my jurisdiction from attending the movie, under pain of mortal sin. What do you think?"

He stood there, calm and alert, turned half sideways, waiting intently for my reply. I weighed the question cautiously.

This was a severe censure, the most powerful in the episcopal arsenal. St. Louis was a heavily Catholic city, and the imputation would probably saturate deep into the population. But a spirit of independence was creeping into the air. What if the proclamation were ignored? There was a famous axiom that applied in these circumstances. It states, "Never slap a king in the face, unless you're sure you are going to knock him off his throne."

But gamble or no gamble, the die would have to be cast. I concurred in the thinking of the Archbishop. "I think it's a good idea," I said.

"Very well, then," he accepted. "If you think it's a good idea, I'll do it. You *do* think it's a good idea?"

"Yes."

He nodded. "I'll publish it Sunday," he said.

An odd sensation coursed through me. In those days, the values represented by this action were still alive to me, even though slightly raveled. I felt strangely responsible. From this point on, should some Catholic go to hell as a result of my back-room manipulations, I would not be uninvolved. The thought that there might be an enormous disproportion here had to be suppressed. That the eternal fate of a human being should have to be connected to Jane Russell's mammaries, no matter how heroic, was a bit much.

As it turned out, the Archbishop did in fact publish his interdict, and his intuitions of shrewdness were rewarded. The picture was not all that good that it attracted bonanza crowds, despite the lure of controversy. Hughes, in an unaccustomed mood of concession, finally allowed the film to be trimmed and to be resubmitted to the Code office. It was approved and finally taken off the Legion's "C" or Condemned list.

The success was not only a compliment to the Archbishop; it was Joe Breen's last small triumph before leaving.

A most involved observer of these processes was Martin Quigley. He had been a principal creator of the Code and, even though Joe Breen had stolen the play from him in a great act of friendly larceny, Martin was implicated in everything concerning the Code down to the very depths of his soul. The Code was, in a manner, his lifework, and the question of decency in movies was, in a very real sense, his vocation. I believe that in order of importance the Code work transcended in Martin's mind even the publishing empire by which he supported himself.

What was it that Martin wanted?

It is far from certain that, as a man, he could have defined this even for himself. To stumble over Martin was like stubbing one's toe on an insignificant pointed rock in the desert, which, when cleared away, would appear to be larger than suspected, and then larger and larger still, until at last it became apparent that it was the tip of a giant pyramid buried in the sands. The pyramid of which Martin was only the ultimate point was the Church. Martin was the very synthesis of the Catholic Man. He wanted what the tenets of his religion wanted. Thus, to cross forces with Martin was no mere personality conflict. It was a head-on collision with a massive and formidable way of life.

Martin reflected the Church's jaundice about human nature. Their mutual assessment of man reflected the belief that humanity was under the blight of Original Sin, and thus weakened and fallen in quality. Human nature was corruptible, and easily so apart from the aid of Grace. Therefore, it must be protected from the "proximate occasions" of sin. The motion picture, which enlarged reality, was an aggravated source of seduction to the enticements of this world.

To the Church, in those years at any rate, and through a substantial portion of its history, the "world" was foreign country. It was not the destiny of man to feel at home in the universe. Life in the grip of matter was a state of exile, *in hac lachrymarum valle* (in this vale of tears). The pure Catholic Man would have a personality that would feel disenfranchised about physical reality. He did not spontaneously "inherit the earth." That part of it which was his birthright was apportioned to him by authority, and the remainder could only be coveted, but not touched.

The crisis was precipitated when the "rest of reality" somehow thrust itself through the veil and imposed itself on the benumbed gaze of the Good Man, like Duchamp's "Nude Descending a Staircase." A case in point of how this exact issue was forced on people through the movies, was in the notorious scene of Stella descending the stairs in *A Streetcar Named Desire*, the brilliant film by Elia Kazan.

Stanley, the brutish Pole, was suffocated with lust for his wife. Standing at the foot of the stairs outside his house, in torn shirt, with the sweat standing out on his bulging muscles, he emits an animal cry for Stella. She hears the call, and comes. Underneath her slow, provocative, knowing descent the sound track was filled with grinding gut-bucket music. It was a moment as devoid of spirituality as it is possible to get.

When Martin Quigley walked out of the projection room in New York after viewing this picture, his face wore the ashen look of a man who had seen IT. He flicked his dull agate eyes at me and painfully drew a cigarette from a silver case, while he let words and emotions roll through his mind. When he had finally fitted the cigarette into a long holder, he lit it, inhaled with slow deliberation, and uttered his verdict. "Jack," he declared, "I tell you, this fellow Kazan is the type who will one day blow his brains out."

Geoffrey, who was Martin's counterpole, was for taking the world as it was given. He did not try to shun the presence of evil, or of the dangerously alluring. He was more optimistic about human nature, or at least more matter of fact. His philosophy was that if the world were a large tantalizing pastry shop, in which a man was forced to work despite a compulsive desire to gobble goodies, the solution was not to wipe out the bakery. It was to let the poor benighted fellow take bites out of tarts until he had convinced himself that there was nothing in it for him but a sick stomach. Then he could walk among the temptations with comfort and without a twitching hand. If, in the indoctrination process, the man got killed, it was a pity, "poor dear," but he could not have been saved anyway. No drunk was ever cured by closing all the bars. Often and again Geoff would fly off the handle and refuse to prohibit, let us say, the portrayal of a corrupt clergyman. "If the Catholic Church (or the Protestant, for that matter) is so weak that it cannot stand to see a little vice, then *we* cannot preserve it by hiding our heads in the sand. Let the producer have his scene. If people don't like it, *he'll* learn."

Geoffrey would not take responsibility for obliterating either the sight or the fact of evil in this world. That was God's problem. Who did people think he (Geoff) was, asking him to lift the load off of God? Neither would Geoffrey take the responsibility for steering producers away from the exploitation of evil, nor audiences from the confrontation with it. "We've changed their diapers and wiped their asses long enough. I'm damned if I'm going to handle their shit. Let them grow up."

Thus, the situation was cast with two men who were diametric opposites. Shurlock operated out of a clear make-or-break philosophy, attributing evil to God, in some meaningful sense at least, and refusing to accept the role of Eradicator. On the other hand, what Martin wanted, whether he would define it this way or not, or even like it stated in this manner, was to reshape and remake the human frame until, in the long run, he could look about and see his own countenance reflected back at him an infinite number of times. In the multiple mirror images of himself he could feel comfortable in the center of reality.

It was not long before Martin's concern erupted into the open. He was on the West Coast on one of his periodic visits to supervise the affairs of his Hollywood office. It was an excellent opportunity to court his good opinion, and toward this end I had arranged a private showing of a film at MGM for himself and a cluster of friends. In the group was Monsignor Tom

Little, Executive Secretary of the Legion of Decency. The film was a sample of which I was very proud. It was the handiwork of a writer with whom I was more than passing friendly, named William Ludwig. It was entitled *Interrupted Melody*.

There was nothing in the picture about which to be apprehensive. Basically it was biographical, being the life story of the opera singer Marjorie Lawrence, who at the height of her career is struck down with polio. It was filled with glorious music and animated by noble emotions, such as her stirring struggles to rejoin the human race and to find her voice again.

Martin accepted the invitation with eyes that gleamed like frosted light bulbs.

That evening after dinner, we convened at the studio for the red-carpet private showing. It was all very elegant, and I was beginning to feel my oats. The projection room went dark, and we were off and running.

The high point of the story was the low point in the life of the opera singer. In utter desolation, she determines to try suicide. Wheeling herself into the bathroom in her hospital chair, she makes a pitiful effort to reach up into the medicine cabinet and lay her hands on a bottle of sleeping capsules. The bottle, just off the tips of her fingers, tumbles into the sink, and spills out its tablets. As her frantic hands scoop up the loose pills, we see in close-up the label on the bottle, lest there be any doubt of her intentions. As she is drawing a hurried glass of water for herself, her husband bursts into the room, discovers her, and brutally wrests the pills out of her clenched fists. If I remember correctly, he overturns her in her chair, and she lies sobbing pitifully on the floor.

So stunning was the sequence that you could have cut the silence with a knife. I was simmering with elation, sharing in Bill's achievement by proxy.

There was a stirring, and Martin came out of his rapt immobility. He reached across my wife, who sat between us, and touched me gently on the arm. I leaned forward to accept plaudits in the name of the film community. "Jack," he rasped in an audible stage whisper, "where was the Production Code Administration when *that* scene was shot? On *vacation?*"

I flushed so that I almost glowed in the dark.

I knew what the impolite man meant. All through the rest of the picture the nightmarish thoughts tumbled through my mind in fierce disorder. In the Code there was a certain provision covering the depiction of narcotics. Traditionally, it had been interpreted to exclude drugs of all sorts, including sleeping pills. It is doubtful that its original intention extended beyond opium or heroin or other such destructive habit-forming drugs; but since the motion picture theater was not discriminate in its audience, it was thought better not to bring to the attention of children (either the calendar children, or the psychological children) the uses to which any "illegal drugs" could be put. To show, then, a woman attempting to commit suicide (painlessly) with sleeping pills was a departure from respected practice.

Quigley was stung to the quick by the innovation. It was a symbol to him of what was going on in the Code. Perhaps he knew also the rumor that a pact had been struck by the Motion Picture Industry with the famous Harry J. Anslinger, Commissioner of Narcotics for the U.S. Treasury Department. It was Anslinger's philosophy that the less said about narcotics the better. To bring the subject out into the open was only to stimulate morbid curiosity and to increase the problem of addiction. This is something about which Anslinger knew best, of course, even though he would hardly deny that there were two schools of thought on the subject.

Be that as it may, it was whispered around that Anslinger had discovered that the Picture Industry was planning to revise its Code prohibition against narcotics, allowing for more freedom and candor in their presentation. To this he objected. And his objection was backed by a handful of face cards. His agents had unearthed a serious problem of dope addiction in one of the big studios and were ready to splash the news into the headlines across the country. It would have been a serious blow to the prestige of the Industry, perhaps causing another period of public revulsion against films. The Industry could ill afford the hurt at the box office.

Therefore, the rumor went, Anslinger had proposed a bargain to the Industry. He would handle the dope problem at the major studio with tact and without flamboyance, if only the company presidents would leave the "dope clause" in the Code intact. The presidents quickly agreed. All of this had transpired under the administration of Joe Breen, and it is on his recital that we are dependent for the authenticity of the facts.

With the passing of a few years, however, Geoff began to writhe under the inequity of the prohibition. He felt that the producers were entitled to use narcotics, within limits, since they afforded valid dramatic material. And once Geoff had made up his mind, he would assuredly find a rationalization. So that when the question of sleeping pills arose in the case of *Interrupted Melody,* he snorted and said, "If the people of this country are so near to suicide that the mere sight of Seconal will drive them to destruction like the lemmings, then we cannot save them merely by hiding the sight of pills from the screen. Why, my God, *anybody* can get a bottle on prescription from his doctor! We're being made to look ridiculous."

It was against this sort of revisionism that Martin was now reacting. It was indicative of things to come. That he lacked the most rudimentary of manners, when he ordinarily was impeccable in his comportment, did not matter. Error enjoyed no rights, including those to the amenities.

Therefore, when the picture was over, I tried to get out of his presence as quickly as possible. But before I did, he buttonholed me for one question. "No, really, Jack," he wheedled, "how *did* that scene get through the Code?"

He stood there, his clam face expectant (this was his own description of himself), and there was no answering him

without going all the way back to Adam and Eve, and instructing him from the beginning. I shrugged in inability. "I
dunno, Martin," I said. "They were just lucky, I guess."

As they say in the Westerns, Martin did not "take kindly" to
an answer of this kind. He would bide his opportunity.

At the same time, the Code was being subjected to pressures
from another quarter.

The American Left, which had submerged during World
War II, because Russia needed the U.S.A. as an ally, surfaced
after the surrender and became activist again. The campaign
to downgrade all departments of democratic-capitalistic life
was both highly organized and completely saturationist.

The Code was not immune from this onslaught. In fact—not
to aggrandize it—it was one of the favorite targets of the
dedicated Left. It was dubbed an instrument of "thought
control," the ugly phrase of the moment; but generally by
people who, one suspected, would not hesitate to use the same
methods were they to get in power. Thus, the word "liberal"
became a dirty word, since it was assumed by people who were
not liberal at all, but as doctrinaire as those they were trying to
dislodge. The ominous Senator McCarthy sensed this and
capitalized on it.

The standards of conduct for which the Code stood were
labeled "middle class morality." Somehow this was made to
sound cheap, as though the bourgeois were not as sound in
their instincts as either the aristocracy or the proletariat. But
the silly deification of the earthy intuitions of the "common"
man was under way, and there was really nothing to strike out
against in this roomful of feathers. And lastly, the truly shallow question began to be raised as to "who was going to
judge?" It took away from any human being the possibility of
making a human judgment about human acts, on the grounds
that such judgments were self-appointive and messianic. We
will come to grips with this idea in the end, when we make our
summation.

The Code reacted gingerly to these irritations. It had not been brought into being to act as custodian of political concepts or economic theories. Nevertheless, the Left hardly left room to distinguish. It was all one big ball of wax, to fall back on Washingtonese. Capitalism was somehow wrapped up with militarism, and these two, in turn, with a partisan court system that meted out injustice, with the whole interlocking apparatus supporting and being supported by an image of a tribal Deity who was cruel, capricious, and a member of the Club.

I remember very well how inklings of the "party line" seemed to seep through in a script that was sent to us soon after the war. It came from RKO and was entitled *All Brides Are Beautiful*. It was the story of a young soldier who came back from the service, and of the power of his love for his young bride to overcome the "unfairness" of the system.

Very likely the elements that made us uncomfortable at that time would be subscribed to by John Birch himself now. But Al Lynch and I passed on our vague apprehensions to Joe Breen, who attended to them with a sharp ear. Without further ado, he picked up the phone and called the head of production at the studio, a Mr. Charles Koerner, who was Joe's successor in the post. Koerner assured Breen he would look into the matter.

In a short while, he called Breen back and told him that key members of the production staff had been removed from this enterprise, and that the project had been handed over to the skyrocketing young architect, William Periera.

Periera, for his part, had been counseled by his medical advisers to seek an outlet for excess tensions by finding another temporary occupation. When he heard the Code objections, he ran his hand through his handsome shock of wavy hair, shook his head dolefully, and exclaimed, "I feel like I have a tiger by the tail! This work is supposed to cure me. I think it's making me worse."

Even so, he must have cured the script, because no reference was made to its social content by even the most sensitive reviews of the day. The picture was ultimately released under the changed title *From This Day Forward*.

The same issue, relatively, was joined when Charles Chaplin came into the Code office with a script quaintly called *A Comedy of Murders*.

We took the position that it was a tirade against the System. Chaplin denied everything.

A great point was made of the windup speech of the leading character, Monsieur Verdoux (after whom the film was eventually named). It was the Code contention that the dialogue clouded the distinction between right and wrong. "These speeches," we stated, "indicate what purports to be the inconsistency of applauding those who kill in war as great heroes and, at the same time, condemning to death those who murder." Latent in this line of reasoning, too, was the sentimental argument that the murderer himself was the product of injustice, having been forced to kill in order to raise the money to support his needy household.

Chaplin retorted that we were indulging in a philosophical question, not a moral one. He doubted that anyone, including the devisers of the Production Code, could determine exactly what is right and what is wrong. "The Dialogues of Plato have struggled with that question."

With such arguments did Chaplin dig his grave as a would-be intellectual. He left behind him an image of a smallish man, brisk as a cricket, with beautiful silvery hair, and somewhat sensual lips—but stubborn, as only a person with limited academic resources is apt to be, and, in his style, narcissistic.

The picture was accorded only a mild reception by the public.

Not all experiences in this particular area were distasteful. At least one was on the genial side. This one occurred with a producer at MGM by the name of William Wright, who was anything but far left, as far as I could judge.

Bill was a very intense man, slim, dark, and bristling like a bale of barbed wire. One could feel the fury of his glare, even over the telephone. Nowadays he just smiles serenely, like a man whose demons have all been exorcised.

Bill had sent a script into our office for a musical he was producing. In it there was a child's ballet, of sorts. At the conclusion of the number, one of the little girls who was doing a tap dance, front and center, does a pirouette, whirls out her cape, reverses it and, lo and behold, it has turned into an American flag!

At that time, the war was hardly over; the American Legion was very active; and the Veterans of Foreign Wars were afire with patriotism. Millions of recently released servicemen were still very cognizant of flag rubrics and were quite sensitive on the point. The Red Menace was felt everywhere and might easily be felt in such tactics as improper esteem for the flag. Therefore, it seemed an inappropriate time to be abusing the national symbol by turning it into a dance costume.

I looked in the back of the Code and dug out a more or less obscure provision which stated: "The use of the flag shall be consistently respectful."

I quoted this provision to Bill in my letter on his script, and questioned whether this exploitation of the flag were not disrespectful.

He certainly did not need the phone to convey his howl of irritation to me. He protested that this was witch-hunting. He said that he could see my point if a bevy of dancers were prancing all over the flag, singing the "Internationale." But this was just a little girl with innocent intentions, and the ending gave her dance a patriotic flair. He was going to keep it in his picture, whether it technically violated flag and Code rubrics, or not.

When I hung up, I wished I had never brought up the point. It seemed to me he was right and that I had been too evangelistic in dragging up a hardly used Code clause to apply in this case. I decided to forget the whole thing.

Such was not my luck, however. A copy of my letter had

gone to New York, following usual procedure, and had been spotted by an alert officer of the corporation who was very Commie conscious. At once, he dug out his old Army manual and searched it for the rules and regulations governing the handling of the flag. To my distress, he discovered that I was correct, and that it was forbidden to use the flag as part of a costume. He called me on the phone and quoted the passage to me, commending me for my vigilance and urging me to stand fast.

Now what was I going to do? I didn't want to foul up my reputation with our East Coast offices, creating the impression that I was a parlor pink, as they said in those days. And I did not want to pursue the issue with Bill, with whom I had to live, and whom I was certain to meet again on another picture.

Therefore, it was with divided mind that I went into the projection room to review the film when it at last arrived. I was turning my will into iron to make a decision on the spot, when I saw the scene. The ballet number began, and the reasons pro and con were still oscillating back and forth like busy electrons. The tap dance began. My brain clicked with resolution. To hell with the Eastern offices, I determined. Bill was correct. And correct is correct. I'll glare down those fellows in New York. I'll pass it! Go ahead, little girl, pirouette!

She did.

The costume was the same on the inside as on the outside. Solid navy blue!

Bill, for mysterious reasons of his own, had changed his mind.

Is this not justification for indulging in the obvious pun and saying that, for once, Wright was wrong?

One experience in this area became very personal. A script called *Trial* arrived one day from Dore Schary, who was then head of production at MGM.

A primary perusal seemed to reveal glaring streaks of party-line propaganda, in a story about the politico-legal structure in the State of California pitted against a Mexican-American youth being tried for murder.

Apparently nobody at the studio wanted to drag a red herring across this project, because of Schary's eminent position and the clearly inferred risk of reprisals. Since nobody else would speak up, I began feeling an invisible tap on the shoulder. Without pleasure, I had to face the fact that I was elected. However, I had always liked Dore, feeling that he had basic gentility. Therefore, I took the phone to tell him I wanted to see him privately, about certain matters of grave importance in his script. He consented, possibly because of the giveaway tones in my voice.

When I entered his lush office, I noticed that the dominant colors were red, white, and blue—a carpet red enough to make one blink, white walls, and blue decor, with a great gold eagle on the walls. Even the furniture was provincial, in a sort of early-American mood of patriotism.

"All right, Jack," he said, with clear, even, ominously soft tones of voice, "what is it?"

"I want to take a chance on you," I said.

He nodded.

"You know what your political reputation is," I began. "You have not exactly been attacked as a conservative."

He reddened, but he accepted the first gauche gracefully. In actuality, he was probably nothing more than a Stevensonian liberal. But at that moment, it seemed like a lot more.

"With that as a background," I continued, "what I want to stress is that you are prone to easy attack, you are vulnerable, whether the grounds for attack are just or not. And, from what is in your script, I think that you are exposing yourself to attack. More than that, I think you are inviting it."

I waited again, while he calculated this. "Please go on," he invited.

"It is my belief that you will hear that you are sponsoring a script that is filled with party-line propaganda. I don't know if it *is* party-line propaganda. But it is what will be *said* to be party-line propaganda. It is what is popularly *thought* to be the current party line. Therefore, you are playing into flaming contemporary prejudices, and you are liable to get crucified for it."

He sat there for a steely moment, considering, I think, the simplicity of my motives.

He broke the silence. "Jack," he said in a kindly tone, "I thank you for what you have said. Nobody else has spoken up, probably because I am the boss. But I like you better for stepping forward, and believe me, I understand what you are intimating, and I agree with you about my vulnerability to attack.

"Now I wonder if you'd do me a favor? Will you go down through the script with me and show me the spots in which this impression is created, and we will correct them together?

"This is a risk everyone encounters when he tries to make a picture about a social injustice, on the side of the underdog. I'm afraid I may have let my enthusiasms carry me too far."

I was so relieved that I nearly broke out into a chorus of "The Star Spangled Banner." What held me back was that I wasn't exactly "in voice" at the moment. In fact, the only sound I felt capable of emitting would have resembled the squawk of a chicken.

Dore very nicely reciprocated some time later, rescuing my face when I had blundered into an embarrassment with the eminent writer Helen Deutsch. Helen had just scored a triumph in the lyrical film *Lily* and was working on her next assignment for Joe Pasternak. I had overcommitted myself in registering an objection to a detail in questionable taste. She, stung, retaliated with some sharp remarks. Dore put a stop to it with the comment that the line in question would be changed, and that Helen was "being much too fatuous about her own writing."

She had to bite her tongue, and I think I passed over the next several objections in the script.

· · ·

It was clear that the Code was in a dubious plight, caught between the forces of conservatism and of liberalism. The days of honeymoon, when it was on the side of the angels, were over. A note of disenchantment might even be heard at the local cocktail lounge: "What was that you said you did, fellow? The Motion Picture Association? Oh. That's nice. Doing what? The *Production* Code? No, never heard of it. Hey, wait a minute, you mean you're one of those *censor* guys? Jesus, you don't *look* like a censor. George! Hey, George! Look what we got here. A *censor,* by God! Yeah, this is the guy who takes all the *good* parts out of pictures. I bet you have fun, huh? I'd like to see your collection of all those dirty parts, I'll bet it's a dilly! You *do* stick them in your pockets, don't you? You'll have to show them to me some day. You will? Say, wait a minute, aren't you guys getting a bit *liberal* these days? I mean, it doesn't bother me, you unnerstan, but what about the kids? What's that? An example? No, I'm afraid I couldn't give you an example, I couldn't even remember the last movie I saw. No, I don't *go* to movies any more. How do I know about them then? Well, from the *ads,* that's how. I mean, they really tell you the whole story. What's that? Go *what* myself? Whatzzamatter feller, you getting thin-skinned or something? I mean, if this guy can't take the heat, what's he doing in the kitchen?"

And so it went.

13 Dissension in Eden

JUST AS Joe Breen had scooped up Martin Quigley's invention, the Code, and run away with it, so also the reverse happened in the case of the Legion of Decency. In a large and consequential sense, the Legion was Joe's creature, but it was Martin who seized it and scampered to glory with it. Martin had the ear of the Cardinal. He also had ready access to the Power House, Spellman's residence immediately behind Saint Patrick's Cathedral in New York City. From this position of influence, he had next to exclusive say concerning the Secretariat of the Legion. It was he who gave the numen to the appointment of Father Little, after the handsome and virile Father Masterson died of an untimely heart attack.

Martin parlayed this inference of power over onto Eric Johnston. Thus, when it came time to nominate a new Code Director, it was Quigley's candidate, Judge Jackson, who was given the preference.

As an *eminence grise,* Martin was one of the most spectacular successes in this century.

He was not long in striking out against the Code. The spot he selected was high up among the charcoal cliffs of Rockefeller Center, behind the anonymity of a molten window, lost in the midst of myriad others. He was seated behind an impressive desk in his executive office, drawing thoughtfully on a cigarette and scanning me with slow, penetrating eyes. I was hunched forward on a straight-back chair, trying not to look at the buildings turning pink in central Manhattan.

"Jack," he finally said, probing with each sentence like steps on a snow bridge, "I had expected that you would bring your influence to bear on Geoffrey, to keep him more moderate. I am disappointed."

By this time I had ascended our little corporate ladder until I stood on the rung of Assistant Director. I, too, felt that Geoff was dealing away his deck of cards with slightly manic haste. I rankled over the fact that a definition of myself was inextricably tangled up with what Geoff did, without my having any control over the factors that affected my fate. "Martin," I protested, "Geoff's in *charge* now. You seem to speak as though that's a fiction."

Martin took each word in, one by one. "Yes, I see your point," he conceded. "But a disturbing thing has happened. At first, Geoffrey acted nervous, as though the job were more than he wanted. He conducted himself as though he were an interim appointee. But now some time has passed and he has gotten used to authority, and has found that he likes it. Now he's settling in for a long stay, and he's beginning to pull back on the delegations he made to you fellows. I can see this makes it awkward for you. But at the same time, the powers that be are dissatisfied with him. And if he goes down, so will you."

I spread my hands helplessly. "What can I do?" I asked.

"There are things you can do," said Martin enigmatically.

"Well, what, for instance?"

"Is there no way you could make minority reports, in cases where you disagree with him?"

"Martin, when an issue arises where I disagree with Geoff, I speak my piece. But once Geoff has decided, I keep my peace."

"But nobody knows about this. Is there no way you could put it into the record? Respectfully, of course, in the mood of His Majesty's Loyal Opposition?"

"You mean make a Memo for the File?"

"Yes, that sort of thing. Then, when the day comes to review Geoff's record, your statements will have a cumulative effect. They can be used by those of us who have our eyes on you, to point to you and promote your cause."

This bald-faced proposal was too much. "You mean like Steve Jackson?" I asked scoffingly. "That's what ruined him. I'd be fired."

Martin tipped the ashes off his cigarette into a glass tray while he gave this his consideration. "I know it is hard to ask you," he said. "But it may be your duty."

"Martin, listen. I'd rather be a live jackass than a dead lion. I'm not going to be any good to anybody selling apples on street corners."

"Why do you not do what you're supposed to do, and for the remainder, trust others? There are other people concerned with this operation of yours, you know. And there are things they can do. You might say, 'What if they fail?' Well, I would say that is none of your concern. You are only asked to do what you are supposed to do, what you've been hired to do, and you have to leave the rest in the hands of fate. I know you've devoted a number of years to this work now, and it's hard to just let it go and find something else to do. Especially when you have a family dependent on you. But at least you'll know that you've done the right thing, the thing that is right. Couldn't you settle for that and take a chance?" His eyebrows were two large Byzantine arches.

"No, Martin. I'm afraid not. I couldn't do that. I don't think I'm in that much disagreement with Geoff when you come right down to it. And anyway, I'm something like Joe Breen. I don't commit suicide on myself."

Martin absorbed this impassively. "I see," he said at last. He drummed his fingertips quietly on the tabletop, like a poker player gauging whether he should turn over his last card. "Yes," he said, and up it came, wild. "Well, in that case, let me put it to you in another way. The Code is operating at variance with the Legion of Decency. The spread is becoming wider, to the point that it is becoming a matter of conscience."

"In what sense, Martin?"

He looked at me curiously. "The voice of the Legion is the representative voice of the Hierarchy in the United States. That is an obediential voice. You are obliged to accommodate it. Is there not some way you could get this idea over to the members of your staff who would be affected?"

Here, at last, was the latent equation in all that had been said. Now it had been spelled out without frills. The business of the Code was to bring Hollywood in line with Church standards. But, as Martin himself was the king maker and the king breaker of the Legion, this meant, more or less, getting in line with him. To vary from Martin was to run afoul the obediential voice of the bishops. In a word, it was to put oneself at odds with God.

There was no breaking through this lock-chain at this time and in this place with this man. To have grappled with the argumentation would have been to come to grips with the whole presumption on which the Code-Legion complex was structured. It would have been nihilistic. Martin had me nicely cornered, and he knew it. There was a quick instant in which eyes clashed, to measure the depth of resolution in the other. Having no alternative, I bobbed my head slowly. "I'll talk to them," I conceded. Martin nodded sagely, as though he understood that I would make conspiracy with him. But in my heart I maintained a dumb insolence. This man would, in some manner, have to be destroyed.

On the way out of his office, I saw a framed testimonial, gilt on parchment, on his wall. It was from the leaders of the Movie Industry, in tribute to his Statesmanship. He had led the Industry out of the land of bondage and into the hilly country, flowing with milk and honey, of higher moral excellence.

In the skies, on the way back to the Coast, I weighed the dilemma. Martin could not intelligently be rejected out of hand. He stood for much. The picture business needed a refining force at work in its midst. As a medium which reached for the greatest common denominator, it frequently succeeded only in finding the lowest common denominator. And so, some pressure on it, to force it to lift itself by the bootstraps, was tolerable. Even the company presidents knew this. Their realization was behind the testimonial on Martin's wall.

But Martin was a man who had inherited a vast culture; and that culture was making of him a driven man. Now his urgencies were beginning to verge on the messianic.

Martin's whole program would have been much more acceptable had his style been less conspiratorial. He gave the impression of a wand of seaweed wavering under water to the touch of incomparably subtle tides. As opposed to him, Joe Breen cleared the air with a storm of raw bumptiousness. He left no doubt that he was throwing the meat on the floor and was willing to fight any mongrel for it.

But more than this. Martin, while maintaining an air of aloofness toward the industry, was at the same time wresting a living from it, not in the sense that it was a source of news for him, but a source of advertising revenue. The flavor of perfidy involved in this came to the surface in the Legion offices one day. I was discussing with a key woman on the Legion staff Martin's distemper with the Code administrators for passing a picture that had also been condemned by the Legion. I think it was *Son of Sinbad* with problems on the order of *French Line*.

"He's upset with you?" she queried. "Well, let me show you something." She picked up a folded copy of the *Motion Picture Herald,* one of Quigley's publications. She tapped a two-page color spread with the backs of her fingers. It was a great sexy carnival-like splash. "This costs *money,*" she emphasized. "If he's so offended with what you did, why didn't he turn down the advertising for it? It seems he has no objection to giving the picture wide popularity."

Martin was always able to claim that he never came to the rescue of any picture as a negotiator for the company with the

Legion, unless he was requested to do so by the corporation. He worked for nothing. But was the *quid pro quo* a greater spate of expensive advertising in his journals than those of his competitors for the controversial film? A top Legion executive thinks a comparative study would point to this conclusion.

Once again, I was beginning to feel the invisible tap on my shoulder.

When I arrived back in Hollywood, the first thing I did was to saunter into Geoff's office and say, "Guess what? You are supposed to be my cat's-paw."

Geoff looked up with a confused grin. "I am? How nice. To what purpose, might I ask?"

"To achieve the purposes of the Legion of Decency. You see, it all comes out that you're going to be bounced and I'm to take your place, and in order to make myself a right proper candidate, Martin Quigley wants me to make up Memos for the Files, in which I go on record whenever I disagree with you. Then, when the day comes for the big accounting, I parade all these files out and demonstrate that I didn't want to be lax, it was all you."

Geoff, for one of the few times in his life, turned purple angry. "Martin wants you to do this?"

"Yes."

"The sonofabitch!"

"I thought you'd like to know."

Geoff rubbed his hand over his mouth. "He's acting like the typical Irish politician. Get the boys individually and split them. Divide and conquer." Suddenly he tilted back in his swivel chair, cocked his arms behind his head, peered at me quizzically, and a slow grin began to appear on his face. "Well," he said, "what are you going to do?"

A leery smile worked its way on my features. "Have you gone out of your *mind?*" I asked, in a friendly way.

He grinned more broadly. "I just wanted to know."

"You mean you'd like me to be another Steve Jackson?"

He poised the question in the air before wording it softly.

"What's to prevent you?"

"My common sense, maybe."

"Maybe it's not so smart as you think. Maybe Quigley's right. Maybe you *should* keep notes. Then when I get thrown out on my ass, I'll tell Johnston you've got them and you can show them to him. It might work in your favor, after all."

"Geoff, that's so dumb a suggestion I just might take you up on it, for perversity. What do you think Johnston'd say when I came trotting into him with all my little notes? That's a *sure* way to get scrunched."

Geoff shrugged. "Have it your way. I certainly wouldn't object if you wanted to put things into the files."

"Yeah," I said. "I'll do that."

On my way out, Geoff stopped me. "Say, Jack," he suggested, "would you mind if I told this to Johnston?"

"Certainly not," I said. "Be my guest."

"I'll spike that guy," muttered Geoff with grim intent.

The disclosure to Johnston was a revelation about Quigley. Martin had woven a thralldom over him, largely through the editorials in his journals, which were read by the company presidents to whom Eric was answerable. But now it was as though Johnston were delivered. He started to dismiss Quigley. The first step had been accomplished.

It did not take long for the next opportunity to make its appearance. Martin had come to the Coast on one of his cyclical visitations, and we had invited him to lunch with the whole staff to discuss the state of the union. We convened in a fern-and-rock restaurant on La Cienega Boulevard, popular with the movie crowd, called "The Tail o' the Cock."

Martin good-naturedly commented on the phallic potential in the name of the restaurant, and Geoff immediately used this to counterattack. "You see what a tough job we have out here?" he charged. "How do you expect us to keep the movies clean when even the restaurants have dirty names?"

Martin's grin was slightly lemonish. "Now, Geoffrey," he

chided, "I hope you're not taking that as justification for some of the things I've seen in pictures lately."

"No. I guess not," conceded Geoff sheepishly.

To break the ice, Martin asked, "What's this I hear about Murph?"

Everybody looked at one another. Murph had been engaged in a rather colorful bar incident at a restaurant on Ventura Boulevard, called "The Pump Room."

Doc, who had been present, took over. "You mean about the fellow he cooled at the bar?" he asked Martin.

"Then he did . . . ?" quizzed Quigley, finishing the sentence with vague gestures.

"Knocked this guy right through the air into a padded booth," affirmed Doc.

Martin grinned wryly. "It seems we have a gang of roisterers administering the Code," he commented to Geoff.

Geoff dropped his fork and began wiping his lips with his napkin. "It comes mighty close to fisticuffs out here on occasions," he assured Martin. "The producers'll try to provoke you. It's just as well we have fellows on the staff who know how to handle themselves. Joe Breen had to slug a director once. Did he ever tell you about it?"

"Oh, yes," said Martin. "In great detail. And with different embellishments every time." He returned to Doc. "But tell me," he continued, "surely a nice good-natured man like Murph would not strike someone without provocation?"

"Oh, he had provocation, all right," Doc explained. "What happened was this." He paused to light a cigarette and blew the smoke straight out. Some of it caught Martin's face, and he winced discreetly. "It was a Saturday," he went on. "We were coming back from a wedding reception for Emily La Rue. It was still early, so we thought we'd stop by for a final-final. We were sitting on stools, quietly reminiscing, when all of a sudden we hear this awful noise at the other end of the bar, and WHAP! It sounded just like someone spanked a piece of wet meat with his open hand, and then WHAP again, and this dame tumbles off the barstool, and this guy's standing over her yelling for her to get up off the floor so he can hit her again.

"Murph takes on a sudden look like he's got a turd for a stickpin and stands up. 'Leave her alone,' he says.

"This guy looks at Murph and snarls, 'Whyn't cha mind your own goddamn business?' and then does a double take when he sees all six foot five of Murph, but it's too late to back out now, and anyway he's obviously too angry.

"Murph draws himself up in indignation and points a finger into the air and says, 'Anybody who strikes a woman has me to answer to.' When nobody pays any attention to him, he realizes he is standing in a pretty silly position with his finger stuck up into the air, and sounding like he's repeating dialogue from a bad movie, so in order to have an excuse for getting his finger down, he starts to take off his coat. He folds it carefully, and puts it on top of the bar. Then he takes off his glasses, folds them shut, and puts them on top of the coat. We asked him afterwards why he did all this so deliberately, and he said he'd just gotten a new suit and was too cheap to get blood all over it. Anyway, he takes one more nick off his drink to get courage, and walks over in his shirtsleeves, and plants himself between the fellow and this girl, who is whimpering on the floor and bleeding all over.

" 'Get out of my way, you big boob,' this fellow says, 'I'm gonna beat her brains out, she's a lousy tramp.'

"Murph is offended now, but he has to admit that he admires the fellow, who's only half his size but feisty as a rooster. 'You're not going to do anything of the sort,' warns Murph. 'You lift a finger and I'll knock you into that booth.'

" 'Try it!' yelled the rooster, leaping up on a stool so he could get a better swing at Murph.

"The temptation was too much. Murph can move, you know. He uncorked one all the way from his knees and caught this guy right on the point of the chin, just as he was about to start a roundhouse at Murph. The fellow *flew* through the air, about two feet off the ground, just like in a Jack Ford movie! He landed in a heap in the middle of the booth and slid to the floor, out cold.

"Another fellow shouldered up to Murph and said, 'Why don't you hit someone your own size?' Murph stares at him and says, 'You're my size,' and CLOP, hits this other guy. 'Hey, wait a minute!' screams this other guy. 'I'm on *your* side.' 'Oh!' says Murph, as though this explains everything."

Martin's curiosity made him ask, "Was the fellow in the booth hurt?"

"Hell, no," assured Doc. "I guess he was too loaded. He was just coming to when the cops arrived—the bartender called them. He wanted to fight the cops, too. They had to handcuff him and drag him out screaming and kicking."

"Did the girl thank Murph?"

"That was the payoff. It seems 'the girl' was this guy's wife, according to the bartender. He said the husband was right, she was the biggest whore on Ventura Boulevard. She had two kids at home, but she must've been some kind of nympho. She just walked out on them and catted around with any guy she could pick up. The poor husband had just found out where she was spending her time. He was coming to take her home by force.

"When Murph found this out, he wanted to run down to the jail and apologize to the guy. But we talked him out of it. He'd done enough good deeds for the day. He'd probably end up in jail with the guy, charged with assault and battery. If he stayed out of sight, the guy might not remember when he sobered up. And anyway, it was just as well Murph stepped in. The guy would've killed the girl, he was practically insane."

Martin ran the thin tip of his tongue around the edges of his lips. His fondest fears had been satisfied. "Well!" he half gasped. He turned toward Geoffrey, as if appealing to the only civilized member of the group. "Aren't you a little apprehensive, living with this band of roughnecks?" he asked.

"Not at all," said Geoff. "Very comforting, actually."

All understood that Martin liked the narration.

The rest of the meal progressed uneventfully. Martin had clearly not yet come to the *pièce de résistance* on his mind. Suddenly he looked up from the business of stirring his coffee. "Are you acquainted with a certain novel called *Heaven Knows, Mr. Allison?*" he demanded.

Geoff and I reacted to the ring of brass. Here is where the challenge was going to be made. "Yes," we answered in uneven unison. "Why?"

"You know this book," Martin picked us up, "and you ask why? I'm told that one of the companies plans to make a picture of it."

"That's correct," I said. "Fox. Why not?"

Martin accepted the provocation. "It's clearly a Code violation."

It was not that I didn't understand what he meant. The novel was about a nun and a Marine stranded together on a desert island. It had a certain snickering sound to it, even in reciting the premise.

But it had been picked up by Buddy Adler, then head of production at Twentieth-Fox and, dangerous or not, stood a chance. Buddy had had an outstanding success with a novel of similar flavor while still a producer at Columbia, called *The Left Hand of God*. It dealt with a soldier of fortune (the famous Humphrey Bogart) who, in order to escape from the clutches of a Chinese bandit chief, disguised himself as a priest, and performed the functions of the priesthood. This involved such delicacies as hearing confessions, saying Mass, and the complication of falling in love with a missionary nurse. The man finds that in putting on the Cloth, he is unable to escape it, and it makes of him a good man.

Doc Dougherty had pitched in and given many good suggestions to Adler, with the aim of refining the harsher or more embarrassing elements of the story, and his contributions helped make this film an outstanding success. In fact, it was partly on the strength of this triumph that Adler was nominated head of Fox studios. It was only understandable that he should like to try the same gamble again.

But Martin was digging his feet into the ground. To exploit the fragility of a nun, in those days before the great change, was to flirt with being called despicable. Nuns are relatively defenseless, and an abuse of them tends to bring out the masculine instincts in the Catholic man. He cannot be expected to be rational and impartial in an area that is very personally emotional.

That chord had been touched in Martin.

"Do you know it is based on a true story?" I asked Martin.

"How would that change the state of the question?"

"Well, if it were a pure invention, the intentions of the author might be more subject to suspicion."

This was not enough. "I'm told that they die in each other's arms, with their spirits arising and joining together in heaven. So that the love they had to forgo on earth is theirs throughout eternity."

"Is that altogether wrong?"

"It's silly."

Again, I knew what he meant. To make nuns the object of romantic involvements did not seem exactly fair. It tended to break down well-guarded reticences about them, which they had earned by their sacrifices. If they wanted privacy, why not allow it to them?

But, on the other hand, there was something at work here that was more important than the sensibilities of nuns. Martin was trying to spell out, in words of one syllable, that it was the function of the Code to keep things "nice," which meant, in the concrete, that people were to be presented without exposures, in a posture of perfection, semitriumphant over life, slightly elevated above it, relatively disembodied. Ah, yes, that was it! What the Code was supposed to achieve was the Jansenistic imagination about life which, at that moment in history, was the core of the Catholic concept of Man. The "inconveniencies" of the flesh were to be swept under the carpet, and that process was called "morality." It was a cruel enterprise, for it engendered aspirations about life that were angelic, which could never be achieved by mortal men, and which led, eventually, to discouragement and despair. Never show the "invasive" of the sacred Enclave of the *Good* life. The theologians had a word for it. They called it "offensive to pious ears." That was a minor grade of scandal, and scandal tended to break down the resolution of Good people. "Better to have a millstone attached to one's neck and be cast into the sea . . ." than to contribute to the weakening of an innocent soul.

Thus, whenever an area of the sensational was encountered, it was the duty of the Code to intercept it, to prevent it from coming to public notice and inspection. That is why the Code was a "moral" document. It safeguarded morality. In the Jansenistic scheme of things, this meant being the guardian of Angelism.

So, keep the nun looking angelic.

I tried to turn Martin's thought a little. "The ending about being united in heaven is only in the British version of the novel, as far as I know. There is an American version in which both the nun and the Marine live. Historically, of course, the two were killed. Their bodies were found on a beach by mop-up troops of the American Army. They were wearing Japanese uniforms. The guess is that they had stolen them from the occupying troops from Japan, but forgot they were wearing them when they rushed out onto the beach to welcome their saviors. They were shot by those they thought were coming to their rescue."

"That is very touching," said Martin sincerely, beginning to see the story in a new light.

"What provision of the Code does this story violate?" I asked.

Martin bristled a little. This question, so legalistic in approach, was contrary to established usage. If a subject were found that was annoying, it was automatically included among those things which the Code prohibited. The legalistic question was simply not asked. It put a man on the spot. It was destructive of the *spirit* of the Code. The Code was a catchall and was not limited to the narrow confines of the words that were written down. It was primarily a buffer against the embarrassing. To attempt to bring it down to chapter and verse was a declaration of a new concept of the Code. It was to diminish its size, its scope, its original function.

"Surely you can find some provision that is violated by this story," replied Martin.

"Why? It is a valid story."

"I cannot imagine it being passed by the Legion of Decency."

"The Legion of Decency is narrower in its focus than the Code. The Legion is concerned with the Theological Man. It is founded on Revelation. The Code has more liberty. It is concerned with the Ethical Man. It is philosophical rather than theological. The functions of the two cannot always be expected to mesh."

"But you are dealing here with a person of the Church, a nun."

"There is nothing immoral about being exposed to temptation. Suppose she overcomes it?"

"But in the meantime, you are exploiting the sensational elements of her temptation."

"Does the Code say a nun cannot be *tempted?*"

Quigley had been ground to a halt. Of course he could not answer this question in the affirmative. "Very well," he conceded reluctantly, "but if, in the course of telling this story, there is any indulgence in the lurid, in bringing her through her temptation, it is likely to be condemned." He peered significantly in my direction to underline the consequence.

I accepted his gaze without expression. Yes, sir. I knew what that meant. Loud and clear.

The issue had been joined.

14 A Tough Trilogy: *Baby Doll, The Miracle,* and *Heaven Knows, Mister Allison*

GEOFFREY SHURLOCK had gone off to Europe to make a survey of the foreign censor boards. The export market was expanding as Eric Johnston had predicted, so that the standards and regulations in the principal consuming countries were becoming more important.

I had observed Geoff boarding the jet at International Airport with eyes jeweled with envy, because the changes in the foreign field were producing transformations of a deeply intimate character in the local industry. Since the only thing the motion picture sold was an ephemeral shadow on the wall, dollar-poor countries were falling back on self-protective measures and were freezing the profits within the limits of their own borders. The only way these funds could be recovered was by spending on the spot.

This lured many producers abroad. They were sometimes able to buy impounded dollars at a discount from the major companies, thus lowering their production costs. There were also the bonus attractions of inexpensive extras (large segments of the Spanish or Yugoslav armies could be had for little more than the military "exercises" plus the publicity), cheaper animal fees (highly trained animals had become veritable prima donnas), and especially the refreshing of the screen with new and beautiful background settings. No longer was the old slogan valid: "A rock is a rock, a tree is a tree. Shoot it in Griffith Park."

But it was a peripheral consequence of all these fluxes that was, perhaps, the most important. Picture makers were being exposed to whole arrays of new values, new humanisms, and new storehouses of story material. A process of cross-pollination was taking place, out of which a new and robust hybrid was starting to blossom. Producers were starting to come back from abroad with deep suntans, jingling change in their pockets, and wearing faraway smiles on their faces, as though they had seen things and done things to be coveted. Suddenly those of us at home felt strangely diminished and inbred. We felt like colonials in our own domain. An internationalization was going on. We began to secretly sigh for the Via Veneto, and fell under the influence of the fiction that sex with girls with an accent was more exotic and, for some mysterious reason, not so immoral.

And so it was that we stayed home, geldings guarding the sacred flame.

I was in charge.

In the autumn of 1956 *Baby Doll* arrived.

In the writing credits, it is claimed that this material was derived from a fifteen-year-old vignette by Tennessee Williams called *27 Wagons Full of Cotton,* but in actuality this is to stretch it. It was a tour de force of creativity by Williams, in some kind of conjunction with Elia Kazan. Williams is, in my opinion, one of the most important writers in English of our time. I don't know that he has the most important things to say, but he is the master craftsman and the great portraitist. In the case of *Baby Doll* the fundamental story he is trying to tell is worthy of more credit than it gets, and I can vouch from personal knowledge that Kazan, even ten years later, still thought it was one of the best films he had made.

What is the plot? Borrowing from the tight capsulation of *Daily Variety,* it is the story of "an immature teenager [Carroll Baker], married to middle-aged [Karl] Malden, who owns a cotton gin lying idle. When their on-credit furniture is carried away, Malden sets fire to the syndicate cotton gin that had taken all his business. Suspecting Malden, [Eli] Wallach—owner of the gin—carts his cotton to Malden's gin and then proceeds to seduce Miss Baker, who signs a note confessing that Malden committed the arson. Malden, who has agreed not to touch his young wife until one year after their marriage [the year is almost up as the picture starts], finds Miss Baker and Wallach together in the house and goes berserk with jealousy."

What this story was all about, in theme, was revenge; but the type of revenge that is typical of the Sicilian mind. Once Wallach, the Latin, has his piece of paper implicating Malden, he taunts the fellow until he is almost insane with the thought that he has been robbed of the sex for which he waited so long. He takes out his shotgun and drunkenly starts to shoot at anything in sight. He is led off under arrest by the sheriff and his "friends," whom he had counted on to protect him from the wily outsider.

In its depths, however, this story makes other commentaries. It is a sly exposure of the Tobacco Road mentality of the South. It lays naked the arrogance by which trashy whites try to sustain the status quo economically, and the cruelty to which they will go to keep it intact. It shows the evil masonry of the stupid, and its impotence to cope with innovations. It is a social document of no mean power.

The first script for this production had come in to the Code office over a year before. In letter and in multiple conferences we had agonized over an entire spectrum of elements that were clouding the moral equations of the planned film. The problem was not with the basic plot nor with the theme, but with the terms in which this story was told. It was steeped in a heavy sexuality, especially in the areas of the frustration and the lust of Karl Malden, and in the vividly detailed and protracted sequences of the "seduction" of Baby Doll by the Sicilian. The entire plot to awaken her sexuality in order to make her subservient (and sign the confession about the arson) was as "raw" as had been attempted in American pictures, at least up to that time.

When we reviewed the picture in our projection room in mid-September, the print was so crude as to be almost indecipherable, but it was evident that it suggested trouble. We were used to "eating off the kitchen sink," as it were, looking not at polished prints, but at what were called "work prints," full of marks and scratches and blurred sound tracks. The sexual impact of such a piece of rough carpentry was diminished almost to the point of nonexistence. Even so, we took exception to certain items, and especially to the eroticism of the so-called swing scene. Silva the Sicilian had cornered Baby Doll—who sucked her thumb when she slept and caressed the mouth of a Coke bottle with her lips in a manner hardly to be misinterpreted—in a garden swing and purred at her and stroked her skin until she went into reactions that were nothing if not orgasm.

Elia Kazan resisted our interpretation of this scene. It was probably his favorite scene in the picture, and he felt we were laying barbaric hands on one of those fantastically intricate traceries that are the dream of every artisan. Inviting Dougherty and myself to Warners' studio, he sat down with us in the dark of the projection room and went over the footage frame by frame, showing why he could cut nothing and pleading that the texture of the fabric would be damaged. In the end, it was I, as temporary Mexican General of the Code operation, who yielded, and gave "Gadge" his sequence. I was to learn a lesson. In the case of motion pictures, the whole is greater than the sum of all its parts.

There was another famous scene of Silva falling asleep in Baby Doll's crib in the attic. At first, it seemed to convey the idea that a sex affair was consummated here, but Kazan argued that this would be physically absurd, since there was no room for gymnastics of any sort. In addition, he added a disclaiming line by the girl that "nothing happened" and had cut out a facial expression by her that had negated this dialogue. We were content and approved the film, ignoring such minuscules as "wop," and double-meaning gestures of defiance, and even an embarrassing scene of a hound-dog, sitting straight on into the camera, with his conspicuous waterworks palpitating right under the viewer's nose. To have picked on that item would have opened up a whole new thing and introduced the blight of scurrility into the solving of questions that were much more important.

As so often happened, however, the Legion of Decency viewers saw the film where we had left off, an almost infinite number of words and manipulations later; and their shocked reaction was in the order of Quigley's reaction to Kazan's *Streetcar*. So aghast were they that they got word to Cardinal Spellman. This prelate, who was not, unfortunately, most happily gifted with a sense of "issue," flew up into his pulpit, some say without bothering to see the film, and condemned it in the strongest terms. He imposed an interdict on it, exhorting Catholic people not to see it ". . . under pain of sin." He added, "It is the moral and patriotic duty of every local citizen to defend America from dangers which threaten our beloved country from beyond our boundaries, but also the dangers which confront us at home."

Kazan, exhibiting the spirit of self-assertion of the new independents, flashed back at the churchman. He stated, "I disagree that *Baby Doll* is immoral. I am outraged by the charge that it is unpatriotic, and I fail to understand this."

The Legion of Decency itself, echoing the mood of the Cardinal, released a hotheaded condemnation of *Baby Doll* as follows: "The subject matter of this film is morally repellent both in theme and treatment. It dwells almost without variation or relief upon carnal suggestiveness in action, dialogue, and costuming. Its unmitigated emphasis on lust and the various scenes of cruelty are degrading and corruptive. As such, it is grievously offensive to Christian and traditional standards of morality and decency." It appended an all-important slap at the Code proper. "The subject matter of the film indicates an open disregard of the Code by its administrators."

Now the cat was out of the bag. The Legion had thrown sham aside and had assumed a proprietary stance over the machinery of an American industrial entity.

Quigley jumped into the fray. In his influential *Motion Picture Daily* he charged that the film contained violations of all three of the General Principles of the Code—in its ability to lower the moral standards of many who will see it, in its almost total disregard of "correct standards of life," and in its ridicule of both natural and human law. It surely did nothing of these three, but the picture had the ability to blind sober people and make them rage in the same way in which it jangled Karl Malden within the framework of the film itself. But the interlocking triumvirate of the Legion, the Cardinal, and the Quigley complex were revealed—as well as their efforts to intertie with the Code and to force it to their will.

The situation was compounded when James A. Pike, then Dean of The Cathedral Church of St. John the Divine (New York's Episcopal headquarters), scorned Cardinal Spellman's attack by calling it "the efforts of a minority group to impose its wishes on the city." This had the effect of further contradicting the feudal power structure that had been relatively unassailable since the middle ages. It was an evidence of Individualism raising its ugly head. Papal tracts had been written warning of this. What made the System work was compliance; or at least a decent reticence.

The Europeans did not see the case in such monolithic terms. The picture was advertised on the subway kiosks of Paris with the single blurb "Condemned by Cardinal Spellman." This brought in the Catholic crowds. Cardinal Feltin refused to go along with his Prince-Brother's condemnation, overseeing the application of a 4-A classification of the film "strictly for adults, with some reservations."

But when the British Jesuit Father J. A. V. Burke, director

of the Catholic Film Institute, gave it as his view that the film was "a powerful denunciation of social and racial intolerance and as such is something for thoughtful people to see," he was blackballed for singing outside the chorus. Over a lugubrious bottle of wine which we split in the Dorchester Hotel in London, he told me, as an equal "patsy" of the film, that the long arm of clerical vengeance had reached across the waters and touched him. Spellman had asked a fellow British Cardinal to back his action in the name of Church unity, and the British prelate had obliged. Burke was sacked as head of the Film Institute.

There were three areas in which the film showed a capacity for making people blind. The first was very close to home. It would seem that Kazan, by some witchery, had created the suggestion that something else went on in the crib in place of "ordinary" sex. This intimation went completely over my head, but not that of Geoffrey Shurlock, who later said with an agreeing grin that the word around town, in the movie crowd, was that Baby Doll had given Silva (to use his phrase) a "blow job." That was what all the Coke bottle and thumb-sucking symbols may have been about. Neither did it escape the shrewd observation of the critic of the Los Angeles *Times,* Philip Scheuer.

It also, apparently, made the Legion of Decency opaque. That they should have blundered into a coarse personal attack, calling the Code conduct "open disregard" of the document, showed an insensitiveness to the growing reality of the new breed of moviemakers. It was almost as though the Legion were striking out blindly to punish individuals on the Code staff for the existence of the mavericks who were a threat to Authoritarianism. They showed, on the Legion staff, no comprehension that the Independents were the result of the evolution in American tax laws. These laws were forcing individual performers and creators out away from the corporations, where they were salaried and governable contractees, and into private ventures, where they could take advantage of the capital gains loopholes. This broke up the studios, which, in their initial conception, had been monarchical in structure, and devoted to production-line mass turnout of films. The days of the Elephants, as Dore Schary called them, were over, and none of the great beasts knew where to go to die; so they just hung on, being bullied by the new masters. But with their demise, the authority of the Code began to drain away, slowly, almost imperceptibly, like the leakage of sands in an hourglass. But the Elephants had brought it on themselves. Otto Preminger, one of the most conspicuous of the Independents, made the acid remark that the Motion Picture Industry was the only business in which it was more expensive to make production-line goods than it was to turn out custom-made products.

But there was a third area of density and of misunderstanding that *Baby Doll* was able to produce, and this is probably the most important of all. It had to do with Kazan's statement that he could not understand what the issue had to do with patriotism. Had he been tuned in to the overall realities of the case, he would have understood what forces were operating, to the degree that they made prudent men and groups foolish, stinging themselves with the tails of scorpions in their exaggerations. An understanding of what was moving the Cardinal in particular, but the Legion and the Quigley Thing secondarily, can only be gleaned by stepping back a few years and taking a look at another controversial picture of immense impact on American culture, *The Miracle*.

To summarize *The Miracle*, we are fortunate in having the brief that was used by the Supreme Court of the United States in their review of this case, and which is attributed to "a practiced hand," Mr. Bosley Crowther:

> A poor, simple-minded girl is tending a herd of goats on a mountainside one day, when a bearded stranger passes. Suddenly it strikes her fancy that he is St. Joseph, her favorite saint, and that he has come to take her to heaven, where she will be happy and free. While she pleads with

him to transport her, the stranger gently plies the girl with wine, and when she is in a state of tumult, he apparently ravishes her. (This incident in the story is only briefly and discreetly implied.)

The girl awakens later, finds the stranger gone, and climbs down the mountain not knowing whether he was real or a dream. She meets an old priest who tells her that it is quite possible that she did see a saint, but a younger priest scoffs at the notion. "Materialist!" the old priest says.

There follows now a brief sequence—intended to be symbolic, obviously—in which the girl is reverently sitting with other villagers in church. Moved by a whim of appetite, she snitches an apple from the basket of a woman next to her. When she leaves the church, a cackling beggar tries to make her share the apple with him, but she chases him away as by habit and munches the fruit contentedly.

Then, one day, while tending the village youngsters as their mothers work at the vines, the girl faints and the women discover that she is going to have a child. Frightened and bewildered, she suddenly murmurs, "It is the grace of God!" and she runs to the church in great excitement, looks for the statue of St. Joseph, and then prostrates herself on the floor.

Thereafter she meekly refuses to do any menial work and the housewives humor her gently but the young people are not so kind. In a scene of brutal torment, they first flatter and laughingly mock her, then they cruelly shove and hit her and clamp a basin as a halo on her head. Even abused by the beggars, the poor girl gathers together her pitiful rags and sadly departs from the village to live alone in a cave.

When she feels her time coming upon her, she starts towards the village. But then she sees the crowds in the streets; dark memories haunt her; so she turns towards a church on a high hill and instinctively struggles towards it, crying desperately to God. A goat is her sole companion. She drinks water dripping from a rock. And when she comes to the church and finds the door locked, the goat attracts her to a small side door. Inside the church, the poor girl braces herself for her labor pains. There is a dissolve, and when we next see her sad face, in close-up, it is full of a tender light. There is the cry of an unseen baby. The girl reaches towards it and murmurs, "My son! My love! My flesh!"

This condensation by the dean of New York movie reviewers gives us the facts, but it does not give us the factors which would explain the great flareup of feelings provoked by this picture. Some said it was just a peasant allegory, conveying the idea that the Godhead lies in all human beings. Rossellini himself, the maker of this film, claimed that the "miracle" was that a demented girl regains her sanity in her eternal love, which springs up at the birth of her child.

The clue to a contrary interpretation, however, is afforded in an action taken by the London County Council sitting in review on this film, after it had been rejected for certificate by the British Board of Film Censors. Three members of the L.C.C. approved *The Miracle* for adults, provided that deletions were made on the sound track of verse 20, Chapter I, of the Gospel of Matthew:

> But while he thought on these things, behold, the angel of the Lord appeared unto him in a dream, saying, Joseph, thou son of David, fear not to take unto thee Mary thy wife: for that which is conceived in her is of the Holy Ghost.

Additionally, the appeals body asked that a mocking chanting of "Ave Maria" be cut from the stoning scene when the woman is driven from the village, as well as a reference by her to her "blessed infant."

Thus, the inference is clear. This film was taken by many—not limited to the U.S.A., but including Italy as well as England—to be an effort to secularize the story of the Virgin Birth. Worse yet, it gave the appearance of being a mean attempt to reduce this tenderly held belief to the level of mockery. It had the effect of playing for fools those members of the audience who might feel that the doctrine of the Incarnation was a matter of supernatural truth.

The Catholic entity in the U.S.A. reacted to this challenge in keeping with its inbred instincts. These instincts were at least partly formed by elements in its heritage. By the terms of the Lateran agreements, for example, the Italian Constitution and the Italian Government were bound to bar whatever was offensive to the Catholic religion. In the case of *The Miracle,* the Catholic Cinematographic Center did not invoke any governmental sanction thereby afforded. Undoubtedly, the same kind of arrangements existed in Spain. It was tradition, even if broken and fragmentary, to fall back on the agencies of State to act as tools for the implementation of Church views.

The highlights of what happened in the case of *The Miracle* can be sketched by borrowing freely from the Supreme Court document setting forth its final opinion.

The film was passed by American Customs and was twice licensed by New York State, once without English titles, and a second time as part of a trilogy with English subtitles. Just before Christmastime in 1950, it was released at the Paris Theater in Manhattan. It was promptly attacked by the Legion of Decency as "sacrilegious and blasphemous." On December 27 the trilogy entitled *Ways of Love* was selected by the New York Film Critics as the best foreign language film of the year. Just prior to this, Edward T. McCaffrey, Commissioner of Licenses for New York City, ordered the film withdrawn from exhibition on the grounds that it was "officially and personally blasphemous." There was the threat of the risk of suspension of the license to operate the Paris Theater. The New York Supreme Court judged that the Commissioner had exceeded his authority, in that he had no powers of movie censorship, and the program was restored to the theater.

Pickets from the Catholic War Veterans, the Holy Name Society, and other Catholic organizations—reaching about 1,000 persons during one Sunday—paraded before the Paris Theater. A smaller number of counterpickets appeared on several days. The movie house was emptied on two different evenings on threat of bombing.

Several days later a statement by Cardinal Spellman condemning the picture, and calling on "all right-thinking citizens" to unite to tighten censorship laws, was read at all masses in the Cathedral. Even though Catholic opinion generally supported the view of the Legion and of His Eminence, a storm of controversy arose from other religious quarters. In view of this dispute, the Chairman of the Board of Regents of the State of New York appointed a committee of three members to review the issuance of the two licenses by the Motion Picture Division. Agreeing with the dissidents, the Board rescinded the licenses. The Board's action was upheld by the courts at different levels.

On the West Coast, Joseph Burstyn, distributor of the picture, had received lucrative offers from theater owners in the art circuit in downtown Los Angeles. The offers melted away, however, when a meeting of these operators was convoked by Mendel Silberberg, powerful figure in the Jewish community and attorney for the Motion Picture Industry, as well as sometime adviser to Cardinal Francis A. McIntyre. All the inferences were clear.

The real, buried, and ultimate feelings about this matter, however, came to the surface in a lead editorial in the *Motion Picture Herald,* Martin Quigley's prestigious periodical. In deploring *The Miracle* as an "outrage," Quigley probed into the heart of the suspicion. "Its thinly veiled symbolism is an attack not only on Christian faith, but on all religion." It was produced in that period of Rossellini's life when, claimed Quigley, he was flirting with the extreme Left, and some of his associates, including Anna Magnani, were active Leftists. Fundamentally, the story was "repugnant to the American instincts." It is at this point that we harken back to Elia Kazan and cater to his puzzlement. The idea for *The Miracle* could only have had a logical birthplace in Soviet Russia, although it was possibly too daring for even these Communists.

Thus, we see what was the core of the issue. The Catholic Church had pulled out all the stops in the case of *The Miracle.*

In its attempt to employ naked civil power, it was defeated. The Supreme Court ruled that the notion of sacrilege was too vague to be a term of law. It was still stinging under the embarrassment when the provocation of *Baby Doll* came along. *Baby Doll* was a socioeconomic commentary. As such, it seemed to have the earmarks of the great Conspiracy. This fear would account for what, today, would be a reaction of overkill. The Church was at bay.

Things were not going well with *Heaven Knows, Mr. Allison,* the project Quigley had warned us about. The title, incidentally, explains much about the quality of the problems that were latent in this novel. It stemmed from the fact that the Marine, thinking that he and the nun were permanently isolated on the desert island, had proposed a man-woman relationship to her. She had refused. He argued, "Why not? The world's passed us by. Who'd know?" She smiled and said gently, "Heaven knows, Mr. Allison."

John Huston, the director whose credits were more lavish than the campaign ribbons of General MacArthur, had agreed to tackle the book. At that particular time, however, he could not come into the United States, for some reason having to do with taxes. Therefore, he had come as close as he could, taking up residence in Ensenada, Mexico, about two hundred miles below Los Angeles. With him was an old hand at screenwriting, John Lee Mahin, who had won the Oscar for his version of *Quo Vadis.* From that time on he was tabbed as a "religious" writer. Between the two of them, they were mailing pages daily of a first draft script to the studio, but Buddy Adler could see that they were bogging down. He called on the phone. Would I go down there and help?

"Geoff's not back yet from Europe," I explained.

"I'll get you back in a couple of hours any time you want," said Buddy. "I'll send a private plane for you."

This sounded more like the Hollywood of fiction I had used to hear about. "Well, in that case . . ." I agreed.

I was met in San Diego by a smartly uniformed Mexican chauffeur who stood by a black Cadillac limousine. We purred down the well-paved highway to the border, seventeen miles away, and slid under an archway. The chauffeur waved familiarly to the police, who wore dark glasses. He called them *viejos* (old guys) and they waved him on nonchalantly with a "keep the traffic moving" gesture. I was in Mexico. For the first time, I had crossed an international border. In the back of the limousine, blowing out cigarette smoke as though I did this every day, I began to feel very much like a man of the world.

When we arrived in Ensenada, we cruised slowly through the old town, with its rutted streets and an unpainted building labeled "Hospital." I felt that were I a fly, I could hardly have resisted an exploration of this unsanitary-looking place. A dog loped stoically in front of our car, made us wait, and stared at us blankly as we passed on.

We turned a corner and came into the new town, a mélange of motels alongside a jade-green bay. The beige-colored strand curved sharply, like a Moorish scimitar. On the smooth waters rode an occasional fishing cruiser.

The chauffeur deposited me at the best motel in town, and left with a friendly *hasta luego*. The minute I got to my room, I seized the phone and asked for John Lee Mahin. I was familiar with him, but had never met Huston. "Johnny?" I asked, in tones filled with happy assault.

"Ye-es," replied the voice at the other end.

"Johnny? This is Jack Vizzard! How the hell *are* ya, y'old scoundrel?"

The other voice filled with the sunshine of recognition. "Oh, *Jack!* Hi! I'm *fine*, thanks, fine. C'mon up."

"Y' near Huston's? I oughta check in with the old geek, y' know?"

There was a small beat, like a stumble.

"This is the old geek. Who were you calling?"

I swallowed the blunder like it had never occurred. "Oh,

Johnny!" I enthused, "I thought I had John *Mahin* on the phone. *Hi* ya! Thissiz Jack Vizzard."

"So I gather," announced Huston. He decided to forget it. A warm note flooded back into his voice. "C'mon *up,* Jack," he invited. "Dying to see you."

I'll bet he was. "Be right up," I promised. I could see him putting the phone back on its cradle and scratching his head.

When I got to the room, I met a lanky man with a well-seamed face who was standing like a question mark with his hands thrust in the pockets of a bathrobe. Somehow he gave the impression that he had just stacked his squirrel gun and raccoon hat in the corner. He was smiling in a queer, expectant manner.

"Well!" he exclaimed. He came forward with hand extended and a hearty expression on his face. "Welcome, welcome. Glad to have you. Sit down." He waved at a wicker chair. He made a few aimless moves, as if looking for another place to deposit his Deerstalker frame, and finally cast himself on the edge of a couch, with one leg tucked up under his haunches. "Well!" he said again, when he had finished perching.

At this point John Mahin came into the room, and we went through the welcoming rubrics again. John took a chair a little in the background, as though to obliterate himself.

Huston balanced an elbow on his knee, and held his chin between his thumb and forefinger. His eyes looked countersunk behind high cheekbones. "Tell me, Jack," he began, "have you read the script?"

"Yes, I have."

"Good, good," he approved, in a voice that sounded like he had just eaten a chocolate bar. "H'mm. What did you think of it?"

John Lee Mahin stared from the background in an owlish manner. He wore horn-rimmed glasses, which he rode on the end of his nose while gazing over the tops.

"You are cautious with your material in the wrong places, and a little forward with it in the wrong places," I began.

John Mahin blinked like a slow lizard.

Huston let the statement roll around in his mouth like a wine taster. "Ye-es," he said with calculation. "Good, Jack. Very good. Now tell me. Where were we too cautious?"

Just as I opened my mouth to speak, Huston said, "Pardon me," and went scrambling pell-mell in the direction of the bathroom.

"He has 'Montezuma's revenge,' " said Mahin.

"Oh!" I said. That explained the bathrobe.

The next I heard, Huston was calling out, *Lorrie!* in tones that were slightly panic-stricken. The implication came through quite clearly that poor Huston had not altogether made it to the bathroom, for he could be heard telling Lorrie Sherwood, his secretary, to dig a fresh pair of pajamas out of his dresser drawer.

"He's not supposed to be working," said Mahin. "He was so God-awful sick last night that they had to fly in a specialist from the Scripps Clinic in San Diego. They thought he was going to die. They woke the doctor out of a sound sleep and chartered a private plane to bring him here. Can you imagine the bill?"

"Wow!" I breathed.

"He's still running a fever," John continued. "The doctor told him to lie quiet for a few days, but he won't. He insists that we keep going."

Huston eventually came back into the room. "I'm sorry, Jack," he said, without further explanation. "Now. What were you going to say?"

The hub of the long dialogue which followed revolved around a single axle. Huston had one set idea about the constancy of the nun; I had another. The only thing remarkable about this was that Huston tended to favor a more conservative point of view, more like Quigley's, actually; while mine tended to be a little more familiar. It was Huston's fixed conviction that this woman would, and should, persevere in her vows for the remainder of her life, come what may.

I disagreed. If time had passed these two people by and there were no prospect of rescue, what else was there to do but to consider herself absolved? I drew upon my vague acquaintance with Canon Law, which said that when the original circumstances in which vows were pronounced have drastically and essentially changed, the vows themselves automatically melt away. I knew I was playing fast and loose with a sensitive area of doctrine, but the alternatives seemed to me to make God incredible.

Huston was intrigued, but he would have none of it. His idea of the girl was more rigoristic and, in the final analysis, more romantic. She had given her heart to her Beloved, and it was once and for all, as far as he was concerned. Even if all hope were lost, she would remain faithful.

"That's very beautiful," I argued, "but what about *him?* Has the Marine no rights? Doesn't this woman have an obligation in charity toward his feelings, his needs? He didn't *put* himself there, you know. He was fighting for his country. His sacrifice was equally as great as hers. Is he to be left to suffer, just so she can follow the safe course?"

This gave Huston pause, for a while. He kept looking off into the distance, his brown eyes full of contemplation. "Very interesting, Jack," he muttered. At last he shook his head. "These two people are too incompatible," he pronounced. "Had they met in the normal course of life, there would have been nothing in common between them. It is unsuitable to imagine them coming together, even in these exceptional circumstances. No, it would never do."

"If they were alone and together for any protracted period of time," I countered, "their differences would begin to fade. *She*'s human and vulnerable, too. What if she should be caught up in a state of passion for him? *He*'s not all *that* unattractive."

"She would not give in," said Huston. "She would go about her daily tasks and suffer. But, she would remain faithful."

"*What* daily tasks?" I demanded, sensing an opening. "Saying her rosary and planting her vegetable garden? And what's *he* supposed to be doing in the meantime, besides providing meat and protection for her? Going down to the far end of the island and running through the manual of arms?"

Huston looked up brightly. "Say, I think we can use that," he said to Mahin. "That's good."

John Mahin nodded and made a note.

The remainder of the dilemma was solved in a very satisfying way—in this sense, that the solution served the story. It was agreed that the nun, in common with usual practice, had taken her vows for a fixed period of time only. That time was expiring. She was on her way home to take her final vows when she was marooned by the war. An explanation of this fact led to a misunderstanding on the part of Allison, who exclaims, "Then you're not *in* yet?" or something to this effect, but full of hope. She replies, kindly, "I'm *in,* all right. It's just that I'm about to re-enlist for life." This definition of her situation, in terms that were understandable to the Marine, gracefully opened up for discussion the question of what would happen to her if the time expired. It led to one of the more poignant moments of the picture.

There were many other items covered, but I think this one example will give an idea of the delicacies through which we traveled. I was armed not only with my own inventions, but with many valuable suggestions which had been made by Monsignor John Devlin, the representative of the Legion of Decency in Hollywood, in an earlier conference in the parlor of his rectory. He had first spurned the script, with the comment that it "oozed sex." One of the things that particularly offended him was a "shower scene" in which the nun undressed and cleaned herself. A plausible excuse had to be concocted in order to get this poor woman into the nude. To oppose the scene put one in the position of seeming to be in favor of bodily odors. Devlin was not to be fooled, and he firmly rejected this scene. But, when the studio bent to his indignation and cut the scene along with other troublesome spots, the Monsignor became more cooperative and dipped into his own store of experiences for many deft suggestions. He was well equipped to do so. He was the guardian and superior of a group of nuns who taught in his school, who had been trapped in the South Pacific during the war, isolated in the mountains by Japanese forces, and who had been led to safety in a long march through the jungle by a group of American Marines!

That night I felt like I had been put through a wringer. The discussion had lasted more than a few hours, and it had involved a maximum of mental exertion. I wondered how Huston, with a fever, was able to stand the gaff, and what would be the measure of his resiliency when he regained his full health.

John Lee Mahin stopped me in the lobby of the motel and invited me to dinner with himself and his wife. "We know a little place out on the rocks," he said, pointing to a headland in the darkening distance. "I'd like to introduce you to Margaritas."

I was unable to resist the pun. "You mean *Margaritas ante porcos?*" I asked. John clasped his hand to his brow and groaned.

We sat down in an intimate candlelit restaurant, with fan coral decorations and a blue curving sailfish on the wall, and the waiter brought the cocktails in chilled glasses with a rim of frosted salt around the top. When I tasted the tequila and the lime and all, I felt like crying out, *"Olé!"*

"I think once in a while Huston's putting you on," said Mahin. "But on the whole, keep going. You're doing fine."

"Thank you," I replied. "Tell me, did Huston get sick just last night?"

"No, it's been creeping up on him for several days. In fact, I think it's shattered his whole dream of an adventure in Ensenada. He's had a fishing cruiser standing by for several days, at thirty dollars a day, and he missed out on a hunting trip into the mountains for bighorn sheep. He's mad."

"Are the mountains that high around here?" I asked.

"I guess so. And no roads, either. It was all arranged with the Army to bring a half-track up into the back country to haul the sheep out. The rest of the party, whoever they were, went anyhow and they came back with a couple of big specimens. John was so miffed he wouldn't go out on the street to look at them. They were lying on their sides on the bottom of the truck, with eyes the size of saucers and big swirling horns, all full of flies and blood. John said, 'Who wants to look at a coupla dead sheep, anyhow?' He wouldn't go."

"He strikes me as the type who'd want to do the things a character in a Hemingway novel would do."

"That's pretty close to it."

We spoke of many other things, and when we finally decided to order chicken about midnight, all the waiters shrugged their shoulders. The kitchen was closed and the chef had gone home. We didn't mind. By this time we had accumulated plenty of anesthesia. On the way back to the motel I noticed that the stars in Mexico are very unreliable and tend to reel a great deal. *Caramba!*

I climbed into bed, and my mind wandered back to the men's room in Chasen's restaurant on Beverly Boulevard, not far from our office. There, over the urinals, hangs a classic picture. It is a colored drawing of a fellow floundering in an ocean of breasts, big breasts and little breasts, soft ones and firm ones, round ones and elliptical ones, all in endless confusion like a satyr's dream. And across the top, in a reckless scrawl, were the words "To Hell with the Johnston Office!"

Me too. I was in the business now with both feet. To hell with tits and trivia!

I slept well.

15 The Legion Tightens the Screws

WITH THE SPECIAL ORIENTATION of the Legion, and the mood of provocation on the part of the liberal camp, it was only a matter of time before another symbolic case occurred. Today the picture is all but forgotten, but for a moment in the late fifties it flared into prominence like a pyre of burning books. The picture was called *Storm Center* and dealt with the touchy question of the right of access to information in American libraries.

Remarkably similar to a real-life case that had erupted in the little picture-town of Santa Rosa, in north-central California, it was a story of an idealistic librarian (Bette Davis), who has a dream of opening a children's branch of her revered institution. She fondly studies the blueprints, and has applied to the city council for funds to begin building. A lifelong friend, Judge Ellerbe, visits the library and in browsing among the shelves finds a book titled *The Communist Dream*. With heavy heart he brings this news to the City Fathers, who give Bette an ultimatum. Take the controversial book off the shelves and she will get the money to build her children's branch. She refuses, and the dilemma is joined. What are the citizens going to do? The Gordian knot is cut for them by a precocious young boy, Freddie Slater, who had been a favorite of Bette's, and to whom she had opened up the wealth and the wonders of the world of books. He is caught in the raging tides of controversy that surge back and forth, and is agitated to the point of distraction. He climbs into the library through a window one night and, while he is scanning the troublesome books, begins to hallucinate. The books turn into nests of writhing snakes, and the matches he holds up for light turn into torches. He sets the whole building aflame. The shock of the holocaust brings sobriety to the citizens. The boy is rescued, and Bette comes back fighting, determined to rebuild the library even if she has to do it with her bare hands. She vows that anyone who tries to take a book off the racks in the future will have to do so over her dead body.

As corny as this plot seems today, it had caught an issue of the moment, and in so doing had scraped a sensitive nerve of the Legion of Decency. The Legion, in some qualified but real sense, was a continuation of the tradition of the "Index" of forbidden books, and, in a more limited manner, of the Inquisition. Therefore, *Storm Center* touched them where they lived.

Knowing, however, that in a pluralistic society they would be walking into a certain blackjacking to condemn the picture, they employed for the first time a new device, called the "Separate Classification." In thus rating the picture, they expressed their pique in the wording of their accompanying comment:

> The highly propagandistic nature of this controversial film (book burning, anti-communism, civil liberties) offers a warped, over-simplified and strongly emotional solution to a complex problem of American life. Its specious arguments tend seriously to be misleading and misrepresentative by reason of inept and distorted presentation.

The "Separate Classification" was defined in an appended note as that which was given "to certain films which, while not morally offensive, require some analysis and explanation as a protection to the uninformed against wrong interpretations and false conclusions."

The action of the Legion had about the same effect on Hollywood as scratching a fingernail on a blackboard. The Motion Picture Industry Council, a representative group made up of various factors in the film business and headed by Lou Greenspan, a one-time editor of *Variety*, flew into session and drew up a resolution, which it cast back into the teeth of the Legion. The resolution, which was published, read as follows:

> We do not question the Legion's right to offer normal and religious leadership nor do we approve or disapprove the film at issue. However, we believe that by implication and inference, this action by the Legion goes beyond normal criticism and spiritual advice and is a form of censorship with the purpose of dictating and controlling the content of motion pictures contrary to American principles of freedom of thought and expression.

Such public chastisement of the Legion was uncommon, to say the least, and was another sign of the times. The truth of the matter lay deeper than the actual words used by the Legion. A secular community recognized the European quality of the approach and of the theory behind the words, and reacted accordingly.

In the interests of impartiality, it must be said that the picture received good critical acclaim in England, as well as in France. The critic of the influential *France-Soir* turned around and scolded the United States for its timidity. He said, "What is most difficult in a free country is not freely expressing one's own opinions, but respecting the opinions of others. Americans are not the only true democrats to suffer this sectarianism disguised as vigilance and good faith, but they are perhaps the only ones to denounce and fight it in their films." As opposed to this view, weekly (or "Big") *Variety* said that the picture "never gets the grip of reality on the viewer."

Of considerable significance, however, was a second-wave action taken by the Motion Picture Association itself. A brochure was prepared by the Community Relations Department under the directorship of Arthur DeBra, brashly promoting the picture in a clear exercise of sycophancy to popular sentiment. Even General Eisenhower was requisitioned. His famous "book-burning" speech at Dartmouth College was quoted: "Don't think you are going to conceal faults by concealing evidence that they ever existed." These words, which helped earn the President the suspicion of the far Right, were attached to the plug for the picture, to give it borrowed import.

In close consequence, I began to be the recipient of a number of comments from people in the picture business about the Legion getting too big for its pants, and suchlike. I recoiled from these remarks with a "Listen, don't blame *me*. I have nothing to do with the Legion of Decency." However, the resentful looks I received made it clear to me that many thought I had some responsibility, being a Catholic and all, and it was my business to get the word back to my acquaintances to play it cool. I began to search my imagination. I agreed with the basic complaint. Something ought to be done. But what? The Legion is relatively immune to frontal assault. To take it on is to tangle with the whole apparatus of the Catholic Bishops of the United States. One does not twist the tail of this lion with impunity. For the beast which seems to be moribund may only be sleeping and is quite capable of waking up and clawing its tormenter to shreds.

I was saved from making a decision by the timely intervention of Buddy Adler, calling again about *Heaven Knows, Mr. Allison.* He was pleased with the way things had gone in Ensenada. The revised version of the script had been shown once again to Monsignor Devlin. He was beginning to thaw out and could see the possibility of making an acceptable film of this material, but he still had many reservations and objections. However, there was a difficulty. John Huston had left for location on the island of Tobago in the West Indies. To transmit to him cold, in memo form, the long list of items remaining to be corrected was too great a gamble. About three million dollars were riding on this venture, and the Legion of Decency was clearly waiting to pounce on it in New York if it should go sour. Would I take up from where I had left off and join John in Tobago until the wrinkled areas were ironed out? In short, would I assume the role of "technical adviser"?

I said, "Buddy, twist my arm. But, convince Geoff."

It took one quick telephone conversation to persuade Geoff, who had just returned from abroad. His immediate reaction was "What's to hinder you?"

I rushed to my atlas. I found that Tobago was a tiny island in the lower West Indies, a satellite of the larger island of Trinidad. It stood just off the coast of Venezuela, a mere twelve degrees north of the equator. I wondered where I could buy a pith helmet. Some knowledgeable soul warned that it is necessary to guard against fungus in the tropics. I bought a bottle of Clorox and stuffed it in a shoe in the bottom of my traveling bag. I was ready.

It was a sunny afternoon in September when the two-motored British plane curved in for a landing on the hilly hyphen of land in the Caribbean called Tobago. We bounced to a stop on a rutted dirt strip half-covered with grass and lined with tall coconut palms. Offshore, a quartz-blue surf creamed into a sandy lagoon. A limpid wind spilled down out of the skies like a decrescendo of violins. A cascade of blue flowers stirred on a jungle bush.

I was met at the airport by Harold Nebenzal, the son of the producer of *M*, who was an expert on Japanese language and customs. He suggested we have a local drink while we waited for the baggage to be unloaded. This was more like the movie business of my fantasies. We had a rum and Coke each.

At the baggage rack, they had just finished unloading two enormous turtles, which were to be used in the picture. A crew had been sent into the Caribbean to catch them, and had immobilized the poor creatures by keeping them on their backs in the cargo compartment of the plane. They were still floundering vaguely with their feet while a couple of native boys trussed them and threw them into a jeep. Someone asked me which bags were mine, and I pointed to two or three. "This one, suh?" asked a porter, holding up a scotch-plaid foldover. "Yes," I confirmed. "Trouble, suh," he said dubiously. He turned the bag around and exposed the bleached and burst bottom. The cargo hatch had not been pressurized, and the altitude had exploded the Clorox bottle in mid-air. The shoe in which it had been stored looked like a boiled delicacy out of Charlie Chaplin's *Gold Rush*.

I found John Huston running busily around the middle of the island in a pair of safari shorts and a straw ranchero hat. He had started shooting the day before, and it was clear at once that his whole demeanor had changed. He was now a study in concentration and keen anticipation.

The rumor was already circulating around the location that a match between professionals was in the making. John had begun his camera work with a shot of Bob Mitchum landing on the island, tossed up by the surf from a rubber raft. Mitchum had made it clear that he was not afraid to get wet or dirty, or to use his muscles. It was almost as though he were taunting Huston to test him. John sensed the challenge and accepted it.

To his satisfaction, John had gotten the first scenes on film with an absolute economy of takes, a fact which continued to give him pleasure throughout the remainder of the film. The Huston I saw was a direct and lean man. When he saw what he wanted, he would declare, "That's *it*. Print it!" He felt no need to "cover" himself with a few "insurance" shots. There was no "Let's take one more 'for the camera,' " which tends to wear out the actors and make them soggy for later scenes.

Huston ended up with a considerable esteem for Mitchum. "Some day I'd like to direct him in *Othello*," he said. "He's the perfect Iago."

The "location" itself was a little village constructed of bamboo and thatches and coconut logs, and set down in a clearing of the palm jungle. To one side flowed an inlet from the ocean, where the salt shingles mingled with the fresh waters of a mountain stream. Over the little estuary stretched a bamboo bridge on palm piles, which reached out for a finger of land to seaward. In back of the village a series of soft slopes flowed upward toward the backbone of the island, a long mountain ridge covered with rain forests. On the shoulder of one of the hills stood a wooden chapel with a modest spire. It was the only building of milled wood in the cluster.

It was in this setting that most of the exterior shots were filmed.

Many of the interior shots were in an elaborate cave, which the Marine had supposedly found up in the mountains. To erect this cave, the town hall of the city of Scarborough was rented and turned into a set. It became a corrugated-iron horror. With the heat of the equatorial sun boring straight through the metal roof, and the thermal waves pouring from the arc lamps indoors, the temperature would quickly fly up to the level of a furnace once the doors were closed and shooting began. Several times scenes had to be broken up on an emergency basis so that the coolers could be turned on and the doors opened, lest the cast suffocate. If I acquired nothing else on Tobago, I at least came away with an increased respect for the physical hardiness needed to make pictures.

I found out another thing, too, which I think it might be interesting to note here. I discovered that one of the greatest problems in the making of pictures has to do with the art of coping with boredom. Strange as it may seem, tedium is the most formidable enemy.

The reason for this is that pictures are made according to the old Army maxim of "Hurry up and wait." There is no avoiding this technique. A scene has to be rehearsed again and again and this in itself is stultifying enough, especially when one is familiar with the script. But, before rehearsal the set has to be "dressed" with lights. The arranging and the filtering of the lights, which is the function of the cameraman working together with the director, is *the* most time-consuming factor in the making of pictures. It is also the least interesting. It is a technician's occupation. Oddly enough, the cameraman scarcely ever touches the camera. This great contraption, with its exquisite precisions, is handled by the camera operator, who is usually called the "second cameraman." But, in watching the functions of these professionals, one gradually comes to the realization that the business of making a movie is a technique of painting with lights and shadows, be they colored or otherwise. This is essentially what is meant by "making a movie." Up to this point I had only thought of it in terms of "telling a story." It is a mistake to think of a film in such narrow terms. The story is the soul of it all, true. But the soul has to be incarnated into a body before it acquires a life-as-a-whole. The camera is the magic filter through which this incarnation takes place.

My first item of business with Huston was to present him with the letter containing the remaining objections of Monsignor Devlin. It was by no means a short document.

I felt somewhat like a process server handing over this paper. John was sitting in one of the thatched huts while a scene was being lighted by the first cameraman, Ossie Morris. One could not help feeling very much aware that he was in Huston's bailiwick now. He shoved his ranchero hat to the back of his head, took a blue bandanna from his neck, and wiped his brow. He stuffed the bandanna in his pocket and fished out a flat cardboard box looking like it had come from an exclusive tobacconist's shop in London. He slid open the box and dug out a long oval dark-brown cigarette, which he thrust in the corner of his mouth. He lit the cigarette with a tarnished silver lighter with a windproof chimney around the wick. He rested his arms on a pair of bony knees and began examining the letter. His reading was punctuated by a series of intent "Mm-hmms" and an occasional "So!"

"Tell me, Jack," he said, with a peculiar fishing tone in his voice, "what does the Monsignor mean when he says that the nun would not have been living alone with the priest on the island?"

The explanation was easy. I tried to point out to him that for reasons of decorum, the nun would have had at least one companion to keep her company. It would be incredible to think that the nun would have been serving a missionary priest in some far-flung outpost all alone. Such a setup would have been a subject for scandal.

"That is a good point," conceded Huston, "very good. Yes indeed. It helps us. But it gives us a problem."

"What is that?"

"It makes it necessary for us to explain how the nun was deserted on the island. If there were others, did they just run off when the Japanese landed and leave her there? Something will have to be worked out that will be brief but plausible. We don't want the others to look callous, do we?"

"The other nun could have been killed during the invasion, or carried off prisoner," I suggested.

"Ye-es," he said, riding the word thoughtfully. "Something like that. I wonder if you'll plan to meet me at the hotel tonight, after the shooting, and we'll examine that? We'll find something."

I agreed readily. My position on the picture was nicely defined in that single sentence.

John ruffled the letter. "Now there's another point, Jack, that I don't find so easy. It's the 'dream sequence.' What about that?"

The dream sequence was important to John because it was connected with the crisis of his story. It had to do with the nun working out her dilemma in the form of a dream in which she transplants herself into common woman's garb and out of her habit. It had the effect, though, of trying to treat the nun as a laywoman, while at the same time keeping her a religious. It was against Monsignor Devlin's instincts, however, since it broke down the walls of privacy around a nun, and dealt with her not as someone special, but as a mere woman. It had somewhat the same effect as the shower scene, although not so aggravated.

The Monsignor was the only one who stood firm against this sequence. The rest of us all felt that the sequence was respectful, even though it took liberties. John Huston tended to be resentful against what he considered an excess of zeal on Devlin's part.

"I may shoot it anyway," said Huston. "If I do, do you think we can get away with it?"

"I doubt it," I said. "Devlin may be in touch with his counterparts in New York, and they're apt to back his action. If it were an inexpensive sequence, I'd say take a chance. But it isn't, is it?"

"No."

"And if they object to it in New York, you'd have nothing to replace it, would you?"

"No. It couldn't be cut. It would break the top of my picture."

"Can we get something else, now?"

"I don't know," he said, worriedly. "We'll have to give this some serious consideration. But this Legion of Decency annoys me."

"You and all the rest of the chorus," I said.

"I once had a story by Marcel Pagnol," he continued. "It was based on the character of Judas. It intrigued me. It was a sympathetic treatment of Judas. I thought it would make a very interesting film. I showed it to Monsignor, and he objected. I want to tell you something, Jack. That's not right, not in a democratic society. The story had nothing to do with dogma. It was simply an untraditional way of looking at a controversial character, that's all. I don't like it."

We met that night on the veranda of the Blue Haven Hotel, where most of the crews were quartered. The great open porch seemed to hover over the ocean like a flying carpet, with the surf breaking on the rocks like shattering crystals. A species of small bird flew in from the ocean and scavenged crumbs from the floor and tabletops, securing their welcome by filling the air with music. Huston sat in a canvas chair with his legs propped up. Against his thighs he rested a pad of yellow foolscap paper on which he idly sketched while we talked. We rummaged through an assortment of suggestions to account for the presence of the nun on the island alone, and John finally fixed on an explanation that was adequate. He began to jot it down, and when it was finished he asked, "How's this?" and he undertook to read it to me. "That's *it!*" I said, clapping my hands for emphasis.

Almost instantly, a native in a white coat materialized at my side. "Suh?" he inquired. I looked at him blankly. "Yes?" I wanted to know. He tilted his head to one side and said, "You clapped, suh."

Huston glanced up and laughed. "It looks like you buy the drinks," he said. "If you clap, it means you want a waiter around here."

After the waiter had served the refreshments, Huston put the pad of paper aside. "That's enough for tonight," he said. "But there's something else I'd like to talk about. You know, there's a moment in this picture when the nun and the Marine think that all hope is lost. It seems that the nun will not be able to renew her vows. At this point the Marine asks her to marry him. It's supposed to be a pretty scene, rather innocent, motivated by an unsure love on his part. She accepts it as a compliment, even though she refuses. Now I want to get that scene right. How would the nun feel about being stranded? After all, she has dedicated herself to God, she has given herself to Him, and He is putting Himself outside of her reach. She has chosen Him, and He has withdrawn. How do you think this would make her feel?"

"I think you've said it backwards, John," I suggested.

"Oh, really? In what sense?"

"The nun would not feel that she had chosen God. She would feel that He has selected her. She is the bride that has been summoned by the Bridegroom. She is not honoring Him. He is honoring her."

"Ah!" said John, "that's just what I wanted. You're sure of this?"

"Positive."

"In other words, she'd be doubting herself," he continued. "She might begin to think that she's not acceptable to God, that maybe she's not a good enough nun."

"Yes. That could be her feelings."

"That's very touching. It gives me something to work with. Her position is more delicate when the Marine proposes to her. That makes her resolution all the more moving. She will not lose faith in God, even though He seems not to want her. I like that. Maybe He is testing her."

"That has a correct ring," I assured.

"Maybe this is her trial to see whether she is worthy of her final vows."

"It all sounds good to me."

"Very good, Jack. Very good. I'll try to write it up when we get closer to the scene, and we'll go over it together. In the meantime, keep thinking about an alternative for the dream sequence. That disturbs me. If you get any ideas, write them down. You want to be a writer, here's your chance."

Back at my hotel, colorfully called the "Robinson Crusoe" after a certain famous inhabitant of the island, I encountered a few members of the foreign press, who closed in around me and began to ply me with questions about my presence on this location. I sparred with their insinuations as best I could, but made an incautious remark at one point. In trying to define my position as a molder of scenes, I pointed out to one fellow that it made a great difference whether some of the scenes were played in a mood of innocence, or with "bedroomy eyes." He immediately seized on the phrase, and quoted me as accusing Mitchum of having "bedroom eyes."

Mitch stood in front of me the next day with a wry but

dangerous grin and said, "So you think I have bedroom eyes, huh?" He really didn't need an explanation. He had had sufficient dealings with the press to know how some reporters are able to put you on.

At this moment, another British newspaperman had the misfortune to appear. "Tell me, Mr. Mitchum," he asked, a little pretentiously, "what do you do to perfect your art?"

Bob cocked his eyebrows at the fellow. "Art?" he asked, feigning an expression of stupidity. "What art?"

The newspaperman's voice bobbled; he recovered and said, "Why, the art of acting, of course!"

Mitchum curled his lip. "You mean like Lassie?" he demanded. "Or Trigger?"

As the reporter cringed and started to back away, Mitchum snorted, "*Art*—for Christ's sake!"

In addition to the quaint rubric of clapping hands for the waiters, there was another little custom that had colonial overtones, but which was more charming in character. Just as the men were called "mister," in like manner the ladies were called "mistress." It was "Yes, mis-truss" or "No, mis-truss" or "As you please, mis-truss," as pretty as an antique harpsichord. "I just *love* to be called 'mis-truss,' " exclaimed Deborah Kerr. "It makes me feel so—so *kept!*" She looked friendly daggers at me. "And don't you dare tell me that's against the Code," she warned.

As the production began to make headway, there were other small points that needed special handling. For example, there was one scene in which a Japanese plane flies over the island on a reconnaissance mission. Hearing the sound of the motors, the nun rushes out into the open to wave the pilot down. Mitchum, realizing this would be tantamount to suicide, rushes to the nun and hurls his body over her white habit to hide her. It was a question of bodily contact with an inviolable person. Monsignor Devlin had made the alternate suggestion that the Marine grab up a few palm fronds and throw them over her.

The feasibility of the suggestion depended entirely on the skill of Bob Mitchum. It required him to indicate very quick thinking to the audience, and to get over the clumsy instant of bending down and seizing the stalks of the great fronds. It then called for dexterity and grace to overwhelm the nun by his headlong bodily approach, and to cast the covering over her all in one motion. The entire action had to be accomplished in the few split seconds before the shadow of the plane passed directly across their bodies.

So masterfully did the actor perform this complicated maneuver that it is to be doubted that audiences appreciated what they saw. Mitchum made it look natural and simple. I began to realize that a really excellent actor has to have the agility and the sense of timing that is little less than that of a Nijinsky. And, because the pilot of the plane was almost equally as skilled in getting the shadow to pass over a pinpoint of ground at two hundred miles an hour, the fantastically intricate scene was achieved in one take. Such a tour de force of accomplishment was this, that Huston emitted a spontaneous shout of acclaim.

"How's that, Jack?" he asked me triumphantly.

I raised my hands like a boxer and shook them in congratulations.

At another time, we were on the set eating salt pills to keep our energy up, and watching Deborah rehearse a scene with Mitch. It was one of those subtle duels of dialogue that exposes the mettle of two professionals. None of us were making a sound.

The chief grip (electrician) sidled up to me. "Watch that woman *listen*," he whispered in my ear.

The whole secret of the excellence of the scene unfolded with that remark. Deborah was giving herself over to what Bob was saying, as though her reply had not yet come to her mind. From time to time, her lips moved, forming the words he was uttering. When he was finished, she had to rake her consciousness for a reply. The result was that her delivery was

natural, both in its rhythm and in its inflection. It had none of
the cadence of being memorized.

When the scene was all rehearsed, the grip had more freedom to talk. "I've seen movies made all over the world," he
amplified, "and I've seen all kinds of actors and actresses. I've
noticed that the difference between the hams and the great
ones is that some listen, some don't."

Meanwhile, back at the hotel, a new British newspaperman
had arrived on the scene. His name was Eric Bennett. He wore
long white knitted socks and smoked a succulent pipe. From
behind the pipe, he kept surveying people with plaintive eyes.

He quickly began floating into my orbit, trying to stir up a
story from my presence on this location. Legally and technically, *Mr. Allison* was a British production. What was an
American censor doing on the spot? Were the Yanks now
trying to impose their moral standards on the English?

Any unguarded word on my part could have been blown up
into an inflammatory article, so I shooed him away. I told him
I had been stung before. "Fool me once, shame on you. Fool
me twice, shame on me."

One morning I arrived on the set in the town hall and I
noticed a certain indefinable withdrawal in the members of
the crews. Arty Ibbetsen, the second cameraman, greeted me
with a sarcastic, "Hello, boss." I thought he was joking. "Hi,
Arty," I replied.

"Would you like to approve my camera setup?" asked Arty
provocatively.

"What the hell are you talking about?" I wanted to know.

"Oh, haven't you seen?" he persisted.

"Seen *what,* for Christ's sake?"

"Show him, somebody."

From behind the plaster of paris walls of the cave, the Best
Boy produced the morning newspaper from London. I unfolded it, and my eyes almost fell out. The screeching head-
line, in letters which, I see now, were only an inch high, but

which seemed then as big as a row of houses, read, "THE CENSOR GOES TOO." The subcaption read, "Kerr, the Nun, Meets Marine Mitchum . . . Mr. Vizzard Watches."

On close examination, and on the whole, the article was not as bad as all that. But Bennett had managed to scatter his little droplets of venom. He instantly endeared me with Huston by saying, ". . . the most important figure in the set-up is not director John Huston, fresh from his triumph with 'Moby Dick.' Nor is it Britain's most risen star, Deborah Kerr, or Hollywood's tough Robert Mitchum. The man who matters is a handsome, soft-spoken American named Jack Vizzard." He ended with ". . . the unadvertised appearance of Vizzard in Tobago may mark the beginning of a new era in film-making and picture-going in both Britain and America. For though these precautions [against bad taste] are taken to protect the American box-office returns, this, remember, is a British production in a British Colony."

I looked up at a lot of unfriendly faces. I saw now that I had paid for my trip.

"Judas, this is terrible," I said to Arty. "Has Huston seen it?"

"He's late. That ought to tell you something."

"God."

"Yeah."

I rustled the paper in anger. "Well, you don't think *I* gave this to the sonofabitch?"

"Maybe not."

"Well I *didn't!*"

Arty began to smile. "Well, while we're waiting," he said, a bit easier, "do you mind approving the camera setup for me. I wouldn't want to shoot without your okay."

"Aw, stuff it."

Arty laughed, and the atmosphere became less tense.

At this moment Huston came striding onto the set, his jaw locked, and his eyes looking neither right nor left. He greeted those he passed with a curt "Morning," until he encountered me, when he became more formal. "Good morning, Mr. Vizzard," he said coldly. He kept moving.

There was nothing for it, except to seize the bull by the horns. I followed John to his canvas chair in a corner. "John, I've got to see you for a moment."

His eyes scanned me from head to toe before he said, "Yes?"

"I want to talk to you about that thing."

"What thing?"

"You know. That article in the papers."

"Oh *that!*" he said, as though it were the farthest thing from his mind.

"I wouldn't want you to think *I* gave that to Bennett," I said.

"No?" he asked in an odd tone. "Well then, where did he get it, Jack?"

"He's been hanging around me trying to gouge a story out of me, and I wouldn't talk to him. So he just turned around and made up *this*, out of whole cloth."

Recognition came into John's eyes. "A-h-h-h," he expired. He scanned me over again to see if I were telling the truth. I obviously looked too naïve to be playing a double game. He summed up his satisfied feelings with an expressive "So!"

I opened up my palms in a gesture of reasonableness. "You don't think I'd be so dumb as to try to promote myself in this way—on *your* location?"

He weighed this. "No."

John reached out and put a hand on my shoulder. "There's one thing I've learned, Jack," he said paternally, "and that is, let a newspaperman have his story. There's really nothing you can do about it."

I shook my head in relieved agreement. I had heard this theme before. Pious and profane old Pat Casey, the labor negotiator with the Hollywood unions, used to startle everybody with the advice: "Never engage in a pissing contest with a skunk. You're bound to lose."

John quickly became his old self, and the set relaxed and became good-natured. It was just as well. We were at a touchy part of the picture.

The setting was in the abandoned officers' quarters of the Japanese camp. The nun and the Marine were left on their own again. They had come down out of the cave in the hills and were rummaging around for supplies. In the course of the foraging, Mitchum had come upon a bottle of saki hidden in a sack of rice.

He offered a small cup of the wine to the nun, and she accepted, with the careful admonition that he should not press more than one on her.

Near the wine bottle, he had also discovered a game of draughts, which was a puzzle to him, but which the nun was glad to explain to him, for she saw that he was getting drunk.

As the game progressed and the alcohol went to the Marine's head, the situation became progressively dangerous. All the animal instincts of this man, so well suppressed when it seemed there was a slim hope of rescue, now began to flow to the surface. The nun knew she might be attacked.

In a rage of frustration, the Marine hurled his empty pipe against a door, and it shattered. The nun was offended. She had given him this pipe as one of the few remaining possessions of the priest. It was a rare meerschaum. She stooped to pick up the pieces, asking him why he was so destructive. Through his gritted teeth, he rasped, "Because there's no more tobacco!"

The line was nicely symbolical. All the man's resources had been exhausted. She looked up from her task to see him looming over her threateningly.

As she stood up, he made his move. Again, with the sense of timing of two ballet dancers, the two entangled for the briefest instant; but before the Marine could more than grapple with her arms, the nun broke out of his grasp and escaped through the door and out into the night.

It was a tense moment, executed to perfection. Once more

the same old hobgoblin had been defeated, namely, the fear that profane hands be laid on a sacrosanct person.

John had been observing with some amusement how this fear haunted me. He was also pleased at how well his inventions, catering to this fear, had worked. He had really racked his talents to accommodate the pressures I represented.

He came over to my side. In the most confidential way, he said, "Jack, now that I've shot it *your* way, I'd like to try it *my* way. I don't think I really have what 1 want in this scene. It isn't rough enough. I'd like to do a little more coarse version. If it doesn't work, well, we always have the first take, and we can use that. Okay?"

"Of course," I agreed. "It's *your* picture."

"Good," he said. He walked over to his position alongside the camera. "All right, places!" he commanded.

When all was ready, he made an announcement. "Now I want you to do the last part of that scene again," he told the actors, "but this time a little more realistically. Don't be so refined. Go at it! Deborah, start from where you're picking up the pieces of the pipe. Bob, you start getting up from the table. All right. Camera!" The cameraman called out, "Rolling!" The mixer called out, "Speed!" Huston picked up the cadence. "Mark it!" he cried to the slate boy. The slate boy snapped his clappers into place, and ducked out of range of the lens. "ACTION!" ordered Huston.

Deborah looked up to see the hulking form of Mitchum looming over her. A look of panic came to her eyes. She stood up, watching him fearfully. "Mr. Allison," she asked, "what are you doing?"

Bob said something like, "I'll show you what I'm doing," and grabbed for her arm.

"Let me go!" she screeched, twisting to get away.

Mitchum kept her wrist in a tight grip and moved in. "Now, Sister," he said soothingly, putting his arms around her shoulders.

She struggled more violently to break loose. He merely drew

her into his close embrace, trying vainly to kiss her. "Let go of me, you sonofabitch," she gritted. In one lurch, she brought up her leg and kneed him in the crotch.

Mitchum made a grunt like a wild boar and bent over double, holding his privates as he limped in circles. While he was distracted, Deborah fled through the door and out into the night.

When the action was completed, there was dead silence. All eyes snapped to me. In the tomblike quiet, Huston intruded his voice. "Is that all right, Jack?" he asked loudly.

I was so flabbergasted that all I could do was flap my hands. "Well . . ." I began, but it dribbled off into a weak "heh, heh . . ."

"Come on, Jack. Is that acceptable?"

"Well, John"—I squirmed—"I *doubt* it."

"You don't think so, huh? Ha, ha, ha, ha." He looked around at the cast and the crews in merriment. "Ha, ha, ha," he continued. Everyone began to laugh nervously and uncertainly.

When he had had his fill, Huston brayed, "Don't worry, boy. There wasn't any film in the cameras."

The laughter became more general as the apparent madness melted away. Deborah came up alongside and said gently, "I'm sorry, Jack."

Huston had balanced things up for that article in the London newspaper.

Well, they finally got the poor nun out of her clothes, as had been their intent from the beginning. However, the excuse that was concocted was so powerful as to finally dispel all accusations of bad taste. The sequence itself was invented by Harold Nebenzal, in large measure at least, and it was used to replace the troublesome dream sequence.

It took up from where the pipe-breaking sequence left off. The nun had fled out into a rainstorm and taken refuge in a swamp. The Marine, sobered, had searched for her and found her sick with a raging fever and delirious. He had tenderly carried her back to shelter, where she was in danger of death.

Realizing he has to get dry covering and medicine for her, he sneaks down to the reoccupied Japanese camp and steals blankets and pills, as well as food. He brings these back up to the cave, where, with the greatest of care, he takes her out of her heavy habit, and wraps her in the blankets. She eventually recovers, and, in the end, the two are rescued by an assault wave of American troops.

So tasteful and so successful was the finished film that the Legion people put it in Class "A-I," the highest possible rating, with no objections for anybody. They even considered for a while to celebrate by issuing a special recommendation of the film, encouraging their constituents to see it. In the final analysis, the picture grossed worldwide some $11,000,000. The studio got $6,200,000 of this; and we got to eat one of the turtles. It was delicious.

16 The Moment of Truth

SEVERAL THINGS now happened in quick succession that brought matters to a head.

It was clear that there was no more ducking the question of encroachments on the part of the Church. It was nearing the point of open scandal. Even men of stature, who were willing to concede that the Church was in the throes of a struggle with inimical forces, were becoming resentful at being reduced to the level of "some pastor in the Middle West" who might complain.

I boiled the whole case down into a brief and sent it to the Chancery office in downtown Los Angeles. There sat Bishop Manning, Auxiliary to the Cardinal, and a member of the Episcopal Committee, which was, in practical fact, *the* Legion. He had been among the youngest prelates ever consecrated in this country, and the reason given had been his intellectuality. This seemed to suggest an open door.

The gist of my little "white paper" was that the image of the Church had been subjected to distortion. It seemed to be unacquainted with the forces of self-determination and self-actuation. In assuming the guise of a cop, it had lost its much more attractive role as the dispenser of Grace, and the cultivator of Charity. Its negative psychology was producing a mentality of ghettoism. A mood of discontent was growing among those who resented excessive pressures for conformity. A priest had recently been barred from the pulpit and silenced for telling his congregation that there was no obligation for them to take the annual Legion "oath," nor to consider the "pledge" binding in conscience, if one had been dragooned into taking it.

About three days later I walked into the Bishop's office. So elevated was I with a feeling of self-congratulation for my "statesmanship" that I thought he would anoint me with the Oil of Office right on the spot. I think I had been expecting to see the equivalent of an Inca chief, sitting on his throne in golden cope, with his Bishop's crook glittering in the morning light. Instead, what I beheld was a mild, gentle, and impassive man, who looked younger than he appeared in ceremonies. He was sitting behind a plain large desk, in stark and simple "sacerdotals."

He glanced at me through dark-framed glasses and greeted me with politeness. When I was seated, he picked up the wad of pages I had submitted to him and held them by the corner, like a physician hoping to avoid contagion. "Did you write this?" he asked.

I looked at my document dangling precariously between two fingers, and my feelings sank into my shoes. "Yes," I admitted.

"Are you a Catholic?" was his next question.

Had a needle been recording my pulse, it would have shot off the chart. "Yes, Bishop, I think so."

"If you keep writing like this, you're in danger of turning into an anticlerical."

My heart was now flopping like a bewildered fish on the shore. "It wasn't intended to be a scientific statement, Bishop. It was written loosely, with the idea that we could refine it as we went along."

"Yes. But if you continue writing things in this vein, you'll turn into an anticlerical."

His inability to get the point began to stir indignation. "But I thought I had made clear the spirit in which it had been written."

He put the pages down. "Why did you send this to me?"

That was too much. "Because I *wanted* to, Bishop," I emphasized. "Are you trying to tell me you're unapproachable?"

"No. But why me?"

"Because you're a member of the Bishops' Committee on Motion Pictures. You have an official capacity."

"Why didn't you speak to Monsignor Devlin? He knows about these things better than I."

"For a very simple reason, Bishop. I didn't want to explain the whole thing to him, and then have him tell me there was nothing he could do about it, I should talk to you. I didn't want to have to repeat it when I'd have to come to you eventually anyway."

He registered this. "But I know very little about motion pictures."

I took a long, deep breath, and did a mental balancing act before replying. "If you don't mind my saying so, Bishop, that's a very bad admission. You're *supposed* to know about them. You're a specialist."

"Now, Mr. Vizzard, you're being legalistic. You know very well how committees work. The main burden usually falls on the chairman, who only applies to the others as consultants. This is fair practice."

My voice fluked upward. "Well then, Bishop, I must say that you have a gall. Because every year you see fit to sign your name to a document that blasts *us* for inefficiency and laxity. And now you tell me you don't know what you're signing. You're knocking the daylights out of my professional name, and this gives you no qualms whatsoever. How are *you* exempt from the precepts of justice you're always sticking others with?"

I was so livid that I do not know what he answered.

"If the occasion arises that I could discuss these things with Bishop Scully, would you introduce me to him?" I asked.

"Yes. He's the chairman. He's the proper man to talk to."

"I didn't want to see him cold. He doesn't know me. He might properly ask me if I had exhausted my remedies in the lower courts, as it were."

"I'll be glad to pass you along," acknowledged the Bishop.

"Thank you. I wonder, then, if I might have my papers back?"

"Yes. I wouldn't want to keep them in your file."

"My *file?*" This sounded more like the F.B.I.

"Yes."

"Well, that's right, Bishop. I wouldn't let you keep them in any 'file' you had on me."

"No. We wouldn't want them."

"That suits me too, Bishop. I wouldn't leave them here."

"We wouldn't have them," he emphasized.

It was clear that he was *going* to have the last word, so there was nothing left to do but take the papers from his hand. The good-byes were civil, and when I got back to the Code office I tore up the brief and dropped it into the wastebasket.

I thought I would try the Cardinal. What was needed was a spirit of comprehension and of leniency in these quarters that would fend off some of the heat from the Legion-Quigley complex in the East. Such a relationship had existed previously under the tenure of Archbishop Cantwell, the predecessor of Cardinal McIntyre, who was also one of the principal instigators in the creation of the Legion of Decency. An illuminative little episode is narrated of him in this context. It seems that a delegation of distraught citizens came to him and put to him the situation with the content of films in the early thirties. "Do you know, your excellency," they asked him, "that a survey has shown that ninety per cent of all films are based on the subjects of love, sex, or crime?" The wise old prelate weighed this for a moment. "Tell me," he responded, "what would you make movies about, if not on love, sex, or crime?" He then asked whether the question was not more the manner in which these themes were treated than the naked subject matter itself.

It was this kind of protective mentality that was needed now, in place of a mood of automatic accusativeness. The industry was situated within the jurisdiction of the Cardinal. If there were anybody who had the responsibility and a vested interest, it was he. The only trouble was that his public image did not hold out much promise of relief. He was known to be a hard-line traditionalist, and his public utterances tended to be platitudinous. But it was a simple question of any port in a storm.

The man I found was very different from the ritualistic figure of the podium or the sanctuary. He was tall with long black frock coat and high-necked vest trimmed with little red pipings of office. He wore the great gemmed ring, but he presented it in a very plain manner. He rested in his power with an ease that suggested diffidence, and in his person-to-person manner he suggested a cool shrewdness that was very much up front.

When I gave him my case, he nodded understandingly, but dismissed the possibility that he could get engaged. He stated that he had made it a matter of policy to stay out of the movie business, just precisely because it was in his own back yard. He did not want to create the impression that he was trying to worm in and run things. This would stimulate anticlerical sentiments. It was the classical case in which I was hoist on my own petard.

He asked me what I thought of the new DeMille film, *The Ten Commandments,* and I told him something like I thought it set back religion six thousand years, to the level of magic and legend. He said, "Oh, really? Is that what you think?" and let it go at that. I later found out that he had endorsed it, and that Paramount had arranged a benefit premiere for some diocesan cause.

As a compromise, he agreed that Bishop Scully of Albany was the one to talk to. He had the position.

How to get to Scully? Eric Johnston would not sponsor such a confrontation, since this would seem to make a formal issue out of something that should seem to happen in passing, as it were. A way had to be invented to be "going through town" to keep the semblance of unpremeditation in the air. It was exactly at this point that a *deus ex machina* swooped down out of the rafters.

Geoffrey exploded into my office one afternoon, coatless and in stockinged feet, with a letter crumpled in his hand, and a quizzical expression on his countenance. Without ceremony, he tossed the letter on my desk. "Have you ever heard of these guys?" he wanted to know.

I seized the sheet of paper and examined the letterhead. "The O.C.I.C.?" I asked. "Yes. As a matter of fact, I have."

"Who are they?"

"The initials stand for the 'Office Catholique International du Cinéma.' "

"What about them?"

"Oh—to make it simple, let's say they're sort of an international Legion of Decency. It's a parent body of which the United States Legion of Decency is a part. They have offices in the Vatican. I think Monsignor Little is an officer on their governing body. It's all very complicated, as suits Italian diplomacy. I think, though, the child is father of the man. The American group ranks the parent body, both in terms of prestige and power. The foreign groups are like splinter segments, a bunch of Johnny-come-latelys."

"But if they're connected with the Vatican, they must have some standing?"

"Yes. I'd say so. But I don't know about that. The first I heard about them was from a hush-hush letter sent by Martin Quigley to Joe Breen. The letter was full of suspicions that this might be an infiltration movement of left-wingers, who were to be suspected of a tendency to subvert moral values. I was delegated by Joe Breen to 'keep an eye' on them. I was supposed to be their watchdog."

"I couldn't imagine a better man," said Geoff.

"The trouble stemmed, it seems, from the fact that the

O.C.I.C. gave a prize, at one of those European film festivals, to a picture that had been condemned by the Legion. *La Strada*, I think."

"I saw *La Strada*. And if the O.C.I.C. is in favor of that picture, I'm in favor of the O.C.I.C. Those people give some evidence of being civilized."

"Why do you ask all this?"

"Read the letter. They're having a convention in January. They've invited someone to attend. I think maybe you're the man. How about it? It's in Havana."

"Havana?" I enthused. "Oh, yes. I know all about that place. I was there four hours once."

"Nothing like having an expert do the job."

"You bet."

"Well, dust off your passport. It looks like you're the big traveler around here."

"What'm I supposed to *do* there?"

"You're supposed to be an 'observer.' They're meeting to discuss 'study groups' that sit down and evaluate the artistic and moral qualities of films—sort of like a network of Communist cells, so maybe Martin wasn't far from wrong, you see?"

"Hm-m-m. I wonder if you're doing me a favor? I think you're a Greek bearing gifts."

"You want *me* to go?"

"Oh, no, no, no. I'll take the chance. I'll run the risk. I might be able to get some clue how to bring some pressure to bear on the Legion of Decency."

"Monsignor Little will be there. It was his idea to get a Code representative. I think it'll be a feather in their cap, if they can get an official recognition from Hollywood."

"Right. And, oh, by the way, Geoff . . ."

"Yes?"

"Havana's a long way off. What if I circled around on my way back and dropped in on New York? It'd sort of seem to be on the way. I could visit with Scully."

Geoff rose to the suggestion immediately. His eyes twinkled.

"Don't say it," I cried, raising my hand to prevent him. "Don't say it! I know. 'What's to hinder me?' "

"That's right."

"*Thank* you."

"Yes. Well, good luck, buddy." He waved his hand, like tilting a hat, and scuffled out in his shoeless state.

Elegance is the word for Havana. There is the great circling bay of gunmetal blue, glinting against the white guardian pile of Morro Castle. Tall palm trees sway against the chalk-blue skies, across which thick banks of clouds are driven by velvety winds. Only the drivers of automobiles, down on the streets of the city, are manic. In Havana, no provision is made for contingencies. A bus stuffed with people will charge into a blind intersection as though there is no such thing as cross traffic. Everything is shrieking brakes and honking horns and last minute emergencies. A crumpled fender is an occasion for a convention. All bystanders seem to take sides. There is hardly such a thing as a disinterested party. Arms wave and voices go up in a very carnival of argument. The Cubans are a passionate people.

The delegates came together in the old and honorable Jesuit school of Belem (Bethlehem). The cloisters, lined with looping arches, were alive with little knots of people who bent their heads together and conferred with a peculiar intensity and then swam away, like scattering schools of fish, to join other groups.

The chairman of the English language workshop, the largest study cell at the convention, was Monsignor Little of the Legion of Decency. For openers, he explained the American practice vis-à-vis motion pictures to the group. In a manner that was slightly triumphalistic, he detailed the Code technique of a "voice for morality" and "compensating moral values" which had the backing of the Legion. He couched the entire presentation with references to the Papal encyclical, and to the declarations of the American episcopal body in support of the overall operation.

The American point of view packed great weight. It reflected the mass and the power of the Hollywood Industry, which at that time absolutely dominated the world of filmmaking. It probably consumed three-fourths of the "real" screen time in theaters at home and abroad and, in terms of money invested and money taken in at the box office, was probably the equal of all the other national industries taken together. The delegates themselves, on the other hand, emitted a slight feeling of the throw-the-negative-on-the-floor-and-walk-on-it-for-a-while-to-scratch-it-up school, which had not yet become vogue. They all seemed to be leaning into the wind with anxiety to come to Hollywood, as guests of the Industry of course, to show the studios how it is done. They were contradictions, because on the one hand they stood for the naturalistic rough-hewn humanisms that were starting to gain credence in European films (as opposed to the high-gloss sterilizations of the Hollywood school), while on the other hand they very clearly wanted to regulate and manipulate and dominate a field in which they were themselves barren. The crosscurrents which they created were confusing and irritating.

At the end of the first session, there was a buzzing as from angry little swarms of bees. I decided to take the chance and thrust myself into the thick of it. "You call that morality?" asked one delegate. "This is the production line. And we're all at the mercy of America to set the standards for the free world."

"What, specifically is your objection?" I asked.

A Dominican from Belgium said, "It's a new kind of magic. You know the natives down in Congo—they are afraid to let you take their picture, because they think you have materialized their spirit and are in possession of it. You own them. It is like that. You think if you can 'name' sin, by this 'voice of morality' of yours, you have 'spelled' it, you understand? You have accounted for it, you have frozen it, therefore you have captured it. It's all very tricky. You understand what I mean? And then you have 'compensating moral values'—very American. You have punished sin, therefore you have disposed of it. It makes your consciences quiet."

"In a few minutes, we're going to have an open forum. Are you going to object?"

"No. That is for you."

"Why?"

"Because it will be said to be the business of the bishops in America. It is none of our business. We can't invade another household."

"If you keep your silence, you are a coward. You're not afraid to shoot your face off out here. You think if you raise your voice in an 'official' forum, you'll suffer clerical reprisals. You can't have the luxury of both. Either hold your tongue out here, or speak up in there."

The Dominican turned to the French delegate. "Pierre," he commanded to an adenoidal layman with rimless glasses, "cancel your commitment for the French workshop and come with me."

What happened next was like a furious guerrilla ambush. Monsignor Little, suspecting nothing, made some placid statement opening the discussion to the house. Before he knew what happened, he had a black-and-white Dominican up him, and down him, and around him, and in him, and out him, like some frenzied Dalmatian. The dear Belgian was not the subtle type. He was from the farm country of the lowlands, with bald pate, bushy black eyebrows, heavy horn-rimmed glasses, and a human style that resembled the thudding of a plow horse. "You know me," he later said of himself. "I'm the type of whom they say, 'He begins by putting both feet in the soup dish.'"

The Monsignor defended himself in a dignified manner at first, thinking that this was some kind of frolic. The color began to drain from his face, however, when help arrived from an unexpected quarter. An energetic Canadian Jesuit, sensing the excitement, took a running jump into the fray with a delirious who-are-we-neutral-against look in his eyes.

Even Pierre, who was busy massaging his crystal-and-silver glasses with a clean handkerchief, paused in the midst of his misty breathings long enough to interpose a polite question.

Some ladies from New York scrambled loyally to the aid of the beleaguered Monsignor. They tried to prove the necessity of imposing such a system on the picture makers, albeit mechanical, because of the almost automated tendency of these men to twist things around and profane everything they touched. One of the ladies, call her Mary, cited a recent example that would be grasped by the collected consciences of the delegates. It was an English film that had been condemned by the Legion, although it had been approved by the Code (thus widening the rift). It was titled *Black Narcissus* and starred Jean Simmons. It had to do with an Anglican nun who found missionary life in India unsuitable to her tastes, and left Religious Orders. The example had the advantage of not even being Catholic.

One of the principal reasons for the condemnation had been a "dream sequence" (!). It was in the form of a reverie that came over the beautiful young nun while she was supposed to be absorbed in prayer. It took her imagination back to the days of her girlhood. There were scenes of a hunt, with horses jumping over stone fences and tousled hair flying in the wind and liveliness and color and laughter, all in contrast to the somber mood of spirituality. Mary recited this example with a little "So there!" tone in her voice. It was not that life in the world was wrong, but that the juxtaposition made religion seem unappealing. When she finished, there was an instant of silence, one of those timeless moments the Arabs call "angels passing." There was no voice in the crowd to stand up and say that religious life was less fun than hunting.

From the middle of the group, a meek hand was thrust into the air. A Central American girl stood up and asked Mary,

"What kind of sequence would have been acceptable as an alternative? It hardly seems immoral to show a spirited girl riding a horse in a red coat."

Mary's voice crumbled in all directions at once. "Well," she speculated, "they could have shown her—if they had good will—in a nice kitchen with her mother . . . in a nice gingham apron . . . drying the dishes . . . and smiling and talking to her . . ."

She was interrupted by a scoff of derision from the crowd. The Latin American girl sat down. What was fatally wrong with the whole conceptuality had been amply exposed.

The next day, Monsignor Little resigned his workshop chairmanship. He had seen the handwriting on the wall. A new criterion was in the making. Henceforth, it would begin to become a question of whether the material on the screen shed some light on the human condition, not whether it catered to some abstraction. Before a new mode of thinking could be effective, however, the grip of Quigley, as strong as his sense of stewardship, would have to be broken. It was he who dictated the terms.

As evidence that the delegates of the Legion of Decency were almost as relieved as everyone else, they gave me their equivalent of an Oscar before we left Havana. It was Mary who made the presentation. She slipped an object from her closed fist into mine, and when I opened my hand, I was holding a tiny rubber doll, with arms pleadingly outstretched. It seemed to be begging forgiveness for the remarks about "open disregard" of the Code. It has since been mounted on black velvet behind glass and usually passes for what it looks like, mute testimony to "my first abortion."

The great express plane that shattered up into the air over the Pearl Island of the Antilles was headed first for Washington. Bishop Scully had agreed to a meeting in New York City, where he would be stopping over at the Cardinal's residence. But, considering the delicacy of this talk, I had arranged to have a preliminary council of war with an illustrious Jesuit, Father John Courtney Murray. He was stationed at Woodstock, Maryland, the theologate for that province, and had agreed to come into D.C. to go over my case with me.

We met in the lobby of a luxurious hotel, and went into a thickly carpeted dining room where all the waitresses were dressed in Revolutionary Minute-girl costumes. He was a tall man with a serious face and gray hair. We ordered a bottle of the best Burgundy in the house to go with our roast beef, and got down to business.

He listened attentively while I unraveled the dilemma. To contest with the Church, and to attempt to dislodge some of its hold in the area of what (for a shorthand definition) we will call its Angelic Concept of Man, was to seem to be trying to emasculate it in its conflict with the Far Left.

Like any true intellectual, he asked, "But, according to your accounting, isn't the Legion relieving you of this complicity? Isn't it emasculating itself? What about *Storm Center?*"

I said, "Why is it that every time you ask a Jesuit a question, he answers you with another question?"

Father Murray cocked his eye at the middle distance. "Why not?" he asked.

We both had our grin at this familiar gambit.

He then summed up. "I believe that prudent men would concede that things have gone too far with the Legion. The Legion is not the result of Divine Revelation. The authorities will have to realize this. It is a human institution, and as such, the proper object of intelligent criticism. To lay hands on it is not to wrestle with the Divine Will. But to deal with this situation properly is dirty work. You've elected yourself as tong man. I can't help you. For myself, I'm completely involved in trying to work out a much tougher question. I'm trying to verbalize a Theology of War. (After this, he was to have gotten totally involved in the internecine struggles of the Ecumenical Council, and is credited with rallying a quota of bishops against the surging tide of power from the Curia. The effort was so extravagant that he literally spent himself to death.) Do you want me to spell out the ugly facts?"

I nodded affirmatively.

"Very well, then," he continued. "You are too starry-eyed in your approach. You're trying to hedge yourself with a lot of pious statements about the Church cultivating virtue and all that stuff. What you have to remember is that the bishops are, as a whole, practical men, not theorists. They are occupied with the hard details of administering their sees. They know what the Church is *supposed* to be. Don't fall into the trap of seeming to instruct them. They're jealous of their autonomy. You'll only annoy them. No. What I'm trying to say to you is that you've taken on a mean job. So do it. Don't try to butter things over. If you're going in to kill—kill!" He twisted his fist, as though he were turning a knife.

He paused to take a sip of wine. The perspiration was beginning to glisten on my forehead.

"Now," he finished, "their fierce pride in their autonomy is also where the bishops can be had. You make a very telling point in passing that you tried to gloss over. You said that Martin Quigley is creating the impression among people in the communications world that he is 'the tail that wags the dog.' Tell that to Bishop Scully and see what happens! That is, if you're really serious about doing your job."

I raised my own wine glass to my lips, and our eyes locked. It was like a toast, and a promise.

The Cardinal's residence in New York City, where Bishop Scully had agreed to meet me, is a stone building in the Gothic style. It gives the appearance of a series of steeply peaked roofs, nestling snugly in the flanks of the mighty Cathedral.

A doorkeeper, from whom age had leached all accusation of sex, ushered me into a plainly wooded back room, and left me in silence to go fetch the Bishop. I looked aimlessly around at the cheerless interior for something that would catch my interest, but saw only a disarrayed rack of pious magazines, out of date and littered with trivia for simpletons. I marveled how the Catholic Church could wax so strong on such fare.

While leafing disinterestedly past ads for statues of Our Lady of the Railroad Station, my mind filtered back to the meeting I had had just previously with Martin Quigley. I had been drawn to his tower office as if by a magnet. Perhaps I wanted to gaze on the face of the man I would attempt to assassinate.

He examined me searchingly and then said, "Let me be the first to congratulate you on the success of *Heaven Knows, Mr. Allison*. You took a great chance in trying to help them with that. Had it been a bust, you would undoubtedly have lost your job. But it was a success, a very great success, and you fooled us all. And since I was the one who objected most strongly, I should be the first to offer you my compliments."

I took the kind words with a small inclination of the head, and almost lost my lethal resolution on the spot. He seemed so mild, sitting there in the midst of a certain grayness, as though he had burned out his best energies in the pursuit of his own Holy Grail. But then a sudden realization flushed through my bones. What was the man saying? Was he not describing the very magisterial use of power I was in New York to break? Behind his compliments were the threats of execution that sounded very much like the Inquisition, which would, with great sorrow, "turn you over to the secular arm." I had to hold up this Gorgon's head to my inner eye and gaze on it to turn my heart to stone.

There was a stirring in the hallway of the Chancery, some brisk footsteps, and a fine-looking silver-haired man swept into the room. He was of middling build, portly in a gentle way, and slightly pink of cheek. When he held out his hand with the amethyst ring turned upward, I knelt and kissed it. He took his seat in a very businesslike way, poised a pencil over a pad of paper, and waited for me to begin.

We began with cape work. I was here on a problem of

mutual concern, and blah, blah, blah. He did not seem terribly impressed. I kept watching to see whether he hooked to the right or to the left.

The discussion quickly began to centralize on the question of whether the Code, the principal instrument for achieving morality in films, was falling apart. The symbol of the situation was *Baby Doll*. I tried to illuminate for him the reasons behind this uproar, which were connected to the condition of the country and the changing times. Not enough account was being taken of these very real factors when prelates were running up into the pulpits and blasting the Code for its laxity. What the Code needed was some understanding from the Church. Otherwise it would be crushed into ineptitude.

The picador work was done. Now the banderillas. Hollywood, like the rest of the country, was seething with resentments. The demands of the Legion were out of touch. They were creating hostile images of the Church. The film industry was rebelling against being molded to the scruples of "some pastor in the Middle-West." Rumors were scurrying around Hollywood like mice that people on the Legion staff were straining to become bishops.

("That is a legitimate ambition, Mr. Vizzard." "Yes, Bishop, I know. But the film industry shouldn't appear to be used to this purpose.")

And then the moment of truth. It was time to go up on tiptoes and deliver the sword.

There was a traceable cause for these excesses. Behind the Episcopal apparatus that ran the Legion, there was "a tail that wagged the dog."

I have an impressionistic memory of the Bishop sitting there looking at me with eyes like steel ball-bearings, similar to a Greek statue. A dark glint crossed them. I knew that the thrust had found its mark.

The Bishop struck back. As for Quigley, I should not think that the Church did not "know" its man. Those who had frequent concourse with him were not unaware of his peculiarities and his orientations. He was a human being, and as such, not perfect.

For the rest, he had been a welcome and valuable and indefatigable asset to the forces of decency throughout the years. He was appreciated and cherished by the Church. To intimate that he was the "tail that wagged the dog" was almost an outrage. In fact, his presence on pictures was the direct result of the desires of the producers, who called upon him as a friend of the court to solicit concessions out of the Legion. His opinion was not final, nor was it anything like overbearing. To cite an example, he was in favor of condemning the film *Tea and Sympathy* but was overruled.

("But does not this prove my very case, Bishop? What was a layman doing in a position like that? Did the producers ask him to run to their aid and use his influence to procure a "C" rating for their film? And how is it that you remember this instance, almost as if it were a triumph over Quigley? Ask Robert Anderson, the author of that play, about his experiences with Martin in this case, and see if he thinks that Martin was such an impartial friend of the picture makers. Talk to Elia Kazan about him, and ask who was the 'important Catholic layman' to whom he referred in an article published in the New York *Times,* and whose standards Kazan had to meet.")

Going to the other end of the spectrum for an opposite example, Martin Quigley had attempted to persuade the Legion to look more favorably on a picture of Howard Hughes, *The Outlaw,* and had been refused.

(Touché, Bishop. But the plain fact of the matter still exists. Around Hollywood, the common rumor is that the Legion of Decency is the rubber stamp for Quigley. Real or false, the impression exists, and needs to be corrected.)

The Bishop then turned to the Code itself. If it insisted in following its obstructionist course, there were ways of bringing it to heel. Eric Johnston was not immune to pressures. There was always the option of whipping state legislatures into a mood of indignation, and of getting them to pass stringent censorship laws.

It was obvious from this recourse to triumphalism that the Church had not yet learned much from its experience with *The Miracle*. As for Eric Johnston, he was a man of his vanities, and one of them was his lack of commitment to the Roman syndrome of obedience. I said that he would fight back, and could not be had by threats or snapping of fingers. The Bishop made a note of this, and later tried to intimidate me by charging that I had said Johnston was vain.

And so it was over. I kissed the Episcopal ring, and somehow left with a little less religion in my heart.

Now, there is a little story told about the fly that was buzzing along in the wake of the carriage of Napoleon. Looking back over its shoulder, the fly boasted, "See how much dust I am raising!"

I do not want to create the impression that all of the subtle changes that took place in the Legion, slowly at first and then with crescendo, were the consequence of my battering the air with a set of translucent wings. But I will detail the things that did happen, if not *propter hoc* at least *post hoc*.

For one thing, a shadowy influence that was concomitant with that of Quigley began to disappear. This was the baleful theologizing of the well-known Francis Connell, a Redemptorist priest on the faculty of the Catholic University of America. He was popularly known as the "official" theologian of the Episcopacy of the United States, although, of course, there is technically no such thing. This "tutiorist" (play-it-safer) once published an article in an influential journal in which he raised the question as to whether constant attendance at "B," or "objectionable in part," movies could amount to a grave sin. He came to the conclusion that it might. This treatise was used as a source of reference around Legion offices, and was alluded to in some of the movie sections of diocesan newspapers. It played an important role in attaching an obligation in conscience to the ratings of the Legion. As doctrine, it would be scorned now by the average intelligent cleric.

Bishop Scully himself went into the forum and published an article in the Jesuit magazine *America,* outlining a new approach to pictures. It was an about-face from the negativism of the past, and was immediately interpreted by Hollywood as "liberal" in tone.

An intriguing shift in Legion personnel took place. An assistant to Monsignor Little was a certain Father Hays, who had written a pamphlet on movies, showing on the cover a cartoon of the moviemaker in the form of a great loathsome octopus. Its long tentacles were labeled "Sex," "Crime," "Dope," and the like. This was the caricature of the fellow I had rushed to Southern California to save the world from. Father Hays was politely excused from his duties and sent back to parish work in New Jersey. In his place, a Jesuit theologian from Woodstock by the name of Father Patrick Sullivan was sent to New York.

Ecclesiastically, this was more important than might appear on the surface. At that time, there was a rigorous jealousy against letting "Order" priests get involved in anything that was the proper domain of the "Local Ordinary," as the Bishop was called. That silly day is pretty much past. At that time, however, the appointment of a Jesuit intellectual and specialist in Canon Law had all the earmarks of a turn in the direction of liberalism. It was so interpreted by observers. It was also translated by insiders as being a rebuff to Quigley. Quigley, for intimate family reasons, was considered to be cool to the Jesuits. It was automatically felt that he would have been opposed to an independent, self-contained, and self-sufficient kind of figure, such as a professional with a doctorate and a status in the academic community.

Next, the Legion system of ratings was revamped. The number of classifications was doubled. The "A-IV," or "unobjectionable for adults, with reservations," was brought into existence and used with particular skill. Who would ever have imagined, in the old days, that a bawdy and brawling film like *Tom Jones* would ever have found a niche in this category? Now a grown-up could see a film like this without courting the risk of hell!

Lastly, Monsignor Little himself began to come out into the sunlight and to flourish. His early didacticism began to melt away and in its place a warm humanism began to set in. He showed all the symptoms of becoming a liberated spirit, and of turning into himself. *Variety* eventually credited him with leading the Legion from the days of boycotts to the point where it gave an award for merit to the daring British film *Darling*. This surely was a sophisticated changeover, and it represented a cultural span that would have taken ten generations to bridge in the days before the world got smaller. At a testimonial dinner in his behalf, the Monsignor admitted that when he was young, things had all appeared to him as stark blacks or whites; but that as he got older, issues seemed less simple and more complex, and assumed various shades of gray.

And what, then, happened to Martin?

17 The Closing of the Circle: *Lolita* and *The Nun's Story*

GEOFFREY SHURLOCK always claimed that if you wait around long enough, everything will come full circle. Martin, having been disenfranchised, took into his own hands the torch he could no longer get the Code to carry. He made himself available to the Industry, and took assignments from time to time as the monitor and molder of troublesome films-in-the-making. He even prepared advertising and announced the opening of an office in Hollywood, to perform this function in open competition, I suppose, with the Code itself. Not that he needed this work for money. He still had his publishing empire, and it seems that he had family wealth through marriage.

His transformation did not take place all at once. At first, it was a simple matter of his vanishing as a palpable presence from Legion corridors. He became, without any declaration of policy, a veritable *persona non grata* in the great soot-stained old mansion across the street from the Power House, where the Legion was quartered. To ask, "Where's Martin these days?" was to be greeted by blank stares. The unspoken question "Who's he?" hung in the air. But how effective this alienation became can be judged from a clue that cropped up about a year later. I was having a drink in a room of the Waldorf-Astoria with Joe Breen, Jr., who was at that particular time working closely with Martin on a special project. They were attempting to edit a feature film from a TV series called "The

Mysteries of the Rosary." This was a monumental opus that had been made in Spain by Joe, Jr., himself. I said to Joe, "I guess my name's mud with Martin, huh?" He looked at me queerly. "No," he answered. "I wouldn't say 'mud' was the word. Let's see. The last time I heard it, I think the word was 'satanic.' "

I laughed a little crookedly. "I guess that's lower than being on the Index, isn't it?"

Joe pouted his lips. "Yes. I'd say so. Lots lower."

I reached up to brush back my hair, but actually to feel if any horn stubs were showing.

In the months that followed, Martin receded further into oblivion, like a star dimming in the morning light. Meanwhile, certain changes were being prepared in the Code document to bring it up to date. A vice president in Eric Johnston's office in Washington suggested to Geoffrey Shurlock that it might be profitable to show the revisions to Martin, as a matter of protocol, and to get combat-wise suggestions. Geoff blew up. "Who's Martin Quigley?" he demanded in strident tones. "He's only a magazine publisher. What's he got to do with us regulating ourselves? Aren't we grown up enough, for goodness' sake, to make up our own minds? Do we have to go running to daddy for approval? This is *our* business, and we'd better learn to run it ourselves!"

Time went by, and then one day the word began to leak around. Martin had been secured by the producers of the most notorious book of the day, *Lolita,* to act as guide and advocate in shepherding the property through the Code. The story, about a pre-teenage nymphette, had been rejected outright by the Code office. Now Martin would attempt to insinuate it through the machinery he had himself invented.

Shurlock was clearly inflamed by this turnabout. He called Martin on the phone, and warned him that there was little possibility of tailoring this material in a manner that would be suitable under the Code.

Quigley set the wires squawking in his counterattack. "Look, Geoffrey," he argued, "this picture is going to be made, come what may. Would you just want to turn the producers loose, to make it their way? Or would you rather settle for a silk purse from a sow's ear?"

Geoff fell back into his old habit of spluttering. "For God's sake, Martin," he said, "now you're talking like us. This's what we've been saying over the years, and you've sneered at us for it. You've called it sophistry. Now that you're on the other side of the fence, it's suddenly all right." Off the phone, he added, "The pious prick. He's been accusing us of making it profitable to write a dirty book. Well, when he comes to us with that picture, it better be clean, or I'm going to rub his nose in it."

There was a silent hiatus, and then one day the notice was given that Martin had the finished film to show us. There was a great bustling among the staff members to get a seat in the projection room. The event promised to be a spectacle.

Before repairing to the projection room, Martin paid a small visit of state to Shurlock's office. Circling around him like an inoffensive satellite was the producer of the picture, Jimmy Harris. Jimmy was startlingly young-looking for such a mature enterprise. He was handsome and deceptively mild-looking. The steely quality of his will did not show through.

Martin assumed the guise of a protective father, hovering over Jimmy in a commanding way, and referring with skittish joviality to "this young fellow." He took pains to tell us how "this young fellow" had made changes that were edifying in order to bring the picture into line with the requirements of decency, that "this young fellow" was quite aware of his responsibilities, and that, all in all, Jimmy was a good guy, and had landed on his feet with a pretty good picture.

Having assuaged our anxieties, Martin then shooed Jimmy off to the Beverly Hills Hotel, where he was to sit on his hands and await our verdict. He did not want the father of the baby to be present in the delivery room when the birth took place.

Taken as a whole, the picture was not bad. It had an off-center humor to it that was reasonably interesting. Neither did it have the thick air of sensuality for which the book was famous.

Geoffrey was inclined to be very exacting about it, however, for this was a symbolic case. There were certain blemishes in the picture, and he was not going to pass them up. They were details of a type for which Martin might have scolded us in the days of the Old Testament. Therefore, Geoffrey bounced immediately to his feet when the screening was over and took the middle of the floor. One by one, he solicited the opinion of the staff members whether this picture contained any Code violations.

Martin remained slumped down in the large blue leather chair while the canvassing was going on. Only the tip of his head showed above the back-rest, gleaming from a faint tonsure. Occasionally a hand appeared, waving a silver cigarette holder from which streamed a busy contrail of smoke.

The first scene to come under challenge was a bedroom fade-out between Humbert (James Mason) and Lolita's mother (Shelley Winters). As Humbert sank down on the bed to consummate his marriage with his new bride, a picture of Lolita is in evidence. We last see Humbert gazing fondly in its direction as he disappears below the horizon.

Martin could not tolerate dirty-minded interpretations of this scene. He leapt to his feet, faced the staff, and demanded to know what we thought the juxtaposition meant.

Geoffrey stared back at him coldly. "We take it to mean that the man is fucking Lolita in his imagination while he is having the mother," he said.

Martin put a nervous cigarette holder into his mouth. "That's grotesque," he said.

"What would *you* take it to mean, then?"

"That Humbert only married the mother to be near Lolita."

"Martin . . ." pleaded Geoff, with a withering note in his voice.

"That's exactly what it means," insisted Martin.

Geoff turned to one of the staff members. "Do *you* think it means that?" he inquired.

"Possibly. By a stretch of the imagination," the man answered.

"And *you?*" asked Geoff of another staffer. There was a long pause, and then a little discussion back and forth.

Before the next man could reply, Martin tried to intervene with a strident voice. "You're just *looking* for trouble in this picture," he charged.

"Martin, will you please let us speak?" asked Geoff in a rather loud voice.

Martin was too nervous to contain his feelings. "I can't stand here and listen to outlandish interpretations," he fumed. "I know that this picture is cause célèbre and I think you're all being too solicitous about it."

"MARTIN!" cried Geoff impolitely. "If you'll just *sit down,* and *shut up,* you might get your scene. Some of the people here are disposed to read it *your* way. If you just let us speak, maybe you can have it. But I can't find out if you keep interrupting."

Martin seemed befuddled. He retired into his chair in a grumpy manner.

Geoff continued the canvassing.

When he was satisfied, he decided to take a chance. "It's yours," he announced to Martin.

Martin misunderstood. He got to his feet again and began to explain the intent of the scene from the beginning.

Geoff cut him short. "Martin!" he emphasized, "the scene's *yours.* You can *have* it!"

Martin stood stock still while the idea penetrated. "Oh!" he said, when he had comprehended.

We merchandised back and forth about another detail or two, but the conversation again bogged down at a critical point. The scene in question was the key to the whole picture. It was the seduction of Lolita by Humbert.

Upon reflection, it seems certain enough that it was not the man who seduced the nymphette, but she him. They were in a motel room, and the embarrassing moment of getting into bed had arrived. To spare the man his awkwardness, Lolita suggested that they "play games." The bemused fellow wants to know "What games?" She (fifteen or sixteen years old in the film version) leans over and whispers into his ear. The device must obviously have been for the sake of the audience, because there was nobody else in the motel room to overhear them. We can all guess that she said, "Play house." When a look of vapid delight comes over Humbert's face, the girl says, "This is how we begin." She reaches up, and folds her arms around his neck. Without warning, the bed breaks, and the two lovers go crashing to the floor. Undaunted, they continue on into the night.

In the opinion of the members of the Code staff, this scene went somewhat too far.

Martin took to his feet once more. He protested that it was the only, single scene of its kind in the picture (which was quite an accomplishment in itself) and that it was essential to the plot. It was not just dragged in from nowhere. "If you were going to shoot a scene like this," he argued, "how could you do it with more discretion?"

"By making it shorter," replied Geoff abruptly.

"It can't be any shorter and convey the idea," Martin disputed.

"Martin," sighed Geoff, "now you sound exactly like all the rest of the producers. This is how they argue. Now you see how we pass all the stuff we've passed over the years."

Martin was unimpressed. "Where should it be cut?"

"When she starts to whisper in his ear."

Martin shook his head. "I couldn't recommend that kind of cut to my principals," he reneged. "This scene is constructed very carefully. To cut it at that spot is to destroy it."

After considerable scuffling, a compromise was reached. It

was agreed that it would be cut at a point halfway between what we were asking and what was on the screen.

It was over.

Geoff began scuttling for his office, thinking of Jimmy Harris sitting alone in his hotel room.

"Wait a minute," Martin protested. "You speak to *me!*"

Geoff did not break his stride. "Are *you* paying for the Certificate?" he inquired.

"No."

"Well then I talk to the producer. My responsibility's to *him.*"

"Geoff . . ." begged Martin.

By this time Geoff was at his desk, and was dialing the phone. He cast an unsympathetic glance at Martin. "Hello, *Jimmy?*" he enthused. "Yes, we think your picture's swell. Yes, you're okay. I'll issue a Code Certificate on it. But now look, Jimmy. There's a few details that'll need doing. Yes. You'll have to make a few *cuts!* Get a pencil and write them down. Here they are . . ."

The trauma took its toll on Martin. He retired to bed, sick, for several days.

When he got back on his feet again, insult was added to injury. He brought the picture back to the Legion of Decency and was in the unenviable position of being a petitioner for a controversial picture before them. He got a lesson in how it was with us, for the Legion people put Martin through the most meticulous paces, demanding that he scrub here and sandpaper there, in exactly the spots where he had negotiated compromises with the Code office. He had humiliated himself for nothing.

The whole exercise was no particular pleasure to watch. We need our dragons, as the arresting officer in Graham Greene's *The Labyrinthine Ways* discovered. But Martin was not finished yet. He was to go underground for a while before making his final bid, prior to phasing out.

. . .

Meanwhile, fortune turned my way in its usual sudden manner.

We were sitting on the patio of Fred Zinnemann's home in the hills above Mandeville Canyon, discussing the script for *The Nun's Story*. It was a sunny day, and there were distant views of the Pacific Ocean sparkling between purple bougainvillaea vines. The third party to our troika was Robert Anderson, who had derived a first-draft script from the book that had created such a furor in Europe. Its original title, *Au Risque de Se Perdre* (*At the Risk of Damnation*) , gave the clue as to how the authoress felt about her story. She was a Belgian nun who found herself in conflict with religious life, and left it. At that time, which was the deepest hour of darkness before the dawn of the Ecumenical Council, there was still the feeling of walking out on God, with all the attendant terrors this implied.

In order to justify herself, the nun revealed the whole intimate anatomy of religious life, down to the smallest details. What resulted was a total exposure of the anchoritic concept of existence, all the rules and the regulations being designed to discipline and subdue the flesh in order that the spirit might flourish. But the rules seemed strangely old-fashioned and steeped in inhumanities, so that when the Mother General announces to a group of postulants that they are entering on "a life against nature," this provoked serious objections from the Church. "This would put the sisters in conflict with God," it was argued, "since He is the Author of Nature, and made it in His Image."

On the other hand, Robert Anderson, a graying intellectual with gothic features, was not willing to imply the opposite in his script—that this sort of life was "natural." It was a delicate point.

"I think the phrase bristles with misunderstanding," I suggested, "because the routine of life within the convent is too harsh. It makes one angry. The script leaves plausibility behind. Certainly the life of a nun is unnatural, in a sense. But not in the same sense as we say 'unnatural sex.' That has the feeling of perversion to it."

Fred Zinnemann had been observing with candid, twinkling eyes. He was not a large man, but he gave the impression that his interior personality had the spread of angel's wings. His hair seemed to ripple back from his forehead like a series of radio waves. "Give me an example," he said, "of where the script fails in plausibility."

"In the scene in the chapel, where she faints," I replied. I was pressing a point, and my voice was very intense. "Why, for Christ's sake, you'd think she fell over in the midst of the Coldstream Guards. All the other nuns keep their eyes glued to their books, and continue with their blankety-blank Gregorian chant like nothing happened. Two drones from the back come up and drag the poor girl out by her feet. What kind of people does this make the rest of them?"

"In that case, how would you reword the phrase?" asked Fred.

"Simply say '*In a way,* it is a life against nature.' "

"Will they buy that?"

"Reluctantly. But what choice do they have?"

Fred got up and went to the small bar nearby. While he was mixing drinks, he looked up. "How'd you like to come to Europe with us?" he asked.

My imagination did cartwheels. "Love to. But what exactly could I do? I wouldn't want to be just a spear carrier."

Fred grinned. "What you have is the dialogue," he said. "Bob and I went all through Europe preparing this script, trying to find help. Everywhere we went we were received graciously, everybody was excessively polite. They patted me on top of the head and told me what a nice fellow I was, but I didn't get anywhere. Each time we knocked on a door, we had to spend the first several hours qualifying ourselves and convincing everybody of our purity of intentions. But they didn't know me, so they passed me on to the next one. I've heard about the 'defense in depth' of the Catholic Church, but this is the first time I've ever experienced it personally. I feel like I'm in a roomful of feathers. I can't move, but I can't hit anybody either. *You* they'll recognize. I think you can open many doors for us."

We set up shop in the Palace Hotel in Brussels. The main strategy was to secure the approval of the Sisters of Charity in Ghent, about an hour's drive away. It was our hope that these religious, representing the largest congregation of nuns in the country, would give us active cooperation in making a film that was authentic. To be authentic was almost a passion with Fred Zinnemann. "I could get actresses," he said. "They're a dime a dozen. But, somehow, they don't *walk* like nuns. I'd like to have nuns themselves in the picture, if it's possible. If not, I'll hire dancers who can study the nuns and imitate their walk. But I'll *have* to have a few real faces of nuns. Did you ever see such peace and serenity? I don't want to hire a bunch of old crabapples who'll make convent life seem like a sickness. Half my story will be told in the beauty of the faces of elderly nuns."

In the great headquarters convent in Ghent, we met the Mother General, who will be remembered by those who enjoyed the book as Mother Emmanuel, although this was an invented name. She was a very elderly woman, shrewd and shriveled, and seemingly not very interested. In her company, however, was a spokesman with the beautiful name of Sister Godelieve (Love of God). She was slightly heavy-set, with a great fund of energy, and the most lovely animated features imaginable. She spoke English fluently and could shift with ease into French or Flemish, and possibly other tongues. As a result of years of un-selving, she had a quality of objectivity that was exceptional for a woman. The one feminine trait that clung, of course, was that which is ineradicable in all nuns, the little habit of reaching up in the middle of a sentence, and unconsciously brushing back her veil. This is probably the substitute for brushing back the hair.

Sister Godelieve had entered the Novitiate on the same day as "Sister Luke" (the "nun" of the book). The only personal remark made by Sister Godelieve in the entire opening conversation was the simple "I knew her from the beginning. What did we *do* to her that she should turn on us like this?"

Through the good offices of the Dominican I had met in Havana, Father Leo Lunders, it was arranged that the script should be submitted to Sister Godelieve, who seemed reliable because of her intelligence, and that she should give us her comments.

When she returned the script, the roof nearly fell in. The good nun had a list of suggestions that seemed half the length of the script. Zinnemann nearly lost his unfailing humor and sense of politeness. With all his tact, he was a man of great stubbornness, and concessions that would seem minor to an outsider were major artistic changes to him. Even so, by a combination of bullying, cajoling, and inventing, a series of compromises were worked out, and the script was resubmitted to Sister Godelieve. When we delivered the document, a strange thing happened. She regretfully informed us that it would be impossible for her to continue with her help. All the hard-wrought changes went down the drain, and Zinnemann's prospects of making the picture on terms that were proper to him seemed to have vanished.

When pressed for an explanation, the nun politely pointed out that the book was notorious throughout Europe, and that it was well known that her Order opposed it. It simply would not be understood, then, that they were reversing themselves, and were giving cooperation in the making of a film from it. It might have the effect of seeming to endorse the book. She was sorry, but adamant.

"But Sister," I argued, "the picture is going to be made *anyway*. Too much money has been invested to expect that it is going to be junked now. Would you rather settle for a silk purse from a sow's ear? Or would you prefer to steer and guide this so as to make it come out authentic? Here is your chance. If you have any complaints against the book, here's your opportunity to get your licks in and correct them."

"No," she said finally. "The best we can promise is that we will not object if a picture is made in the careful hands of Father Lunders."

Lunders sensed danger. "That's all right, Sister," he quickly interposed. "We'll do the best we can with that."

Outside, I turned to Lunders. "What was all that about?" I demanded.

"I'll tell you on the way back to Brussels. Get in the car."

With the rich green countryside spinning past our limousine windows, he told the story behind the story. "First of all, a promise not to object is more important than you think. Who do you think stands behind these nuns? Bishop Suenens of Malines. He will be made Cardinal soon, and is powerful. If the nuns send him a complaint, he will forbid everybody in the country from helping you, including myself. Can you imagine your plight if you try to turn to the Cardinal Archbishop of Paris for help? Suenens would simply pass the word along the grapevine, and nobody in France who is qualified would lift a finger to help you. The same down in Rome, only more so. The same everywhere. That's point number one."

I lit a cigarette and settled back.

"Now. I will tell you some of the facts of life," he continued. "I know what's bothering the sisters. Only they couldn't say it. But I felt it coming on from the very beginning. You know, you have two parts to this story, one in Europe and one in Africa. Yes? In Europe our woman, Sister Luke, is in conflict with the Church. She is struggling for the emergence of her selfhood. She is the type of person who crosses her T's and dots her I's. She is always fighting the bell that calls her to other duties. She wants to take her own initiative. As a result, in the lunatic asylum she is almost killed by a patient she has been warned not to trust."

"Yes," I agreed. (So sharp was the distinction in Zinnemann's mind between Europe and Africa that I heard him instructing his art director and cameraman, "I want all the colors in Europe to be *cold*. Emphasize the blacks and the whites. I want to feel the chill of the stone walls. Then, when we get to Africa, I want all the colors to become warm and rich. I want to feel the *heat*. I want all the trees to be filled with green leaves. In Europe, I want the branches to be bare.")

"Very good," continued Lunders. "Now we leave Europe, and Sister Luke carries her problem with her into the Congo. There, a doctor enters the scene. He shows great interest in her. He sees that she is breaking apart, and diagnoses her illness very well. She has contracted T.B., but the disease is the result of the strain she is putting on herself. Right?"

"Correct."

"So. What is happening? You and I are making changes in the script, and we are softening her conflict with the Church. We are bringing it down to size. But, as we take out the harshness, the reason for her leaving religious life is becoming unclear. It is vague, not impelling enough. So what does her motive become? By default, it becomes that she is in love with the doctor!"

"Ho, ho, ho, ho!" I said quietly. "The unpardonable sin. She is under the spell of sex." I drew on my cigarette.

Lunders looked perceptively at me. "That is not it," he said.

"No? It isn't that we're tarnishing the image of 'perfection'?"

"No. Nobody's afraid of that. It happens. Right in my own household. I have a sister. As a young girl, she entered this same Order of nuns. She always had a dream to go to the Congo. She went. She met a doctor there. She fell in love with him. And she left."

It was my turn to be surprised. "Did she marry him?"

"No. She never saw him again. She came back to Belgium,

and she married a man here. She had two children by him. He was killed during the war. I will take you out in the country to meet her, if you want."

"No, I believe you."

"So. Now we go back to Sister Luke. The nuns feel we are giving the *impression* that this is what happened to her. They feel that if this was the true reason for the woman's leaving, it is not our business to advertise it. It is hers. But there is still an added element. Something else."

I waited without comment.

"This Order of nuns is probably the most professional in Belgium. They were founded by a bishop whose idea was that if they were very good teachers or nurses, *that* was their spiritual life. Their *work* was their prayer. In consequence, he put great stress on this, at the expense of their community life. He simply borrowed a set of rules from the past, and more or less threw them together. The rules are filled with practices that are very archaic. Many of them will have to be corrected. Did you notice, while we were talking with Sister Godelieve and Mother General, that there was a stern-looking fellow lurking in the background—a canon?"

"Yes."

"Who do you think he was?"

"I don't know. The Chaplain? Some sort of spiritual adviser?"

"No. He was the *Ecclesiastical Superior* of that Congregation. The Mother General has to take orders from him. He is there to study, and make corrections, among other things. This is very rare. There are only two congregations in the whole Church, to my best knowledge, who are like this."

I whistled softly.

"But now, maybe you see why these nuns were given charge of the insane asylums. Like Lovenjoel. You've been there, haven't you?"

"Yes."

"They have others. They not only have charge of the asylums, but they also train the student nurses. It is from these girls that they mainly draw their vocations. Without vocations, they could not continue, they would die out. Yes?"

"It goes without saying."

"Very well. A few years ago, they had a very prominent doctor working with them at Lovenjoel. He had reason to think that he would be elevated to chief administrator. When the time came to nominate him, the nuns selected someone else. In great anger, he resigned, and wrote a book called *La Nuit Est Ma Lumière* (The Night Is My Light). Because of his reputation as a psychiatrist, the book had a great impact. It was believed. It attacked the nuns very severely. As a result, they began to lose vocations. They were afraid for their very existence. They had just recovered from that blow, when Sister Luke published her book. It seemed to substantiate the first. The first effect of the publication was that certain parents began to worry for the safety of their daughters. They came to the Novitiate and demanded that the girls come home with them."

"What did the girls do?"

"They just laughed and told their parents not to worry. But those who had not entered yet lost heart. Vocations among the student nurses began to fall off again. So you see, there sits the Mother General and Sister Godelieve, and they are wondering what they have done to God that He appears to be so angry with them. They are afraid that He wants to return their generosity with Him by putting them out of existence. Now do you understand?"

"Yes."

"Yes. But not everything. What the nuns fear is that it will seem that they dealt with us to protect themselves. It will look to the world as if they revealed a confidence to us, that the true reason for Sister Luke's leaving was that she fell in love with a doctor. This would give a very bad impression. And so they are *forced* to withdraw from cooperation with us. They would rather bear the brunt of more suffering than to give the impression that they were lashing out at Sister Luke and trying to give her a reputation she did not give herself."

I looked at Lunders with gratitude. "Thanks for spelling all this out for me," I said.

"That's all right. You have a right."

"What do we do now?"

"We will steer our way through it. Zinnemann's a very clever fellow. He's refined, too, so everything will be all right. We may even get the faces of some nuns in the picture for him. But not here. In Rome, maybe."

And that is exactly how it worked out. At least two priests played the parts of priests in the picture, and one nun played the part of a choir director. Fred had to go through with his plan to hire dancers for many of the parts, but he did manage to get the close-ups of nuns' faces that he needed.

It seems to be belaboring the obvious to point out that the finished film was an immense success, both artistically and financially. It was one of those rarities that was well received both critically and popularly.

The full true-life reasons for Sister Luke's having left the convent still remain a mystery.

The couple of months in Europe were one more strong step into the world that I was seeking to join, not dissimilar to the nun. Two or three things happened which left a lasting imprint.

One of the most memorable was perhaps the most simple. I was strolling the streets of Brussels with Henry Blanke the producer. We were out for an after-dinner constitutional. Henry was a man with a remarkable career. He had been responsible for smash hit after smash hit for Warners', over a career lasting too long to recount. All told, he had brought eighty or ninety great pictures into being (including *Anthony Adverse, The Story of Louis Pasteur, The Treasure of the Sierra Madre, Zola, The Maltese Falcon,* and *Robin Hood*). At the peak of his productivity, Henry was one of the three or

four most formidable names in Hollywood. He *was* Hollywood.

We had stopped in front of a department store window, and
were admiring a display of electric trains. "Beautiful, the way
they do things here," he remarked. "We couldn't make things
with such perfection in the States. Do you know this is my first
time in Europe? In twenty years I have never been to Europe,
since I came over from Berlin as a boy. Think of that, darling,
think of that." Excessive terms of endearment were a habit of
Henry's and the butt of many jokes.

"I'm glad I made it," I said. "I've always wanted to come."

"Me, too. But I was always too busy. There was always
something else coming up. But I tell you, sweetheart, I think I
was not kind enough on myself. My soul was not my own. I
was owned lock, stock and barrel, for money. And what did it
get me? Nothing. Zinnemann's smarter."

"What do you mean?"

"He made an issue with Warner. He's got guts. He was
down in the Caribbean making *The Old Man and the Sea*.
Things were not going his way, it was terrible. He saw it
would not be a success, so he went into Warner, right in the
middle of shooting, and you know how he says, he 'threw the
meat on the floor.' Phew! Warner blew up, of course, but he
gave in. He took Zinnemann off the picture and assigned it to
Mervyn LeRoy. Zinnemann knew he was in danger of being
sued. He'd be in hock the rest of his life. He went first to his
wife and said, 'How about it, darling?' She said, 'You're un-
happy. You've fought to get where you are. Leave the picture.
I'll stand by you.' And he did. And he won. Now he's free.
That's why he's on this picture. It was part of the deal to get
off *Old Man*. You didn't know that, did you?"

"No, I didn't."

"Take a lesson from me, darling. I played it safe. I wanted
to protect everything I had. I protected too much. In the long
run, Zinnemann's going to make more money than me, and he
can do what he wants."

There was a certain intense glitter in his eyes as he exposed this inner sanctum of his heart, a very personal chamber which I think few people had been allowed to see.

An episode that was part of my indoctrination into the world occurred in Wiesbaden. I had gone to the Rhine Valley to visit a friend. He was an expert on Rhine wines, and took me on a delightful journey through the vineyards and wineries of this beautiful section of the world. In the space of a day, I was cast back twenty-five years to my Novitiate period, and revivified the warm feelings of walking among the vines and tendrils on the sunny slopes of the California mountains.

I was staying at the finest hotel in this luxurious city. In the evenings, having nothing else in particular to do, I tended to drift around the bar and to strike up a conversation with a congenial companion or two.

This one evening, the bar was pretty much deserted, but the piano player was ripping great chords off the keyboard like rich clusters of grapes. I bought him a drink and leaned over the piano, and pretty soon I was singing along with him. By the second drink, he was joining me, and we were going at the top of our lungs. Now I was feeling very expansive.

In an alcove in a far corner sat an elegant woman at a table. Poor thing, I thought. She's probably an American tourist like me. Probably a widow, revisiting some of the places she had been happy, spending some of her insurance money. She should not be alone.

I sent her a drink by the waiter, and when she acknowledged receipt of it by a little lift of the glass, I waved her over to join us. She demurely shook her head. Too shy, I made a mental note. I became evangelistic about luring her out of her shell. I sent her another drink, and when she again nodded her head to thank me, I called, "If you won't sing with us, at least give us your favorite song so the pianist can play it."

The pianist was darting lively glances at me and cautiously waving his head. I did not understand.

The lady finally tilted her chin upward. "Tell him," she said in a refined voice, "to play 'The Lady Is a Tramp'!"

The piano player immediately dropped his eyes to the keyboard to spare me my confusion.

In the elevator of the Plaza Athenée hotel in Paris, I walked into the arms of my boss, Eric Johnston. He was no less surprised than I. After a series of quick explanations, he said that he was going out on the town for the evening with some of his European representatives, and would I like to come alone? I jumped at the chance.

We all headed for the Lido, where I got my view of chorus girls dancing about in the altogether. I was staring at the catholicism of the shapes and sizes of the breasts, but tried not to look too fascinated, lest Johnston think my interest was not completely professional. One of the party leaned over my shoulder and whispered, "They put wax into them, you know, to make them stand up." I looked around to see him leering wickedly. By the end of the show I caught myself beginning to count the moles on the legs of the girls who were nearest to our table.

After the show, we all climbed into a taxi, and went to a place on the left bank called "La Boule Blanche." It looked like something out of the picture *Moulin Rouge*. It was filled with smoke and had the shabbiness of a cheap dive. The headwaiter jammed us all together around one long table, and there was a scurry among the girls to join us. I was flattered that one girl sat down alongside me, all for myself, and I fell right into the oldest dialogue in the world, "Say, tell me, how does a nice girl like you . . . etc., etc." She replied with her very best story for such an obvious sucker. She had a blind little boy, whose father had deserted her. The nuns at the convent would not accept the child, because his mother had to do work with a bad reputation to support him. I practically gave her the bankroll then and there. Then I spent the rest of the evening trying to convert her, I think, although I can't remember exactly.

Johnston was more relaxed. He turned to me before sitting down and said, "Here, hold this, will you, Jack? I'm going to dance." He thrust his scotch and soda into my fist, and I found myself with two. My girl said, "You like to dance?"

I said, "Sure." What was good enough for the boss was good enough for me. I turned to our London representative, and said, "Here, hold these, will you, friend?" He had quite a juggling act to get a grip on three slippery glasses.

The headwaiter banged several bottles of whiskey onto the table, and we were doing fine, talking and laughing and dancing, when a raucous commotion broke out at the bar. Some fellow was pummeling another fellow, and the second was kicking back in typical French fashion, trying to find the first fellow's crotch. "What's going on?" I asked my girl curiously. She shrugged. "Oh, pouf, nozzing really. The man who is sleeping with the wife of ze ownaire had the bad taste to come into the bar. Now ze ownaire has found out, and is attacking heem."

"Judas, Eric, did you hear that?" I asked.

"Yeah. Very French, isn't it?"

"Yes. It would also be typically French if there was a murder. If that ownaire gets his hands on a knife, there might be a stabbing. Then we'll all get hauled in by the police for questioning. If the newspaper fellows get wind that the two biggest censors in the world are involved in a killing in a French dive, we're going to make awfully big headlines, boy."

"Let's clear out of here, whatta you say?"

"It's all right. I don't mind being in jail so long as you're with me."

"I'm afraid it'd be a little hard to explain. Let's go."

We both scrambled out posthaste, leaving the others to settle the bill. The life of a censor was getting more interesting.

18 The Crumpling of the Doll's House and *Cleopatra*

GEOFFREY SHURLOCK had said, "I don't intend to take this job to ride a sinking ship to its doom." And yet, the Code was being desired less and less by the picture makers. Their attitude was ambivalent. They wanted it, and they didn't want it. They wanted the respectability of it, but preferably without its inconveniences. Nobody could very well come right out against it, because this would be like casting a vote against apple pie and motherhood.

Geoffrey had perfected his dark tactics of reverse English into an art. A scene typical of him occurred in the gloaming of a Sunday afternoon in January, in the early sixties, on the sidewalk outside the theater of the Motion Picture Academy. He and I had gone to attend a showing of the Mexican film *The Paper Man,* which had been submitted as a contender for the Best Foreign Film award.

After the showing, we collected in small knots on the street, and were discussing little nothings. I was trying to insert a favorable word here and there in behalf of the director, Ismael Rodriguez, a good friend.

From out of the dusk, we were approached by Rudi Fehr, the executive in charge of film editing at Warner Brothers. Rudi was the sum of elegance, in his bearing and in his point of view. He had a north German way of carrying himself which, in his case, was only a noble pride.

"Jack Warner's been calling all over town for you," said Rudi. He was looking at Geoff.

Geoff waved his hands in a bothered manner. "I know. I know. There're messages at my apartment. I just didn't answer them."

"He's chasing you because Frank Sinatra's putting the pressure on him."

These were fighting words to Geoff. He was not likely to knuckle under just because a popular actor was showing his teeth. Geoff had held up the Certificate on a picture called *Robin and His Seven Hoods*. The studio had put up the money and was guaranteeing distribution, but in all other respects it was an independent production by Sinatra. In the picture there was a scene of Dean Martin chalking his finger instead of a pool stick, which may or may not have been offensively phallic. Geoff did not much care, either way.

"What does Jack Warner want to do?" Geoff demanded of Rudi.

Rudi drew back in an expression of rebuke. "I beg your pardon?"

"What does *Warner* want?" plumped Geoff. "It's *his* picture."

Rudi's features froze like cement. "Surely that's not the criterion," he corrected.

"No?" asked Geoff with exaggerated openness. "I *work* for him. What he wants is what I do."

Rudi negated the dialogue by rubbing one finger across the air.

"You have a *Code*," he said quickly. "The state of the question is whether it violates the Code or not."

Geoff brushed this off with friendly scorn in his voice. "Don't give me that," he warned. "Where in the Code are you going to find anything about chalking your finger?"

Rudi's voice faltered. "The Code forbids vulgarity. This is a vulgar gag. You said so in your letter on the script. They took a chance and put it in the picture anyway. Now they want to fight for it."

"Does Warner think it's vulgar?"

"Well, he's waiting on you. He'll back you."

"I know. But what does *he* think of the gag?"

"He reserves the right to make cuts for you, or the Legion of Decency. You ought to stand your ground."

"You mean our letter?"

"Yes."

"Did you ever look at the last sentence of our letter?"

"I know. I know. You reserve the right to pass judgment on what you see in the picture."

"Right. And that means we can change our minds. If Warner wants that silly business, I'll change my mind. All of a sudden I'll say it's *not* vulgar."

"But he doesn't want to commit himself until he hears from you."

Geoff's voice began to rise. "What's he waiting on *me* for? Hasn't he an opinion of his own? It's *his* picture. What's *he* think of it? Doesn't he have an opinion? I know he's got eighty million bucks. But does he have an *opinion?* Does he have an opinion on *good taste?* If he thinks it's vulgar, let him cut it himself. If he doesn't, what's he looking for? Someone to fight with? Not me. If he thinks it's all right, I'll pass it!" Geoff's hands were getting very active and expressive. He started to walk away, leaving Rudi frustrated. He stopped and called over his shoulder in a more conciliatory tone, "I know, Rudi. I'll get in touch with Warner on Monday."

And that was the end of it. He eventually approved the gag.

A property that was calling for a lot of attention at just about this time was the immensely popular novel *The Devil's Advocate.* It had been adapted for the New York stage by Dore Schary, and had been a moderate success. It had then been purchased by Warner Brothers, but the studio could not seem to get an acceptable screenplay out of the material. Structurally, it was unsuitable for the screen. Richard Breen, onetime president of the Screen Writers Guild, had done a first-draft script. Eddie Anhalt, who got the Oscar for his adaptation of *Becket,* did a second version, but neither could come up with a treatment that would justify the vast cost of production. The dramaturgy of this story became a matter of discussion among the creative people in the movie colony.

One afternoon, I found myself in the office of a new and brilliant producer, Saul David, who had come to Hollywood from the publishing world. At that particular moment, he was all tangled up with a slightly scandalous best seller, *Sex and the Single Girl.* (He was taken off it before it went on the stages; and he went on to a considerable personal triumph in *Von Ryan's Express* at Fox.)

The conversation fell away from *Sex and the Single Girl* and somehow wandered onto *The Devil's Advocate.* I believe I was trying to persuade him to produce it.

"I could produce that book," said Saul. "I could make a *good* picture out of it."

"How?" I wanted to know.

"Well, it's basically a story of faith, as I see it. And all stories of faith have to be played off an innocent man. The problems that attack his faith have to be made to seem to happen to a 'first man in the world.' He has to be an Adam. Against this kind of man, the problems loom as original. They become startling and acquire vitality."

A gleam of excitement began to course through my spirit. The book was the story of a Church-oriented man who had spent his life locked up in the citadel of himself. He was a theologian in one of those top bureaus in Rome that passes on petitions for the dissolution of marriages. In the midst of his approving and disapproving, of his molding and shaping of the lives of shadow people whom he neither saw nor spoke to, he is suddenly told that he has incurable cancer. In a terrible moment of insight, he realizes that he is empty internally. He has lived by derivative values, but none of his own. He is condemned to die before he has had a chance to live. How will he be able to join the lists of those he has judged? That is the core of this story.

Seeing it in its shattering perspective, the parallels with my own situation were abundantly clear. But, how would I make my way out of Eden? I was blocked by an angel posted at the exit, holding in his hand a fiery sword. The sword was the fear of hell.

"Where, where was a, where was a way out?"

While waiting for a clue, I was having a protracted and invaluable dialogue with the director Richard Brooks. He was helping me from time to time in my efforts to write a novel, which I thought would give me my passport to the "outer world."

Richard was at one time a smoldering saturnine man. People shied from him when he first came to the movie colony from the East Coast, as a novelist and ex-newspaperman. He was fierce about his rights and his liberties. He writhed under confinements he had not put on himself.

"I used to sit in my office at Warner Brothers," he said, "and try to figure out ways of escaping from the studio without checking with the policeman at the gate. All this is when I was supposed to be spending my time writing scripts. And then at last I discovered the perfect way."

"You flushed yourself down the toilet," I said, sparking to the idea.

"No. I heard of the system invented by Mark Hellinger."

"What was that?"

"Well, he had this famous car with the New York license number MH-1. You know about it? The New York police arranged for him to get it because he was Mister Manhattan himself."

"Yes," I said, "I saw it. Who didn't?" I last remembered the car, a leather-topped limousine, sitting in its stall at Universal, waiting like a faithful and lonely dog for Hellinger, the morning after he dropped dead with a heart attack.

"Well, Mark, you know, he was always thinking. Then he suddenly remembered that it was his habit to study the *Racing Form* in the back seat of the car on his way to work. He used to come out of hiding and wave at the cop every time he passed through the gate. Not that the cop needed to see his face. The car itself was passport enough.

"So Mark continued to be absorbed in the *Racing Form* one morning and didn't look up as he passed the cop. The chauffeur did the honors for him, waving politely at the guard, and the guard merely gave a cursory glance at the face of Mark as he went through.

"A week later, Mark's butler was sitting in the back seat, a *Racing Form* hiding his face, and Mark was out at Santa Anita the whole day."

Richard had found his own way "out."

It may have been his triumphs that warmed and mellowed Richard Brooks. He had done *Cat on a Hot Tin Roof* and *The Brothers Karamazov,* to mention only two. As a result of *Elmer Gantry* he had married the supremely beautiful star Jean Simmons, the young girl who had been jumping over the fences on horseback in *Black Narcissus.*

"Have you ever read Ibsen?" he asked one day.

"No." This was 'forbidden' territory.

"You should try *A Doll's House.*" It was clear from his glance that he was consciously steering a course. He was habitually relating the elements of our discussions to appropriate examples in world literature. He was richly read. "Try it," he insisted.

"I will."

"Your promise now?" He asked this most seriously.

"Yes."

It was in the fulfillment of this promise that my own "Doll's House" started crumpling like a cottage of papier-maché.

The moment in which I was delivered, like Eurydice, from the Pit, is still clear and vivid in my mind. It was at the very turning point of the play, when Thorvald, Nora's husband, tried to block her from leaving her home and family by hurling in her path reasons of religion. "Have you no sense of religion? Isn't that an infallible guide to you?"

She replied, "But don't you see, Thorvald, I don't really know what religion is. All I know about it is what Pastor Hansen told me when I was confirmed. He taught me what he thought religion was—said it was *this* and *that*. As soon as I get away by myself, I shall have to look into that matter, too, try and decide whether what he taught me was right—or whether it's right for *me,* at least."

These simple lines struck me with the force of the blow that threw Paul from his horse on the road to Damascus. I was engulfed with the realization that this is all I knew about religion, too: what others had taught me. I knew nothing of its verities from myself. I knew only what Pastor Hansen had *told* me to be true; or Sister Serena, or my friends, or anybody else. But what did they know about it, any more than I? Faith was no more than a multitude of assurances, a chorus of acclaim that had somehow calcified into a form of certitude. That others should *assert* hell did not necessarily bring it into existence. Who was it who said (Voltaire?), "You may *believe* me to be a marshal of France, but that does not make me one."

It was on the crest of the Santa Monica Mountains, on Mulholland Drive west of Beverly Glen, with the San Fernando Valley unfurling below me on the one side, and the Stone Canyon reservoir glistening below me on the other, that I finally put the question to myself. *"Do* you believe?" And from my depths came the answer in all its simplicity. "No."

It seemed as though the music of the spheres welled up all around me.

I had come to Hollywood to keep it, like Prometheus, bound to a rock, the rock of Peter. Instead, Hollywood had showed me how to steal fire from the gods.

Around the Code office, we were beginning to think that the whole operation would end not with a whimper, but with a bang. It would be something big, something with a reputation for scandal like *Cleopatra*.

Rumor had been circulating about this giant production being made in Rome by Twentieth-Fox, for months and even years before its completion. It was bruited about that it had been turned into a device for a systematic bleeding of the corporate assets of the studio, thanks to the ineptitude of some of the top officers, and that things had gone so far that many of the extras were reporting in daily, going over the back fence (in costume), returning to their little pizza stands or other places of business, and then coming back over the fence at night and checking out. It was implied, of course, that there was an "arrangement" to ignore this, because somebody was getting a cut of the "take." True or false, the talk over high-balls was filled with stories like this, and others. The most important among the others was that Richard Burton, a married man, had discovered Elizabeth Taylor, also in wedlock. She, in turn, in a mood of defiance, was cooperating in the creation of certain highly unconventional scenes, in the thick of the picture itself.

One thing was certain. Fox was fighting for its corporate existence. It had something like $33 million invested in a film which nobody thought would be able to be exhibited publicly. It was not going to commit suicide in the Code's behalf, that was sure. On the other hand, if only half the reports were true about the contents of the film, the Code would be asked to annihilate itself by approving it.

The first inkling that *Cleopatra* was ready for review by the Code office came to us in the form of a mysterious letter from Martin Quigley. Addressed to Geoffrey, it announced that the

picture had been scheduled for projection, without our knowledge, for Thursday, May 16, 1963. We wondered how Martin
had managed to get himself into so authoritative a position on
this film that he could start dictating the terms. A review of
the picture was getting to seem a mere academic exercise. We
had been told by an officer of our Association on the East Coast
that Eric Johnston had called Fox about some advertising
material that was being sent ahead of the film for approval by
our New York office. Johnston talked to a high official of this
studio, objecting. The answer, essentially, was that he should
stop bothering them.

Nevertheless, on Tuesday, May 12, two days before the
showing of *Cleo* (which, we found out, had been set for the
big projection room in Fox itself, and not in our own projection room), Martin called Geoffrey on the phone and announced that he was stationed at the Beverly Hills Hotel.
Could Geoffrey and Jack meet him there at the close of the
office day for cocktails and a discussion of the issues? Geoffrey
told him, "Of course."

John the Baptist had arrived, the Precursor, to level the
mountains and to make the crooked ways straight.

In the meantime, Joe Mankiewicz, the director, had also
called Geoff on the phone. "This picture is going to be the
censor's biggest disappointment," he told Geoffrey. "What I
have made is a philosophical tale. It has only been made
famous by the notoriety of some of the principals. Suspend
your judgment until you see what's in the film itself."

At five o'clock that same day, Geoffrey and I were standing
in the heavily carpeted lobby of the Beverly Hills Hotel, feeling important all out of proportion. We picked up the house
phone and asked for Martin Quigley. Martin's metallic voice
came over, a little high-pitched. "Oh, yes. Come right up.
Room 475."

When we got out of the elevator, we saw Martin standing in
the hallway, looking slightly befuddled, with a letter in his
hand. He was searching the walls and the crannies for a mail

chute. He found what he wanted, dropped the letter down the brass slot, and turned to us. "Well!" he exclaimed, *"you* gentlemen look very spruce."

We shook hands and, as we proceeded toward his room, I thought he looked ever so slightly bent, a little feeble.

His room was simple, nothing ornate. "Now," he said, "I think the first order of business is to have a little libation. Geoffrey? Jack?"

He ordered two bourbons and water, no ice, for Geoffrey, and four scotches, two with soda, for himself and myself.

We settled in comfortable chairs. Martin looked at us proudly. "This is an issue," he started, "involving the welfare of the entire Movie Industry. The eyes of the world are on you two fellows. *Cleopatra* has acquired a reputation for scandal from the conduct of certain people connected with it."

I said, "Yes, but also from gossip about what is in the film itself."

Martin agreed with docility. Magazine articles had been printed to inflame the expectation of nudity. "But, on the other hand," said Martin, "the President of Fox tells me there is nothing in the film about which to become unduly concerned. There's a scene of Elizabeth Taylor's backside, and another scene in which you think you see her breasts, but really don't."

Geoff piped up, "I don't think Liz Taylor's rear quarters are going to send the world into a spin of corruption. I guess your President was referring to the 'massage' scene, and the scene of the asp biting Cleopatra."

Martin agreed with a sage nod. "You will be the first people to see the picture," he said. "The reason it has not been seen by anyone so far is that, up to now, a picture simply has not existed. Darryl Zanuck has seen the rushes. As far as I can judge, he came to the conclusion that the picture needed more action, more roughening. It was too philosophical."

I cast a glance at Geoff and he looked back at me meaningfully.

I turned to Martin. "If nobody's seen the picture, how can your President be so sure there's only two rough spots in the film? On whose advice is he relying?"

Martin swallowed this bit of rigoristic logic as though his throat were lubricated with olive oil. He conceded, "Good point. Maybe the President is speaking ahead of himself. I expect there might also be some 'violent amatory encounters' in this film, as the result of Zanuck's entry into the enterprise. We should wait to see the picture, though, before making any judgments—shouldn't we?"

All nodded.

Martin continued. "The President got in touch with me after I had tried to contact him, and he was in Mexico. He wanted my advice. It seems that he had been contacted by Monsignor Little, who told him that a number of letters of protest had been coming into the Legion Offices. The Monsignor said that he had been 'discouraging attendance' at the film. I think this frightened the company."

We all had a sip of our drinks while we absorbed these realities.

"Fox does not intend to show this film to anybody in the Legion," assured Martin, "except Monsignor Little and Father Sullivan. The company officials will refuse to show it to the whole board of reviewers. Fox does not care about a Legion rating, if they can get the picture through the Code. They don't want a Legion 'C' if they can avoid it. About a 'B' they don't care. But they will not go out into the theaters without a Code seal. They feel this is absolutely necessary."

The ploy was suddenly clear. The studio wanted our reputation to play off against the Legion. Suddenly Geoffrey was God, Junior, and his opinion was a dogmatic absolute.

"It's inconceivable," said Martin, "that *some* adjustments cannot be made to bring this film in under the Code. We cannot destroy the Code, but the picture must be passed. The sticky part is that the President has announced that he is showing it to the Code on a 'take it or leave it' basis. He will not change *one frame* of the picture. Mankiewicz doesn't want to show it to the Legion. He's an atheist, but he has a high regard for you, Geoffrey."

Geoffrey accepted the compliment. "But tell me, Martin, why does Fox bother showing the picture to us if we're just supposed to be a cookie cutter?"

Martin's eyes raised in alarm. "Oh, no, Geoffrey," he insisted. "They feel they need you. Without a Code Seal, it'd be a disaster to the corporation."

Geoff's endocrines were beginning to flow. "A disaster? Over nudity? Other films have been going out into the American market with nudity, and not a word is heard. Look at *Boccaccio 70*. What's all the fuss? Apparently the American public is a little more robust than we are imagining. And we may be out of step with the times, and our public. Are we out of step, Martin?"

"Oh, I hope so," said Martin fervently. "I hope so. At least, I hope *I* am. I always used to say to Joe Breen that the Code can be destroyed in two ways—by too much severity, and by too much laxity."

Geoff was shifting in his chair. "All right, Martin. Now that you've brought it up, let me ask you a pertinent question. *Have* we been too lax?"

Martin drew carefully on his cigarette, and blew on the end of it, as on a live punk. "Well," he said, "let me answer you right to the point." He stood up and began to wander around. "My grandfather was born in County Somethingorother in Ireland. And my grandmother was born in County Somethingelse, only twenty-five miles away—no, less, fifteen. Well, whatever. This is all by way of telling you that I come from a background that makes me have a proclivity to have certain tendencies. So that my own personal desires are one thing. But I spare you the family tree. The consequence of these tendencies, however, is to make me have certain desires about the Code, which may be in conflict with the turns of history. And, I think that had the Code hewn to the line, in a manner that would have pleased me, and had I had the responsibility for making it measure up to *my* desires . . . I would have destroyed it!"

He gazed at Geoffrey very significantly. Geoff realized what a tremendous concession this statement was on the part of Martin. To me, at this moment, Martin looked quite human.

The review of the picture was anticlimactic. Joe Mankiewicz came in, burly, shiny-cheeked, with horn-rimmed glasses, looking none the worse for wear. He lit an expensive cigar and settled down on the back of his neck in a soft lounge chair. "This picture is not going to be what you expect," he told us. "You'll be pleasantly surprised."

"How do you know what we're expecting, Joe?" I inquired.

He did a little bump with his head and made a quick laugh. "I know what I've been made to think I've made," he replied.

As it turned out, the picture, of course, was colossal, with moments of poetry, such as the entrance of the Egyptian queen into Rome on the giant float; and moments of questionable taste, such as the famous massage scene, and the equally famous scene of the asp stinging her breast. Neither scene was worth a life-and-death struggle, however; and, although Martin knew that raising no issue about these sequences pushed back the limits of Code interpretation into new, more liberal grounds, he sighed with evident relief when we found no difficulty in accepting what was on the screen. Just for good luck, Geoffrey asked that Mankiewicz consider abbreviating one small scene. At this point, I can neither remember the spot nor whether Joe agreed to trim it or not. In effect, what was approved was what was finally seen in the theaters.

After the screening, Martin insisted that we repair with him to his hotel room. There was one more point to be nailed down firmly. He had his leverage against the Legion now in the form of the Code Certificate. What he wanted to know was whether, in our opinion, there would be an issue made by the Legion. I answered for Geoff. "The people on the Legion of

Decency are not fools, Martin. They'll pass it. I guarantee you. This picture is what, in their parlance, is called 'spotted material.' There are a few places that they will regret, that they might even fight about. But taken as a whole, they don't have a chance, and they're going to know it. Relax. You're home free."

The anxiety of countenance seemed to leave Martin. "You really think so?" he asked.

"It's a certainty."

He handed us each the sociable drink he had been preparing. "Tell me," he asked Geoff, "that's a big job you've just done. You've taken a great responsibility. How much do you get paid for it?"

Geoff half slurped his drink while trying to answer. "The regular fee for any picture costing this much to make. Three thousand dollars."

An infinitesimal smile began to make runnels around the corners of Martin's mouth, and his gaze wandered off toward the ceiling. "I think you're very bad bargainers," he said banteringly. "I could've gotten you a *hundred* thousand dollars."

That was the last we ever saw of Martin.

19 Second Act Curtain: *Kiss Me, Stupid,* Pussy Galore and a Question of Bond-age

ON AN AFTERNOON in the fall of 1964, Geoff Shurlock was walking down the long neon-lit corridor of the Code offices in Hollywood. The footfall that only yesterday had been so perky was now a trifle irregular on the lime-green carpeting, making his progress a little like the pecking of a chicken. One shoulder sloped a bit low. A third of a century had passed, and time was beginning to tell.

Joe Breen had died. In his terminal years he had turned into a specter of skin and bones, with teeth that were loose in their sockets. He did not seem to care especially. His birdlike hands gripped the arms of his wheelchair, and only an occasional flash showed in the pale eyes that in the noonday years had blazed with blue flames.

Martin Quigley, too, had succumbed. A gray disease had made its inexorable way with him and had brought the fierce will, in a terrible attrition, to rest.

And Eric Johnston had been carried off by some kind of cranial disorder that makes one grieve for the human condition. There was no President of the Motion Picture Association. Technically, there was an interregnum.

As he turned the corner to go into the projection room, Geoff realized that he was being separated, little by little, from the original realities and the old familiarities. He knew that he would get no sympathy, one way or the other, for the decision he would have to make in a few minutes on the most recent picture of Billy Wilder. What was it called? Oh, yeah. *Kiss Me, Stupid.*

As usual, there had been no script. Only an occasional news item, like runnels of lightning on the distant horizon, gave any hint of the kind of material the picture contained. Ever since Shurlock had turned down Wilder's application for the popular stage play of several years back, *The Bad Seed,* the offended director had slammed the door on the Code.* When the movie was brought into the projection room months afterward, acceptably adapted by Mervyn LeRoy, Geoff had had to face the disconcertment of issuing a Seal for *Bad Seed.* In so doing, he acquired the enmity of Wilder. So stung was Geoffrey by this experience that he vowed loudly that he would never again give a categorical no on any property. ("And I know that *all* generalities are wrong, including this one.")

Inside the projection room, with its expensive beige curtains and oversize chairs, Geoff found the staff already waiting, slumped down on the small of their backs and smoking cigarettes. Geoff gave a shadowy smile at the assemblage. He knew what they were thinking.

They were in a deathwatch, waiting for a clear-cut issue that would allow the Code to come to grips with basic sanities again. They were still saddled with the responsibility for decent films, but without the cognate authority any more. The apparatus of the Appeal, which was at the guts of the whole operation, had been made so unwieldy that, as a practical matter, it was impossible to convoke it. At Goeffrey's suggestion, the Appeals Board had been widened to give representation to other points of view along with the Executive. It was a well-meant idea. But it involved summoning theater owners from various quarters of the country, and prestigious film makers from Hollywood, so that it all became very expensive, and a bother completely out of proportion to a little nudity here or a little violence there. The result was that the Industry made it known, without coming out with an edict about it,

* See End Note A, page 359.

that the Code authority was to be very chary about making ultimatums. In consequence, the screen was suffering from a mild case of creeping indecency. But life was like that. It seldom afforded convenient black and white issues, as in the Westerns. It required fortitude to wait like a cat at a gopher hole for a first class blunder based on presumption. Well, from the gossip about *Kiss Me, Stupid,* this might be the case.

But it was wrong to prejudge.

The lights went down, and the familiar flick of the projection beam began. What the staff saw is all history now.

Right from the outset, Wilder made it clear that he was not fooling around. The town in which the story was set was called Climax, Nevada. It was the tale of an attractive scamp, Dean Martin, on his way back to Los Angeles from a singing engagement in Las Vegas when his car is sidetracked and sabotaged by two aspiring songwriters who own the local gas station. Dino is worried over the prospect of having to spend the night in this strange hick town, because if he has to go for a night without sex, it gives him a headache. To keep him happy, a waitress named Polly the Pistol is acquired from the local tavern, gently named the Belly Button, in case anyone might not be getting the point.

In a nighttime of confusion, the wife of the songwriter switches places with Polly, and Dino goes to bed with the wrong party. Two weeks later, the songwriter hears his tune being sung by Dino on television. When the naïve fellow wants to know how this happened, his wife says fondly, "Kiss me, stupid."

It was not merely a question of the plot, with its implication of what in the old crass days of the Code used to be called "screwing for the jewels." It was the whole atmosphere of what the London *Times* eventually called "cheery bad taste." When Dino approaches his bed for the night, a pet parrot caws, "Bang, bang!" (because it has been deprived of seeing its favorite Western on TV, the lights being out and all—wink, wink). When Dino tries to get rid of the songwriter, he tells him to make a dozen copies of the tune while he and "the wife" go out into the garden. "She can show me her parsley." When the Legion of Decency balked at the double meaning of this line, Wilder is supposed to have protested with great innocence, "What do they want? Broccoli?"

And so it went. Halfway through the showing, the Code people relaxed. They had their case. There was nothing left for it but an occasional guffaw.

The only unpredictable element might be Geoff himself. He had been manifesting a mood of derring-do lately. It was such a departure from the personality of his early days as Code Director that it did not seem quite real. At the outset, he had been as volatile as a bird hopping from branch to branch in a tree.

Recently, however, he had been acting more tough on the heels of an experience that had firmed up his sense of decision. He had written a letter to England, rejecting a script based on the classic novel *Tom Jones* (despite his rule about all-out statements). The producing company had gone right ahead and made the picture anyway and, as luck would have it, had shown it to the Legion of Decency before bringing it to the Code. The Legion had, surprisingly, withheld from condemning it, with the civilized comment: ". . . this film is an earthy satire about the manners and morals in 18th century England. Although the film may appear frequently coarse, it is saved from being offensive by reason of its fast paced and exceptional comic treatment and its honest portrayal of the period."

It was one of those cases in which liberties are allowed for artistic achievement or, to use the phrase that had become popular through the Supreme Court, for "redeeming social merit."

There was no such pliability under the rigid Code system. The office was supposed simply to approve a picture or declare it unfit for public consumption. This limitation, which particularly irked Geoff, ceased to daunt him when he learned of the Legion's unilateral action. With the expression of one who had just been issued a license to steal, he announced to the Code staff, "Look. Just sit back and enjoy this picture. It's one of those scripts I rejected out of hand. I'll never learn. But if you think now that I'm going to be holier than the Pope, you're crazy. As of this moment, the picture's passed."

Although *Tom Jones* ruptured just about every second precept of the Code, it was clear from the whoops of joy with which it was received by audiences everywhere that the moldy old Code could be honored more in the breach than in the observance. This, of course, gave rise to a basic hypocrisy, since the Industry insisted on maintaining the sanctimonious air of one who still lived up to all the terms of the existing document. In characteristic fashion, it wanted to burn the candle from both ends. Geoff, resenting the pharisaism, sought to burst the bonds of the old taboos wherever it was practical. His liberalizations were met with such yawns of silence as to lead him to the conclusion that the American public did not give a damn, and even that it would hardly be insulted.

Such were the feelings in the breasts of the staff when *Kiss Me, Stupid* came to an end, and the lights came up. Right to the very last frames, Wilder had been cracking the whip. Imposing Dino's image on a whole series of television screens, and repeating it by reflections in the plate glass of a shop window, he has the songwriter's collaborator (and service station partner) coo in admiration, "I guess the bigger they are, the nicer they are." You had to hand it to the director. When he decided to jump off the world, he didn't leave any anchors attached.

Geoff stood and turned to face his associates. "Well," he wondered, with a slightly quizzical smile. "What about it?" Although there was no question in anybody's mind, the staff was beginning to learn to practice cunning. A ragged volley of halfhearted opinions were ventured, all of them negative. "It's funny enough," said one. "Yeah, Wilder's always funny," agreed another.

"I'm going to pass it," interrupted Geoff.

We all heard the sound of hammers on casket nails. "As is?" someone asked with a small voice.

Geoff looked hard. "If dogs want to return to their vomit," he reported, "I'm not going to try to stop them." He stalked out.

It was the end of an era.

It was not long before the Legion of Decency turned its public tongue on the film like a flamethrower. In an unusually wordly opinion it declared:

> Satire on the foibles of its people has always been a sign of the healthiness of a society. Through humor the weaknesses of men can be exposed to a salutary recognition by all—and, many times, much more effectively than by preachment. Mr. Wilder's earlier film, "The Apartment," was an example of such effective comic satire.
>
> In the case of "Kiss Me, Stupid," however, not only has Mr. Wilder failed to create a genuine satire out of a situation comedy about an amateur composer who attempts to sell his songs to a big-name singer in exchange for the adulterous attentions of his alleged "wife," but he has regrettably produced a thoroughly sordid piece of realism which is esthetically as well as morally repulsive. Crude and suggestive dialogue, a leering treatment of marital and extra-marital sex, a prurient preoccupation with lechery compound the film's bald condonation of immorality.

To rub salt into the wounds, the Legion appended a press release to its condemnation in which it made a highly personalized attack on the Code Administration itself. First, it noted its "astonishment" that a film "so patently indecent and immoral" should have received a seal of approval by the Code office. It then went on to level a broadside:

> It is difficult to understand how such approval is not the final betrayal of the trust which has been placed by so many in the organized industry's self-regulation.

It followed with a pitch that can only be regarded as having the taint of pandering:

> Moreover, the release of this film by Lopert Films, a wholly owned subsidiary of United Artists, at any time, but particularly during the holiday season of Chanukah and Christmas is a commercial decision bereft of respect for the Judaeo-Christian sensibilities of the majority of the American people.

At just about this same time, the Legion had coined a phrase, borrowed from the vocabulary of the late Secretary of State John Foster Dulles, in which it had accused movies of indulging in "moral brinksmanship." No observant person would have doubted that this was right. But when the Legion itself pretended to show a solicitude for the sensibilities of Jews during the Chanukah season, then the thinness of its own fabric was clearly beginning to show.

By the time Geoff had read all this, he had had time for reflective analysis. Looking up from the press releases with calm eyes, he said, "Yes, well, I'll tell you what. I passed this picture with my eyes wide open. I did it to precipitate a crisis. Now maybe we've got it. Somebody had to rupture the Code in so conspicuous a manner that they'd have to do something about it. Because if this's the kind of movies they want to make, if the companies're going to put up the money for this kind of stuff, and then expect me to try to stop them, they're crazy."

It was bravely said, no doubt. But, intending to be a Sampson, it turned out that Geoffrey had only knocked over a house of cards. At first, true, there was a squall of indignation on the part of the public, and the outcries reached noisy proportions. In fact, Geoffrey later opined that this manifestation may have been the last random chorus of traditional protest by the American public against an offense to its sense of decency.

The stir reached into the Olympian atmospheres where dwelt the company presidents. They, dimly alarmed, filtered the word down through the organizational structures that the Production Code office was to begin rejecting pictures and sending them back to New York on appeal. It began to appear for a moment that Geoffrey had made his point and had achieved the effect he had speculated upon.

Diligently, he undertook to reject one picture after another and to send them back East for consideration by the Appeals Board.* Virtually none reached this consummation. Most of the pictures were lost in interim committees, which suggested compromises or made token cuts or simply negated the concerns of the Code staff. Eventually the whole futile process fell apart. The ultimate blow was when we were informed that "Seymour's secretary saw that picture in a local theater last night, and she couldn't see anything wrong with it." Everybody on the Code staff blinked and wondered what the hell he was doing there.

In the midst of all the clamor, however, one small voice was raised in sympathy. It was—guess who?

January 11, 1965

Mr. Geoffrey Shurlock
Motion Picture Producers Assn.
8480 Beverly Blvd.
Hollywood 48, Calif.

Dear Geoff:
I have just returned from Europe, and have been briefed on the uproar the picture has caused.

It is obvious that the Legionnaires have been lying in the bushes, biding their time until they could waylay some picture-maker of import and use him as a whipping boy for the entire industry.

At this late date it would be both pointless and useless for me to stand up and defend myself against this vicious onslaught of bigotry. However, I am aware that I must

* See the complete list, beginning with 1964, the year of *Kiss Me, Stupid*, in End Note B, page 360, and the resolution of each case.

have caused you considerable trouble, and for this I am
genuinely sorry.

Let me assure you that I am resolved never to put you on
the spot again.

Affectionately,

BW:RS   Billy Wilder

January 13, 1965

Mr. Billy Wilder
Samuel Goldwyn Studios
1041 North Formosa Avenue
Hollywood 46, California

Dear Billy:
My warm thanks for your kind and generous letter. Basically, I have no right to object to being put on the spot by
any of my friends in the business, because after all that is,
among other things, what I get paid for. But in your case,
please believe me, I was motivated primarily by my esteem
and affection for you, over and above the normal call of
duty. And I hope I can oblige again, some day.

Affectionately,

GMS:a

In every conventionally constructed play there is a moment
at which "all seems lost," commonly called the "second act
curtain." This is the point at which the protagonist has not
only failed to solve the "problem" with which he was confronted at the play's beginning, but is actually worse off than
before he started.

The Code, which was saddled at the very outset with the
problem that it was not wanted by the Industry, was, after the
debacle of *Kiss Me, Stupid,* headed at a full gallop for its
second act curtain. Only one ingredient was missing. That was
the collapse of the human equation.

What happened to Geoff Shurlock was a textbook study in
the stealthy process of aging. When the shades began falling

across his eyes, a twilight mentality began to set in, so that he saw only that which he wanted to see, and lost much of his circumspection about his true and real estate. In consequence he committed the one cardinal sin of show biz: he stayed on "after curtain." And on. And on . . .

It was too bad, because in his earlier days, Geoff used to amuse everybody by likening the plight of those who could not let go of power to the straight man in the old vaudeville routine, the one who shook hands with the baggy-pants comedian only to find that he was stuck to a veritable human flypaper. The line was Geoff's stock in trade, what the Jewish professionals would call his "schtick."

The rationalism which Geoff employed to perpetuate himself in office was simplicity personified. He defined old age in terms that were compatible with his wishes. He likened it to a state in which a person begins to "play it safe," when he loses his instinct for taking a risk and begins to defend the status quo. It did not seem to occur to him that playing the role of "maturing liberal" can begin to appear as the affliction of second childhood.

Motivated by his definition, Geoff automatically gravitated to the side of "taking a chance" whenever a controversial scene cropped up in a film. The result was that he not only started giving away the store, but ended up on the brink of the pitfall for which he had scorned the ancient caricature, Binford.

A prime example occurred in the case of the great money-maker *Goldfinger,* the third in the fabulous James Bond series. Geoff laughed off the first two entries, *Dr. No* and *From Russia With Love,* and in so doing had shown both wit and perception. "It's only a little fucking," he said stridently. "What's all the shouting about?" He would begin to look walleyed and would exclaim to the world at large, "My God, what do women think they are, that to give them a little of what-comes-naturally brings the sky down on everybody's heads—like something out of Chicken Little? This deification of the female waterworks is too much."

When the time came to make *Goldfinger,* however, the producers were beginning to feel the pinch of their own inventiveness. Having expended all outlandishness on the first two fantasies, it was incumbent on them now to top themselves, even though this be at the expense of straining taste along with credulity.

The gimmick in this particular story was an attempt to rob all the gold in Fort Knox. If the villains only knew, they could have done it legally through the stock market. Instead, they enlisted the services of a lesbianlike character called Pussy Galore and her all-girl circus of aerial acrobats. Even Geoff had to wince at the baldness of this cuteness. He also squirmed at the obviousness of a line at the opening of the picture. Bond is in bed with a luscious creature when the phone rings, and he is summoned by headquarters. Speaking into the phone while looking wistfully at the actress Shirley Eaton, Sean Connery (Bond) explains that he can't come now, because "something big has just come up."

Geoff no sooner got back to his office from reviewing the film than the phone rang from London. It was the producer, "Cubby" Broccoli (of the family that had invented the vegetable which Billy Wilder thought the Legion might like).

The promptness of the call, hardly before the staff could gather its thoughts, seemed to reveal an anxiety on the part of the producer.

"What did you think of my film?" he wanted to know.

"The best in the series," Geoff rightly raved.

"Any problems?"

Geoff wiggled uncomfortably in his chair. "Well, yes," he admitted. "What about that 'Pussy Galore'?"

A great deal of static was heard at the other end of the line. Geoff gave an interpolation out of the side of his mouth, with his hand over the mouthpiece. "He says it doesn't mean a thing. Nobody pays any attention to it." His face lit up. "He says it's in the book. It was President Kennedy's favorite reading. On top of that, the British censor board passed it. There was a command performance or something like that, and everybody saw it. Not a voice was raised. Nobody walked out." He took his hand off the mouthpiece, and his voice went up a few notches. "All right, Cubby, all right," he said. "If everything you tell me's true, I'll buy it. Yes. Good luck. Send us more entertaining things like this." With that, he hung up the phone. He turned in his swivel chair and faced the staff members who had straggled in. "Well, there you are," he announced.

In a smothered voice, one of the men asked, "What about that opening line?"

"What line?"

"You know. 'Something big has just come up!' "

Geoff waved a depreciating hand at the questioner. "Oh, that," he snuffed. After a beat, he said, "It doesn't bother me."

That night, a few of the staff members gathered at the bar of the Cock 'n Bull restaurant for a cup of forgetfulness. "You know what he reminds me of?" groused one over his martini.

"No. What?"

"He reminds me of that old joke. You know. The one about prenatal influence?"

"No. What about it?"

"Well, you know. There was this group of women standing around, all talking about prenatal influence, how what a woman does while she's pregnant leaves its mark on the child. Like one was saying it was true, all those things they said, because her mother had been scared by a wild strawberry or something, and that accounted for the strawberry mark on her thigh. Things like that. And there was this one woman standing back, kind of, and not saying anything, so they asked her what she thought. 'Oh,' she said, 'I don't believe in that stuff. It's just old wives' tales. Why, for goodness' sake, when my mother was carrying me, she fell down a whole flight of steps, carrying an armload of phonograph records. Every one of the records broke, but it didn't hurt me . . . it didn't hurt me . . . it didn't hurt me . . .' "

Everybody laughed. "Yeah. It doesn't bother me . . . it doesn't bother me . . . What would, over seventy?"

The producers took advantage of Geoff's ready disposition, as was to be expected, and pressured him for more and more concessions. One of those who came into the office after a noticeable hiatus was Sam Spiegel, who brought along his production, *Night of the Generals*. This must have been one of Sam's "every other" pictures, since it created only a small flurry of conversation, and then was not mentioned any more.

Well into the picture there was a "love scene," which was introduced, if memory serves rightly, on a great canopied bed, across one of those large, old-fashioned European rooms. In the middle distance the two lovers are seen struggling in the early throes of sexuality, with the man bending down to kiss the woman. Since he was partially and astutely shadowed, it was not clear exactly what he was doing, but the impression was evoked that he was, at the very least, feasting orally on her body.

The suggestion was scarcely scored when the camera moved in for a close-up, which corrected this false notion. Now we are able to observe that he was kissing her in a much more conservative manner, so that anyone who wanted to defend the scene could waggle a finger and say, "Ah-ha! You see? You've got a dirty mind."

When Geoff broached this concern to Sam, the entrepreneur brushed it out of existence with a wave of the finger. "It's so quick that it doesn't mean anything," he said with a tiny show of annoyance. "And besides, we come in right away and *see* that nothing's wrong."

"You're right," scrambled Geoff. "I'm sorry I brought it up. Skip it."

A movie executive, subsequently hearing this, turned his

glance indignantly on Geoff. "Oh, I see," he said loudly, "we now have a new criterion. If you only *think* you see it, it doesn't count. It's only your imagination. The next thing we'll have a little muff-diving, but if it's real quick, (he flicked his fingers) and you didn't *really* see him eating her, but only *thought* you did, that makes it okay. Is that it?"

Geoff looked at him, dead-pan. "It looks like it, doesn't it?" he snapped.

The fellow turned and strode away, slowly flailing his fingers in the air, as though he had picked up something too hot.

Geoff, caught now in a vicious circle, was forced to conjure up excuses to pass what he knew he could not stop anyhow. But sometimes his willingness to be simplistic went too far.

A case in point was *The Swinger,* a sexy little soufflé starring the popular Ann-Margret. Somebody in connection with this film must have become infatuated over the actress, because the vulgarities of camera work were glaring. In one shot, in a dance sequence, the camera was mounted underneath a glass floor, and peered without embarrassment right up into the girl's pelvic area while she ground and gyrated.

The *pièce de résistance,* however, was an orgiastic sequence in which Ann-Margret's body was used as a paint brush to create an abstract painting. A huge slab of canvas was spread out on the floor, and buckets of colored paint were splashed across it. Then Ann-Margret's torso was lubricated by squirting it with syringes filled with the colored goo. She was then seized by the male members of the dance troupe and slid hither and yon on the canvas to make the patterns.

When Geoff saw this, his first reaction was to dismiss it as just "messy." As for the dance movements themselves, he said they were "athletic" and "calisthenic," but not sexy.

A vice president of the Producers Association got wind of Geoff's marvelous interpretations, and came up spluttering. "For Christ's sake," he protested, "you know what the Code is? Lissen. I want to tell you a story.

"You see, there was this patient that was going to a psy-chiatrist. His problem was that he felt like a horse. The doctor put him on the couch and reassured him. He told him the problem was not uncommon, and that a little work would cure him.

"The doctor was a trifle optimistic, because it took five years of hard work on the couch before he felt justified in releasing the patient. Eventually, however, he turned him loose. 'Come back in a couple of months and report on how you're doing,' he instructed.

"Two months later the patient was back as instructed. 'How's it going?' asked the doctor. The patient was disconso-late. 'It was okay for a while,' he said, 'but every time I see a horse nowadays, I get that old feeling.'

"The doctor picked up a pad from his desk and started writing. 'Do we have to go through all that again?' asked the patient. 'Haven't you taken enough notes?'

" 'I'm not taking notes,' said the doctor. 'What I'm doing now's writing you a permit.'

" 'A permit? A permit for what?'

" 'For shitting in the streets.' "

A member of the Code staff remained obtuse. "What's that got to do with the Code?" he wanted to know.

The executive looked at him with eyes like the underside of the soap in the soap dish. "You're the psychiatrists," he said.

Stirred by the reaction of this pooh-bah, Geoff decided to retract his opinion. He wrote to the studio:

> This scene of the orgy contains a great deal of material we think has an unacceptable phallic inference. Individual scenes which we think should be eliminated include the opening shot of the man flaunting the syringes, which to us seem to have a definite phallic symbolism; the breast-shaking of Kelly [Ann-Margret]; the scenes of the man shooting the syringe down her breast and into her crotch (symbolic of squirting seminal fluid); the scene in front

of the multiplying mirrors where she does the bumps and grinds; the scenes of her wallowing and writhing orgiastically in the paint; and the final shot of the man flaunting the syringes.

The edited version was called "hyperthyroid" by one critic.

The staff was put to the test in being forced to listen with owlish solemnity to one flimsy sophistry after another in defense of questionable material. They were like the judge on the bench who must lend a serious ear while a stripteaser argues that her act is the "art" of ecdysiasty.

There was a case in a film brought into the Code projection room by the actor Cornel Wilde, a man as personally charming, incidentally, as he is willful and good-looking. I believe the film was *Beach Red*. In the course of this picture there was a scene of a girl in the nude, bending over and just beginning to work out of her panties. It was a reasonably brief scene, and not one that it was possible to dwell upon, but it was a clear technical violation of one of the most hard-and-fast prohibitions of the Code at that moment.

Morris Murphy, who was beginning to turn a trifle silver in the hair and blue in the gills, told Wilde in his great dark brown voice that the scene would have to be sacrificed.

Wilde stammered for a moment, not knowing what to say about a piece of footage he wanted to keep. Reaching for whatever absurd argument that came to his mind, he blurted out, "How do you *know* she's undressing? For all you know she might have been stepping into her panties. You call this an undressing scene. Prove it."

Murph was equally nonplused, because the rejoinder so totally evaded the core of the question, which was the girl's nudity. He held his breath while he fumbled for an answer, then erupted into a complete non sequitur. "Well, at least we know *one* thing," he said in a conciliatory voice. "She's a *good* girl. Because she wears *white* panties (and good girls don't undress in public, so you're probably right, etc. . . . .) "*

Shenanigans like this put the whole discipline of film controls in a bad light, and it was not long before people began making fun of it. An example occurred in the case of the Swedish film *Night Games,* which was submitted for consideration to the San Francisco Film Festival. It was a picture made by a woman, Mai Zetterling, and it set new lows for tastelessness and boldness. Among other things, it had a scene of a boy masturbating beneath the sheets, having been so turned on by his mother that he had to relieve himself. At some point in the review of the film, one of the members of the audience stood up and walked out in public protest. The dissenter was none other than yesteryear's child star, Shirley Temple.

In retaliation, the manager of the theatre in which *Night Games* was showing began playing a record of "On the Good Ship Lollipop" during the intermissions. When asked why he should rub it in like this, he is supposed to have replied, "Why not? She popularized my picture. Why shouldn't I give some advertising to 'her song'?"

The absurdity of the situation began to take its toll on the Code personnel. "To one degree or another," wrote Bayard Hooper, Human Affairs Editor for *Life* magazine, "everyone encounters a sense of despair when he is forced to compromise

---

* This spontaneous, real-life episode is remarkably similar to one attributed to Toulouse-Lautrec. He, drunk, is supposed to have come into an exhibition of his works, only to find a dowager shocked at some of the pictures "glorifying" ladies of easy virtue. She was peering through her lorgnette at one in particular, showing a "date" fiddling with her half-opened undergarment, while nearby stood a gent in swallow-tailed coat. Boozily indignant, Lautrec assulted the critic for her "dirty mind," saying that the picture represented a girl who was dressing, not undressing, the gentleman was her husband, and they were going out to dinner to celebrate the birthday of their son.

his inner vision with the realities of a world he must share with others. It is one of the terms of existence as a social being, and therefore part of adult life. To the extent that a person can overcome these conflicts—or develop internal defenses and disguises to protect himself from them—to that extent can he escape a sense of self-alienation. But for the intellectual, whom Albert Camus described as 'someone whose mind watches itself,' the disease is apt to run rampant."

Watching what was happening to themselves, the men of morality became demoralized.

It was all symbolized in what occurred to Milt Hodenfield. He came out of the Cock 'n Bull one night, his head blossoming with fumes, blinked at the lights along Sunset Strip, leaned against the stucco wall of the restaurant, and slid slowly to the ground. At this moment, along came Gene Dougherty, who saw Milt floundering on the cement. He offered to help him get up, but Milt rejected the outstretched hand with fuzzy indignation. He had something to do first. He had to put on his topcoat. And so Doc stood by and watched with fascination while Milt went through the gyrations of slipping into his topcoat while still glued to the pavement.

When he was finished, he allowed Doc to set him on his feet, and escort him to the parking lot. His car was easy to find, because it was a brand-new beet-red Buick. Carefully Doc deposited him on the front seat and craftily stole the keys. He patted Milt on the shoulder and suggested that he take a little snooze before trying to drive. With docility, Milt agreed and soon was snoring blissfully. Doc brought the keys back to the bartender, Ralph, and left them in his keeping, admonishing him not to let Milt have them until he was in a good condition to drive. Ralph agreed.

"Of course, you know what happened?" asked Doc.

"No, what?" I echoed.

Doc looked at me from a cocked angle. "I'd put him in the wrong car," he said.

It was not long after this that poor Milt stumbled, stepping out of a shower, and struck his head on the corner of the washbasin. For at least three days he carried a great egg on his temple where he had struck it, and wore dark glasses to conceal the glaze of death in his eyes.

One evening he was sitting in a lounge chair watching TV, sipping on a highball while a close friend made dinner. When she came out to summon him, he was slumped down in the seat, a trickle of blood leaking out of the corner of his mouth.

He never regained consciousness.

It was curtains.

20 To the Rescue!: *Who's Afraid of Virginia Woolf?* and *Alfie!*

THE THIN GOLDEN tootling of cavalry bugles began to be heard on the Eastern horizons in the spring of 1966. Rumors began to circulate that the company presidents were looking for a new Czar.

The first names that were given currency were from the Kennedy palace guard. Names like Larry O'Brien's were bandied around, and Ted Sorensen's, but it was quickly leaked that he had a prior commitment to write the biography of his beloved leader.

A figure with political connections was desirable because by now over 50 per cent of the Industry's business was conducted in the world market. This involved import quotas, favorable or unfavorable tax legislation, and sometimes impounded monies that had to be unfrozen.*

The whole process was suddenly reversed by the introduction of a candidate from another quarter altogether, that of Louis Nizer, famous lawyer and author of a best seller called *My Life in Court*. This nomination, too, made sense. Nizer was long connected with the Industry in one way or another, and was fond of it. He had a certain air of rabbinical pomp-and-softness about him that was very Old Testament in character, and very influential with the Jewish elements in the movie business. He was known to be devoted to traditional

* See End Note C, page 364.

decency, and would be a welcome symbolic figure as far as the Code staff was concerned. The conversation involving his name became so common that it was finally printed in *Variety* that his appointment would be announced in a few days.

Abruptly, however, all speculations were canceled. Lew Wasserman, the top executive of Universal-International studios, was quoted as saying that he wanted to give the matter further consideration. The fact that Wasserman was also a key figure in the Democratic Party machine in Hollywood was also noted keenly by close observers.

What we first heard about Jack Valenti tended to make us quail about the comfort of our ways. We were told that he was an indefatigable worker, toiling for the President from dawn to dusk, and that he followed a physical fitness program that called for a two-mile jog around a park in Washington every morning. On receipt of this information, we all got up out of our chairs and put Nizer's *My Life in Court* back on the bookshelf.

In May of 1966, it became a *fait accompli*. Valenti, who had been Special Assistant to L.B.J. and had even married his pretty secretary, was made President of the M.P.A.A. His unstinting loyalty had clearly been rewarded. In no time at all, he was out on the Coast, mingling among the face cards.

What we saw moving through the crowd at the Beverly Hilton Hotel was a crisp, dark, compact man, looking rather remarkably like Alabama's Governor Wallace. He was sartorially immaculate, had a ready smile, and kept turning his glowing dark eyes this way and that like luminous lamps.

When he took the stage to speak, his sentences bore a resemblance to the overture of a grand opera. He was forecasting the career he hoped to accomplish, and he sounded such good phrases as dedicating himself to artistic freedom and "creative excellence." On the other hand, when he came to the Code, he left no doubt about where he stood. In ringing syllables, with appropriate pauses for effect, he declared, "I did not take the job of President of the Motion Picture Association in order to preside over a feckless Code!"

We, sitting in the audience among the stars, imagined that the whole room began to sparkle with the good tidings.

Back in the Code offices immediately after lunch, the executive secretary of one of the major screen guilds looked at me significantly and said, "It looks like you've got your man!" He waited for an answer.

"Deo Valenti!" I aspired.

No sooner had Valenti taken his place in the chair of honor than he was struck his first blow.

Who's Afraid of Virginia Woolf?

It was more than three years earlier, in 1963, that we had written our first Code letter on the famous Albee play. In that pace-setting report, a hundred cautions, objections, and admonitions were listed on words, phrases, sentences, and situations. The letter was replete with "goddams," "bastards," and "for Christ's sakes," but also contained more juicy morsels such as the phrases "monkey nipples" and "angel tits." To traffic in these details too much is to run the risk of harpyism, that is, a proclivity to feast on waste products at the expense of larger issues. Nevertheless, there is no way of telling this whole story, in fact or in truth, without coming out bluntly with a sampling of the blue stuff.

Neither is this to imply that the sordities are in themselves vulgar. It is intention that makes vulgarity, and anyone with one eye in the back of his head would see that the dimensions of this important play are not coextensive with the crudities. The story, basically, is more in the order of a Greek tragedy, and has to do with a New England history professor, George, and his wife, Martha, the daughter of the college's president. Returning home late at night from a faculty party, they have brought along a young couple for a nightcap.

The four proceed to drink heavily, and the intoxication brings on a convulsion of truth-telling that almost tears both couples to shreds. This savage honesty leads to confessions regarding a fantasy the professor and his wife have nurtured, that they have a nonexistent son. The burden of the story seems to be that if we disgorge our falsehoods, no matter how painfully, we can face the dawn of a new reality with at least the hope of love beginning.

When Jack Valenti and Lou Nizer (who, as an alternative, had been hired as legal counsel for the association) saw this picture they were caught almost completely off guard. What they beheld was a scene of Elizabeth Taylor looking straight into the camera and yelling, "Screw you!" Add to this scene a dance in a local juke joint that was so extreme as to be an expression of agony rather than of lust; and such occasional expressions as, "Let's play hump-the-hostess," and one begins to get a measure of the disconcertment of these two men. Undoubtedly they had not seen as many films of current vintage as they might have, and so their surprise was compounded.

Valenti subsequently admitted that his first reaction had been to confront Jack Warner, and to have it out with him then and there. Nizer, whose traditional sense of decency seems to have been particularly irritated, afterward hinted that he had prodded Valenti to throw down the gauntlet and threaten to quit, and that he would stand behind him. Perhaps he knew the axiom that those issues which you do not make in the first ninety days are next-to-impossible to make later.

However, the movie industry is more stubborn and more shrewd than it sometimes allows the public to believe. It knew very well that there was no backing out of the situation now. Warner Brothers had, reportedly, $7\frac{1}{2}$ million in this project. What could it do with the film, eat it? The fact that the studio had put itself in that position with full consciousness, and had taken the risk, was justified by the fact that the play had won the Drama Critics' Award in 1963 and had been seen by countless thousands on the legitimate stage without any undue uproar.

And so, the voices of the statesmen went to work and began

arguing sweet reason. Valenti was in no easy spot. He did not want to seem to be used; to be lending the prestige that trailed him from the White House as a cloak for this film. But at the same time some dim, dark instinct was at work in the man, assuring him that beyond the initial impact of the film, its basic validity would prevail, and it would ultimately—in the theatrical sense—play.

The company presidents used some style. In executive session, they ruled on Warners' Appeal from the Production Code's (mandatory) rejection of this film, and permitted it to have their blessing, with certain saving graces. First of all, some concessions were made by way of editing. The "Screw you!" was deleted, and replaced by a protection shot in which Liz yells "Goddam you!" ("Some improvement," growled certain critics.) Other cuts were made, too. But most importantly, Warners' introduced a new "first" into the system. It advertised the film as S.M.A. (Suggested for Mature Audiences*), but even more, it agreed to insert a clause into all contracts with exhibitors making it incumbent on the retail end of the business to police the box office. The stipulation was that no one under eighteen could see this film unless accompanied by a parent. The word was that this promise was kept, at least initially, by the theater owners, and created an illusion of seriousness and of high tone about the picture. This muted, to use a favorite word of Valenti, the feeling of scurrility about the language.

In an elegantly worded statement accompanying the approval of the picture by the Board of Directors, the Movie Industry took the burden to its own breast. It said:

> This exemption means exactly that—approval of material in a specific, important film, which would not be approved for a film of lesser quality, or a film determined to exploit language for language's sake. This exemption does

* Although not numerically the first. This distinction belongs to British made, Columbia distributed *Georgy Girl*.

not mean that the floodgates are open for language or other material. Indeed Exemption means precisely the opposite. We desire to allow excellence to be displayed and we insist that films, under whatever guise, which go beyond rational measures of community standards will *not* bear a Seal of Approval.

Somewhere along in here the Legion of Decency had wisely decided to take the flavor of militancy out of its name, and had changed over to the title of National Catholic Office for Motion Pictures. This awkwardly abbreviated into N.C.O.M.P.

The N.C.O.M.P., expected to be *Virginia*'s severest critic, screened the film for a special review group of over eighty people, experts and everyday viewers alike, and in sum, took out its finest feather pen, and rated it "A-IV" (morally unobjectionable for adults, with reservations). One of the consequences of this liberal action by the N.C.O.M.P. was a flareup of indignation on the part of conservative Catholics. In La Jolla, California, a group of twenty-one "outraged Catholic laymen" petitioned bishops, newspapers, and Catholic organizations to help them get rid of the "N.C.O.M. Petants" and "to clean house."

Mike Nichols, the director, was accused of not caring ahead of time whether he got a Code Certificate or not, but he denied this politely, saying that he did not want to bite the hand that freed him.

In sum, the industry got what it wanted, and Valenti's sense of honor was preserved. He was liberated now to spit on his hands, as it were, and begin to take a hard look at that baroque old document, the Code itself.

What he saw was not altogether pretty. There was a holdover provision from the dear dead days beyond recall that read, "Brothels in any clear identification as such may not be shown." Any intelligent meaning had been squashed out of this clause by *The World of Suzie Wong*, but it had been the root of such hypocrisies as calling the fun house in *Mamie*

Stover a social club, in which the sailor boys in Hawaii had to buy tickets to "talk" with the hostesses. There were also comic provisions, such as the one "Children's sex organs are never to be exposed. This provision shall not apply to infants." (The secret information around the P.C.A. quarters was that this stricture was traceable back to a fix on the part of Y. Frank Freeman, when he was head of production at Paramount.)

More troublesome were those clauses which represented blanket prohibitions, such as ". . . a story must not indicate that an abortion has been performed." This clause reflected a certain amount of Catholic theology, and was dangerous to tinker with; but the days of blanket taboos were past. This was the sort of thing that could easily come back to haunt you.

In the midst of considerations like these, hardly before he had time to absorb the shock waves from *Virginia Woolf,* Valenti was struck his second major blow.

ALFIE!

What *Alfie* was all about, to borrow the catch phrase from the popular title song, was that nettlesome clause concerning abortion.

Fundamentally, *Alfie* was a morality play. That is, it carried a strong and eloquent message against the bad life. The bad life, in this case, is a life of sex without love. Alfie was a cockney Don Juan who collected women like ornithologists gathered their specimens. He used them, and threw them aside. He referred to them as his "birds," and tabbed them "it"—"It does a marvelous egg custard." Alfie took, and gave nothing back.

This led to a life of emptiness that, in the eyes of the producer-director Lewis Gilbert, was little better than the life of a dog. To emphasize this point, he framed the film with this symbol. In the very closing shot, he had Alfie straying off down the street, without "me piece o' mind," with a little cur, his counterpart, trotting after him. And in the very earliest frames, he forecasts what's coming by showing a scene of two mongrels perilously close to the suggestion that they were mounting each other. This bit, of course, was in proximity to a sequence of Alfie having a go with a married woman in a parked car. Lest there be any doubt as to what he is doing, he finishes the scene by throwing her her panties.

A picture with so strong a moral point is excused for much grittiness that might be intolerable in a lesser work.

Alfie was one of those increasing cases in which the Code office did not have a script. Therefore, it took the staff by surprise. It dropped, quite literally, out of the blue, having been flown in from England by Paramount. Attending the showing in the projection room were both Valenti and Nizer. In the semi-darkness, one could almost sense their indignation. At the same time, some of us on the staff irritated what was already a sore provocation by openly enjoying the funnier lines. It was clear that there were two sets of opinion here that were at odds.

The next morning, in "huddle," we addressed ourselves formally to the contents of the film. There had been a chance to weigh the issues overnight, and everybody had his dialogue ready.

Chairing the conversation, Valenti asked how many men in the room had children. Several of the staff members raised their hands.

"What age?" he wanted to know, pistoling a finger at me.

"In their teens."

"A daughter?"

"Yes."

"How old?"

"Fifteen."

"Very well, then. Let me put it this way. If you had a choice, which would you rather that she see—*Alfie* or *Virginia Woolf?*"

"In the company of her mother? In controversial films like this—"

"No, no, I don't mean in the company of her mother. I mean if she were to walk in off the street with her boyfriend."

I thought hard. "In that case, then—I'd say *Alfie.*"

Startled, he asked, "Why?"

Groping, I tried to explain. "In the case of *Virginia Woolf,* what would she see? A sick and repellent view of marriage. As if a relationship with a woman were something out of hell, leading to two people tearing each other to shreds. In the case of *Alfie* she'd see something that was fundamentally sound, what I mean is—basically moral."

He interrupted with an impatient gesture. "I'm not asking about morality," he said. "I don't think any man has the right to pass judgment on the rightness or wrongness of another man's actions. What a person does in his private life is his own business. What I'm talking about is taste. What about that abortion scene?"

The abortion scene had been protracted and extremely graphic. But it had ended with Alfie peering down in stark horror at the pitiful remains of the embryo, his child, that had just been taken from his friend's wife. The shock led him to a scene in which, for the first time in his life perhaps, he exhibited feelings toward another human entity. It was a powerful therapeutic encounter, and showed the fact of abortion in all its shabby, cruel reality.

Perhaps, due to overexposure to seamy material, those of us on the staff had become too case-hardened to scenes like these. We tended to feel that the very offensiveness of the sequence was its antidote, and its moral quotient. But Valenti was reflecting the reactions of a more normal audience, and did not care for highly specialized reactions on the part of technicians. Therefore he was nonplussed. He did not want to contradict his staff. But neither did he want to get trapped by a second outrage.

In a reversal of roles, it was we, who had been looking for some relief from permissiveness, who were now defending a notorious piece of material. But we were the old order. Before our eyes, a new set of criteria for judging pictures was being created.

In the end, Valenti felt he had no choice but to insist that an Appeal be taken in the case of *Alfie*. If nothing else, there was a clear-cut violation of the Code in the *fact* of abortion. Nobody had given the Code office the right to say it didn't count because the picture contained an eloquent lesson.

To keep the central question uncomplicated, the Studio compromised on a few of the more glaring details. It agreed to remove the hint of the dogs in the act of sex and left only a preliminary shot of them sniffing intimately at each other. It agreed to take out the shot of Alfie throwing the woman's panties at her, as being too specific. Thirdly, there was a line, tossed by Alfie at Shelley Winters, while he is setting her up for a candid camera shot. Seemingly referring to the camera, but actually being on the make for her, he says, "Well, I've got two positions [for taking pictures]—straight up or sideways, depending on your nationality." This, they thought, was too pointed. And finally, there was a line delivered about a bathtub with a mirror in the ceiling, which would not make sense unless told in conjunction with the whole scene; and which, therefore, we pass over.

Paramount, of course, while conceding the technical violation, wanted another exemption just like Warner Bros. In accepting this petition, Valenti must have felt that he had been blindsided by his household professionals; the quarter from which he had least expected trouble. He rather clearly wanted to make the issue of which he felt he had been deprived in *Virginia Woolf*.

The Board of Directors saw it for Paramount. On August 2, 1966, they granted an exception, labeling the film S.M.A.

The manifesto issued to cover the single case of *Virginia* was breached in about six weeks. Talking about making only one exemption is like talking about eating only one potato chip.

Many will remember that *Alfie* competed strongly for next spring's Oscar, and, for what it is worth, it was called a "highly moral film" by the Protestant publication *The Christian Century*. The N.C.O.M.P. rated it "A-IV," with the comment that "in spite of the light treatment of immoral situations, the film develops the theme that an individual must accept responsibility of his actions."

By Indian summer, Valenti had come up with a sleek, streamlined version of the Code that was less nit-picking and more worthy of a grown-up industry than the old document had been. At the same time, he determined to emphasize the "presence" of the Code in pictures. Toward this end he ordered devised a new symbol, to be printed more prominently in the title sheets of Code-processed films. The new logo was an improvement, looking more global in character, but also something like a reel of film that had been loosened and was ready to go.

The Board of Directors, which was in a mood to give him anything he wanted, approved this new document on September 20, 1966, at 12:30 P.M.

They also accepted the S.M.A. as a fact of life. The premium was put upon art, not on conformity. The intellectuals were pleased. But we were instructed at the same time to apply the S.M.A. cautiously, and to invoke it only in those cases in which the subject matter was "blatant."

This, then, was the house; this was the house; this was the house that Jack built.

21 Götterdämmerung: *Blow-Up*, *Charlie Bubbles*, and *I'll Never Forget What's 'Is Name*

WHAT HAPPENED NOW is that Valenti learned a hard lesson.

He had come into the world of the cinema employing a certain theatricality of style that was common to political circles everywhere. He had a natural flair for self-dramatization. His consciousness of his physical presence, for instance, was betrayed by a restless habit of shooting his expensively-linked French cuffs. Neither was he past making an occasional pit stop at the wall mirror in a secretary's office to recomb his thinning wavy hair.

Not that these things were out of place, either in the cosmos he had just left, or the cosmos he had just joined. Both were show business. Valenti made the transition from the one to the other with obvious ease, and in no time at all was gravitating to the glamorous places where the beautiful people gathered.

But there was one critical difference. In the political world, personal fiat is like a magic wand. It is circled around by a double nimbus: the ability to reward, and the ability to punish, both in almost infinite degree. It produces almost instant conformity.

In the entertainment world, however, it is a different story. Personal glamor bumps up against personal glamor; and personal fiat collides with a self will that is almost infantile at times.

Valenti, who desired to make changes, was to get a tough

indoctrination into the narcissism of the "performing personality" and the stubbornness of the "creative mind."

Not that the movie business did not need changes, or even cry out for them. A lot of the feeling of Camelot had disappeared from the air. There was the faint taint of spoiling lilies. Something needed to be done to revitalize and refresh a still young industry. But what? And how?

A lesson in the intransigence of the movie mentality was afforded Valenti almost immediately. It came from the hands of a fellow Italian, with the elegant name that is so familiar to film goers the world over: Michelangelo Antonioni.

The picture at issue was *Blow-Up* (the aptness of the title being, of course, almost oracular).

The script for this landmark film had been practically incomprehensible. But when a document carries the signature of an illustrious master of the new school, the fact that it is enigmatic only serves to make it seem deeper, not more dense. I tried to explain in a staff report that it was about a young erratic photographer in London, who apparently has taken a picture of a murder by accident. He learns of the killing when he starts to enlarge some candid camera shots he has taken of two clandestine lovers. In blowing up these negatives, however, and thus enlarging reality, the myriad dots that in ultimate hard fact make up the print, become bigger, and more dispersed, and less representative, light light-specks in stellar groups flying apart, until they no longer are what they were, until they are beyond conveying the "thing," and the line between reality and fantasy has become blurred. All in all, the script seemed to be filled with the existential agony of "absurdity" and the frustration of distinguishing the "seeming" from the "real." One had a feeling that the author was fishing in deep and dangerous waters for a new and vital truth of some sort.

On November 14, Geoff and I were approached by a representative of MGM, who asked us if we would be willing to go back to New York, at studio expense, to review the rough cut of this film. We agreed. As Ignatius of Loyola used to say, "It is not hard to obey when we love that which is commanded."

"Very well, then," we were informed, "there are certain understandings. Nobody has seen this film yet—but *no*body. Not the President of the company or anybody. The reason for this is that we have a very temperamental director on our hands, who won't let anybody see it till he is ready. He's one of the 'artistes,' you know?

"*Any*how, the point is this, he has said he won't change one goddam frame of this picture for any living soul. His only obligation, by the terms of his contract, is to turn over a finished cut to the company, and until that time we don't have a *!!@??*!! thing to say. You beginning to get the picture?"

I was curious. "Do the stockholders of MGM know that their executives have turned over investors' money like this? What other business would sign away control of millions—without accountability?"

The fellow shrugged. "Good directors are at such a premium," he confessed, "that they can set their own terms. The company's afraid if it doesn't give him what he wants, he'll take his picture elsewhere. There's nothing very complicated about it really."

"So what're we supposed—just to be puppets on a string?"

"Listen, let's not be so logical about this. Just see the film, and then let's talk."

I wasn't going to wreck a trip to the Big Stem, and a chance to meet so intriguing a personality. "Okay," I conceded.

While we were sitting in the cheerless MGM projection room in mid-Manhattan, waiting for the arrival of the director, we received further instructions. "Remember," we were admonished, "if you have any problems, be discreet. This is a tightly wound man, and if you assault him, he might do anything. He might walk out on the picture, or he might insist that his name be removed from it, or he might even faint—I don't know. Be gentle." It sounded like "my first affair."

By this time the waiting was almost unbearable. Frankly, I

was expecting the arrival of some sort of a saint, if such a concept as a corporate holy man is imaginable. Here was an individual who had paid the great price. He had striven for integrity, authenticity, originality; and as a result had gotten his autonomy. These qualities are come by painfully, by dredging one's viscera, but they hold out the hope that the agony might lead to ecstasy, in the revelation of a gleaming fragment of truth. In a basically money-hungry industry, this is what is most admired, and given the most concessions.

My first reaction to Antonioni when he came into the room was one of failing feelings. He was a small, slender man, gray, and with a countenance so cogged with care that he looked like a walking frown.

An interpreter from his entourage introduced us, and there was an awkward pause. We had not yet seen the film so there was nothing to talk about.

"Unfortunately," said the MGM representative, jumping into the breach, "this is not the color print. It's only the mud print. Those who've seen the dailies say the color is simply gorgeous."

Antonioni leaned over to his interpreter, who poured into his ear what had been said. He nodded his head and waved a cigarette that had a long ash. He said something in Italian, and the interpreter said, "Yes. Let's begin." The lights went down.

A needle of doubt had entered my mind. Antonioni was what in show biz is called a "sufferer." Not only did he have a heavy look, but he had tics galore—a facial twitch and a habit of conducting secret dialogue with himself, shaking his head and making silent gestures without reference to anyone present. I shrugged and sat down to enjoy the film. What good has his search done *him?* I wondered.

Those who saw *Blow-Up* know what kind of a picture it was. It was a kaleidoscopic search for the line of demarcation between fantasy and the actual. The color, eventually, was indeed something very special. There were also master strokes in the technique of film-making. For one thing, nobody in the film was given a name. They were all nameless people. Figures. I think the picture also attempted to say something about self-indulgence. The young photographer was a fellow who followed his every whimsey. It was this precise exaggeration of reality that enlarged it and blew it all out of shape, leading to a loss of recognition, and, ultimately, all the way around the circle back to whimsey. And in the final sequence, in which silent people with painted faces, like mannequins, played a game of tennis without racquets and without balls, the sound of the pocking of racquet strings was real, as well as the noise of the bouncing balls. It tended to leave one giggling giddily. But "enlightened"—about what?

When the lights went up, Geoff and I looked at each other like two coral fish suspended in the sky. "I guess it's got some problems?" he suggested.

I nodded my head yes.

"Eh?" inquired Antonioni, leaning toward his interpreter. The assistant translated. The director kept bobbing his head like an alert bird.

"That scene with the teenage girls. And that scene of lovemaking between his friend and *his* girl," said Geoff. The MGM representative remained mute.

Antonioni raised his hands in cultivated despair. In painful, laborious English he tried to explain that there was nothing sexy about the scene of the teenage models assaulting the photographer. "It is—how you say it?—a frolic, like young goats, like young animals."

Both Geoff and I bit our tongues. We thought we had discerned, in a flashing instant of their nakedness, a glimpse of their pubic areas, but we were loath to say so, lest we seem to be foul-minded and censorious. But we *did* insist that the impression was scored that the two gamboling creatures stripped and playfully raped the photographer. Whether this happened "really" or only in the fantasies of the young man is a moot point.

"This is a bit much for us to approve," we said.

Antonioni sucked on his cigarette thoughtfully. "And the second problem?" he asked.

"The sex affair—it's far too graphic. All that writhing and moaning."

In his broken English, Antonioni did his best to explain. "It shows the girl's inability to be moved, even in the middle of sex. She is saturated with life, so she can't enjoy it. She is using the sight of the photographer to bring herself to climax. But he is so bored that he is unmoved. He ignores her. It is very important."

We conceded this. "But it invades intimacies. It transgresses common candor," we insisted.

Antonioni bowed to the inevitable. "Then there is nothing I can do," he said. He looked around vacantly. After a moment he turned to his interpreter. In soft, clear Italian, he said, *"Non accetto—in principio."* The interpreter looked up. "Yes," he translated quietly, "he cannot accept it in principle."

Antonioni, knowing that the situation was the same with us, and that it was an impasse, said in a halting way, "You have your job to do—and I have mine."

That was it.

We shook hands. We separated.

MGM was now on the spot. The ink was still wet on its signature in support of the new Code. But its desires for respectability were all confounded with its fascination in a provocative new film. The Code stood in the middle.

Reaching into its bag of tricks, the studio came up with a device which was purely sleight of hand. It "discovered" on its books an unused subsidiary, wholly owned. If the picture could be dropped into this slot, the technicalities would all be salvaged. Premier Films, the subsidiary, was not a specific signatory to the Code agreement. Therefore, the corporation would not be violating its pledge were it to distribute a maverick film. Of course the ruse was transparent even to the point of being cynical, since all the machinery of distribution employed by Premier would be the same, step by step, as

MGM's. Most importantly, the profits would flow through the subsidiary pipelines right into the identical corporate pot as the parent company. But the trademark would have been saved. Leo could roar without shame and confusion.

With this manipulation, the ideal of uniform application of the Code was forever wrecked. Henceforth, a company, any company, could go ahead and make anything it wanted. If the completed film were too bold to fit even under the S.M.A., it could be bumped upstairs into the subsidiary, which would be held in reserve for "special situations." Thus, it behooved the Code administrators to move cautiously, lest they force the studios to seek the sanctuary of the subsidiaries too frequently, and thus create a plethora of pictures being circulated over the head of the Code. This, it goes without saying, would eventually alienate the Code, and finally reduce it to zero. As a matter of survival, it was incumbent on the staff to begin to stretch the meaning of "blatant," on the top side, lest too many films get away from the system and render it extinct. The S.M.A. was beginning to creak because of the way it was being forced to include not only the outrageous, but even the near-pornographic.

An accidental counterattack fell into our laps, and we tried to use it to forestall the inevitable. We were called back to MGM in Culver City to see a final version of the disputed scenes. This time the footage was in color, and we got some taste of the powers of sublimation from this simple factor. But as far as we could see, the romp with the teenage models was the same. As for the overly explicit sex affair, it appeared that it had been softened by sly editing. Behind the scenes we negotiated with the studio, and offered to issue a Code Certificate, S.M.A., on the polished footage we saw. It is our opinion, backed by some practical facts, that the studio did an about-face and refused this compromise because it might have brought the editorial changes to the attention of Antonioni. This would have kicked up a tempest. The studio said thank you but no thanks.

Jack Valenti got the message. The company managements were beginning to extort from his hands the powers they had so flamboyantly given him. They were not going to permit him to function in the traditional Code sense.

The picture went out and, despite a N.C.O.M.P. condemnation, was a great success.

The state of bankruptcy was confirmed when Otto Preminger, who had twice before put serious dents in the Code mechanism with *The Moon Is Blue* and *The Man with the Golden Arm,* presented the Code office with a copy of a so-so film called *Hurry Sundown.* There was an assortment of details in this picture, but the one item that stood out glaringly was a scene of Jane Fonda sucking on the mouthpiece of a saxophone in a manner that suggested fellatio. We turned the matter over to Valenti, who saw the film in Preminger's New York apartment, in the company of certain other eminent people. Preminger "voluntarily" trimmed some of the anatomical details of a sex affair. But the "punch" scene involving the saxophone was not only left in, but was selected as the highlight of the advertising campaign.

The final film in this cruel chain of cases is *Charlie Bubbles.* For my part, this was a better than average piece of work, even though it got kiss-of-death notices in the trades, and a lukewarm reception out in the theaters. It had something worthwhile to say on the subject of the boredom of success, and its arrogance too, with clever asides about the arrogance of nonsuccess. It was an episodic, plotless portrait of a couple of days in the life of a rich writer of popular fiction, who had his Rolls Royce convertible, ate in the most posh restaurants, and had his apartment wired with a multicamera closed-circuit TV system so that he could see what was going on in every room at once.

He also had his adoring secretary, played by Liza Minnelli opposite Albert Finney as the writer, who accompanies him on an overnight dash to the North Country. There, he plans to pick up his young son from his estranged wife and take the boy to a football game. The secretary puts up with him in the Midlands hotel and, in a spirit of complete naturalness, offers to make love to him. He, however, is jaded to the point of being joyless and is unable to respond. When he senses her slipping below his waist (and below the frame line of the camera), he glances down, and looks only blank when his hand comes upon her loosened "fall." It is the most passionless "going down" scene conceivable.

Geoff, with the wisdom of an old fox, sensed that the scene would not be resented, because there was no pleasure in it. His reaction was conditioned by a realization, over the years, that the N.C.O.M.P., for one, would tend to look more leniently on a scene of sex without joy, because this echoed its basic orientation that joy was given to insure responsibility, not for hedonism.*

Made uncomfortable by his intuitions, Geoff was caught in a clumsy snare. Officially, he had to make an issue of the clearly suggested fellatio. But practically, he felt that he would get no place. In his thrashing about for a solution, he spent a good part of the rest of the day walking around talking to himself, saying preposterous things he half didn't mean. He declaimed that "if we could just forget honor and all that crap, and get pragmatic, we'd realize that the only time the Code got into trouble was when we refused to pass a picture." He was tired of being known as part of the gang that condemned *The Moon Is Blue,* and annoyed by facing the question "Tell me, why didn't you approve *Blow-Up?*"

By huddle time next morning, Geoff had it all rationalized

---

* A recent proof of this had been the reaction to the film *Cape Fear.* This picture contained a brutal rape that stirred a hue and cry in England and was resented by religious viewing groups generally. Not so the Catholic group, however. The Catholics, by long conditioning, took a more easy attitude toward a sex act that was more accompanied by pain than by gratification.

to the point that he was asking out loud, "What's wrong with inferring she was sucking him off? A few years ago we wouldn't even have allowed the inference of *normal* sex. What if that's the way the public wants to go?" Recovering his senses later, he hastened to add, "I'm only playing devil's advocate, you understand."

Shortly after our review of *Charlie Bubbles,* while the question of a Code Certificate was still in abeyance, Valenti came out to the Coast and into the Code office. Geoff, at that precise time, was doing business at the Academy of Motion Picture Arts and Sciences, where he was a member of the Board of Directors. Like the first mate when the captain is off the ship, I was in automatic charge of the bridge, and I took it in hand to outline our crisis to Valenti.

I was ticking off on one finger after the next the growing problem of fellatio in pictures. "If somebody wanted to trace it all the way back to *Baby Doll,* he probably could make a consistent case," I said. "But more recently, we've had the inference or the suspicion in *Torn Curtain,* then *Hurry Sundown, Bonnie and Clyde,* and now this one, *Charlie Bubbles.*

Valenti was listening carefully, a glint of anger beginning to appear in his eyes, when Geoffrey walked in.

"I'm just summing up our current problem," I told Geoff.

Geoff stopped short. He looked straight at Valenti. "Things've come to a pretty pass," he said, "when people like us have to stand here and discuss oral copulation."

At this point, we freeze-cut the action and go back to collect certain factors that enter into this scene, and make it more comprehensible.

It was one year, almost to the day, that the Board of Directors had endorsed the new, revised Code. During this time, certain changes had been taking place, all having a direct connection with the leakage that was occurring in the area of quality controls.

Mainly, there was a process of depersonalization going on in the film companies. The trend toward conglomerates that was so pronounced in the economy as a whole was touching the studios in a special manner. Paramount was taken over by Gulf and Western Industries. United Artists had been absorbed into the huge Transamerica Corporation. Universal-International, already a subsidiary of M.C.A., was to receive flirtations from Westinghouse Electric, and, when this was frowned on by the Justice Department, by Firestone Tire & Rubber. An important position was taken in MGM by people from Schenley Industries. Avco, the aviation conglomerate, was about to take over Embassy Films. And so it went.

The result of this process was a diffusion of interest at the top. Harry Warner, in the old days, used to use the homely Russian adage that "a fish stinks from its head." With the diminishing of clear and sharp leadership at the head of the industry, authority was seized by individual picture makers at the actual shop level. Directors became tyrannous in their demands and in their assertions of rights. They pushed for liberties that were sometimes all out of proportion to their talents, so that men of secondary ability were forced to substitute shock for skill, and to pawn off boldness for inventiveness. And since anything innovative was the vogue, the public was giving the appearance of standing behind these men, making them seem like pioneers in the opening of brave new worlds.

With the power to administer a halfway efficient Code being progressively drained from him, Valenti began to squirm over his connection with it, and then began to show signs of outright disenchantment with it. He began to protest that he was finding it necessary to "dissemble" in his social circles regarding the content of films. Little by little he began to disassociate himself, and started protesting that people thought his whole time was taken up with Code matters, whereas in plain fact less than 10 per cent of his attention was devoted to this subject. To confirm this point, he began ranging abroad, and is said to have negotiated a contract with Italy for the import of American films on terms that were exceptionally favorable. He began redeeming his promise to foment interest in creativity, and accepted engagements at several large universities to participate in film forums in the company of eminent directors. And, although he seemed pleased to step into the limelight of the Academy Awards ceremony his first year, he eschewed it like a disillusioned suitor the second spring around.*

Valenti, in his effort to tone down the image of his involvement with the Code, began to fall back on his bread-and butter topic of conversation and stressed his familiarity with the President, giving inside glimpses of the White House and the awesome office of the Chief Executive. Unfortunately, this had the partial effect of not making him seem his own man, but rather aggravated the feeling of an individual who subordinated himself to others. This made him appear like a creature of those elements in the Industry who wanted to denature the Code. So impoverished, then, did his name become around Hollywood, that, in the fall of 1967, the annual issue of *Variety* undertook to print a poem entitled *Ode to Revised Motion Picture Code*. Excerpting from it, it went:

> *In urban nabes and drive-in glades,*
>   *The screen at last is free,*
> *Four-letter words, explicit verbs*
>   *Titillate tots of three.*
> *With derrières and pubic hairs*
>   *Blithely exposed today,*
> *When they say "he went thataway,"*
>   *Means the hero turned gay.*

---

* This event, incidentally, was dear to the heart of Eric Johnston, who twice bestowed the Oscar for the best foreign film, in enhancement of his image as a globalist. But his Americanistic orientation made mincemeat of such corporate names as Sochiku Co. Ltd., and A. B. Svensk Filmindustri, and, at a luncheon, Jawaharlal Nehru. It came to an end after he broke open the Academy envelope, and announced that the winner that year was *Through a Dark Glassly!*

It concluded:

> *Let villains win and reward sin*
> *With riches aplenty*
> *Now girls can strip or take "a trip"*
> *Thank you, Jack Valenti!*

In hindsight, of course, it appears for what it is; a trifle cruel. But Valenti was now a man at bay.

Thus it was that when Geoff laid it on the line that the Code was faced with an impasse involving oral sex, Valenti answered in anguish, "If your staff thinks this material is unacceptable—and goodness knows you're surrounded by the most liberal group of men ever—then you can't approve it, no matter what. The objections from the audiences may not be forthcoming, but they will be, they will be. And if the roof falls in on these guys' heads, we'll simply say we told you so. I'm going to see Lew Wasserman and tell him this, and see if he's seen the picture. [It was U-I, Wasserman's company, that had applied for a Code Seal on *Bubbles*.] But unfortunately, any muscle we might apply to them now would be inefficient. The public doesn't raise a hue and cry to sex. To violence yes, and the attack on authority. But not sex. I'll tell you, I wanted to go to the mat with Otto Preminger about *Hurry Sundown,* but prudence dictated against it. He *wanted* me to get into a controversy with him, so he'd have an issue to promote his picture. Goodness knows he tried hard enough. He kept running around going on television and making statements trying to provoke me, but I held back because that's what he wanted. I had to swallow it rather than play into his hands."

One can imagine the difficulty a mannered man like Valenti would have, trying to explain the nature of the objections in Otto's picture. Even if he were allowed to use the word fellatio on TV or in the news media, he would hardly be allowed to translate it into its more common and readily understood vulgarisms.

From Lew Wasserman there came complete silence. The request for the Code Seal was canceled, and the picture dropped into U-I's subsidiary, Regional Films. And confirming Geoff's experienced guess, and Wasserman's educated gamble, the picture was not condemned by the N.C.O.M.P. It was rated "A-III." It is a solid surmise that the cheerlessness and the world-weariness of the scene had much to do with this rating. The picture did not seem to do well at the box office, fellatio or not.

The dam now broke.

The picture makers, a substantial number of them anyway, having more or less high-graded the veins of "normal" sex and what one might call "normal" violence, began to erupt toward the peripheries and to exploit the weird and the sick and the fringe of human experience.

We were instructed to forget the "blatant" criterion for the application of the S.M.A. A new semantic definition of this label was found. It was to be considered a sort of "early warning system" to parents who might want to be put on the alert regarding the suitability of the film for their children. The responsibility of controlling the recreational fare of their charges still rested with them. The movie industry was bailing out and trying to disclaim accountability. The result of this new instruction was that we jammed as many films as possible into the S.M.A. category, until it burgeoned into 60 per cent of all films processed by the Code.

Weakness at the policing level produced impudence at the film-making level.

A vivid example occurred hardly three weeks after the discussion about *Charlie Bubbles*. A film was presented to us from England, by U-I again, called *I'll Never Forget What's 'Is Name.*

This film had some merits. It opened with a fellow striding

along the street with a lethal-looking ax over his shoulder. Grim of face, he walks into a plush advertising agency, invades an office, and begins to smash up an expensive desk—his. He is sick of life in the velvet web. He is going to seek out "honesty," which in his state of autism is a job on the small magazine where he started.

The theme of the picture is surely valid, stating that it is impossible to return home, to go back to original simplicity, to find Eden. In the end, the lead in *What's 'Is Name* surrenders, rejoins the exploitation world he tried to forsake, and refinds his wife, whom he has temporarily deserted.

In the course of telling this story, there is a long encounter with a girl who is a virgin, who is afraid of sex, and who is unable to give in. She lives in a houseboat on the Thames River, where our lead joins her.

He campaigns with her, breaks down some of her defenses, and the moment finally arrives when she is ready to surrender. They start to kiss passionately, "eating" each other's lips. The fever mounts and they force each other to the floor. He rolls over half on her, his hand finds its way up inside her sweater, and he begins fondling her breast. As she is going into passion, he slides below frame, with the clear and unmistakable inference that he is "going down" on her, and she goes into orgasm, very specifically and very erotically. In her writhing, she knocks over a can of paint just as she achieves climax, and the white goo spills toward her, and her fingers are immersed in it.

When the picture was all over, Geoff Shurlock stood up and remarked, "What a nasty picture." He then began to suppose that there were some scenes in it we'd be unwilling to approve, even with the S.M.A. "Yes," everybody agreed, "especially that scene in the houseboat."

"Yes," confirmed Geoff, standing with his arms more or less hugging himself, as though he were cold, "all that breast fondling."

"Sure. And the going down on her."

"The what?"

"The cunnilingus. Where he slides down beneath the frame. What do you think he's doing?"

Geoff began scratching his opposite arm, and a simplicitous smile dallied around the corners of his mouth. "Oh, is *that* what he was doing?" he exclaimed. "I couldn't figure it out. I didn't know what was going on."

All eyes flashed to each other. Was he deliberately blanking out his mind, after his good guess about *Charlie Bubbles?* Or had the scene truly gone over his head? He was beginning to show signs of decay. He was starting to cup his hands to his ears and say, "Eh?"

Reading the looks on everybody's face in the projection room, he suddenly discerned the staff's opinion. Whatever the reason for his temporary obtuseness, he instantly firmed up.

Going to his office, he called Bill Hornbeck, the chief editor of the studio. "Hello, Bill?" he greeted him in a raised voice. "Lissen, what's getting into those goddam British? They're going crazy."

Bill must have made inquiries about the scene in question. "That scene on the houseboat," said Geoff. He listened for a moment. "No. I mean beginning with that kissing, where he starts twisting his tongue around to get into her. All those oral shenanigans. Yeah, including where he slides under the frame line and starts eating her. What? Yeah. That. I'll tell you Bill, you'n I've lived too long. We didn't think in our youth we'd be spending our old age talking about cock sucking!"

It was clear that the studio, relying on the correctness of its gamble with *Bubbles,* was not going to yield. It canceled the request for the Code Certificate and slid the picture over into its subsidiary, Regional. It had its "A-III" on the previous picture to prove it was right in taking a stand a second time.

Geoff, trying to figure out what to do about "oral copulation," groped desperately. "Well, they'll put that stuff out in their art subsidiaries, and we'll just wait and see if the public raises any objections," he declared. "If they don't—well, maybe we should just pass it. We're not going to be the guys on white horses, riding around objecting and looking foolish."

Shades of the man from la Mancha in his tatterdemalion, and waving a corkscrew sword.

The N.C.O.M.P. did not react so good-naturedly toward *What's 'Is Name*. It condemned the film, stating, "This film is seriously delinquent in its introduction of a sequence of cunnilingual sex, which can only be seen as yet another instance of the game of one-upsmanship as it is played today by some movie makers in the name of free expression."

Michael Winner, the director of *What's 'Is Name,* was in Vienna at the time this announcement was made. In a fighting mood, he said that the Catholic statement was "unrealistic" and "offensive." Continuing, he translated his own scene. "First of all," he said, "the scene involved is deliberately and totally inexplicit as to what is going on. (One might ask, if it were all this foggy, how did he know so well what scene was referred to?) The photography rests on the clothes, bust, and head of a young girl. If the N.C.O.M.P. wishes to assume that cunnilingual sex is going on off screen, that is entirely a matter of their imagination. That is not what I, or the actors, imagined was going on off the screen, but to each his own."

(Ha, ha.)

Wasserman later admitted the apparent inconsistency of the Legion stumped him. As far as he could see, the only difference between *Bubbles* and *What's 'Is Name* was that in the one case, a woman goes down on a man, and in the other, a man goes down on a woman. Apparently, then, one must conclude that if the man is on the bottom, it's okay. If he's on top, it's not.

A veritable blizzard of cases now descended on the theaters of the land, and the screens were filled with every thinkable subject in a splurge that can only be described as exhibitionism. The material ranged through *The Fox,* as well-regarded import from Canada, based on a novelette by D. H. Lawrence with elements of lesbian love-making and masturbation; all the way up to *I Am Curious (Yellow)*, the Swedish import, which is the current but transitory symbol of the ultimate in screen sexuality. The Federal Government attempted to have this film declared obscene. It was blocked from entering the U.S.A. by the customs inspectors. It was declared obscene under the meaning of the present law by a jury in the Southern District of New York; reversed by a split panel of five judges in an appeal to the Second Circuit. After due consideration, the Treasury decided not to carry the issue any further, and the action lapsed. The picture went into general release.

There were many other cases, but the list is tedious. Bob Hope summed it all up when, as master of ceremonies of the 1968 Academy Awards, he quipped, "Last year we gave you the dirty words. This year we give you the pictures to go with them."

There was a moment of rage and revulsion throughout the land after the assassination of Robert F. Kennedy. The feeling spilled over onto whatever was violent and whatever was opposed to public order. Certain films came under critical scrutiny and were disclaimed for elements of savagery. Most frequently blamed were the spate of "Italian Westerns," a fad in which men were knocked over like tenpins, and sadism abounded. They were easy targets of criticism, because no one was around to defend them, and the distributors were laughing all the way to the bank. But the spate of death-dealing set responsible men to thinking, and to asking, "Are we really that corrupt, that we should leave our houses and go down to a theater and be entertained by all that flowing of blood?" It was a sobering question.

The next two most mentioned candidates in this unpopularity derby were both from MGM: *Point Blank*, which was poisoned by the mental violence that was generated by the acting of Lee Marvin, and *The Dirty Dozen*, a film from the sometimes primitive director, Robert Aldrich, which terminates in a mass incineration of helpless human beings, little less than a Götterdämmerung.

Encouraged by this public revolt, Valenti seized the opportunity to address himself to the companies, studio by studio, and to plead one last time for moderation. He described what was obviously his man-to-man experience with Antonioni. He had apparently begged his compatriot to make some trims in *Blow-Up*, but the stubborn director replied that this would be impossible, "since every frame in that film has been dug up from my guts. [Valenti's hands illustrated.] There's not a single millimeter that's unessential."

"However," went on Valenti with great earnestness, "the film went on to England, where the official censor voiced objections to the scene. The director repeated his protests, and used the same arguments. John Trevelyan, the Secretary of the British Board of Film Censors, bowed stiffly. 'Very good,' he agreed, 'we respect this authenticity. We'd not touch a frame of your work. Unfortunately, you'll have to show it elsewhere, for you can't show it here.' "

Antonioni (presumably) then suddenly discovered that there were certain possibilities that he had overlooked. He found that he could make certain compromises that would clear the way for a mutual understanding. The film was altered, and nobody seemed to notice the difference.

Valenti used this example to stiffen the resolve of executives to exercise their managerial authority and their discretion. They all solemnly nodded and intimated that they were converted. Not all. A few went away muttering. And before the rest of them could say Mrs. Robinson, they had reverted to the sorry old game of one-downsmanship. In the end, Jack Warner summed it up in his own inimitable way. "The studios," he said, "now have clean toilets and dirty pictures."

By the end of 1968, the handwriting on the wall was obvious. Valenti had declared that he would not preside over a futility. For two and a half years, he had struggled to put some sense in censorship. But fate, and the force of events, coupled with the defects of human nature, had reduced the venerable old Code to the condition of a groveling pulp. It shamed those who had custodianship over it.

In an act of mercy, Valenti put a gun to the poor thing's head, and gave it the *coup de grace*.

It went without a whimper.

L'Envoi: "Where Now, Brown Cow?"

WHAT NOW?

Well, nature abhors a vacuum; and the social order is part of nature (animate). Therefore, the question raises interesting speculations in a society like ours.

We are a people in the throes of an intricate experiment in statehood. Some may fall into the trap of thinking that we are, after a couple of hundred years, locked into an eternal orbit, and that we are destined to immortality. Not so. It is a sobering thought that no state ever, from the dawn of history, has lasted as a permanence. In the perspective of the evolution of civilizations, we are still in the experimental stage. We have to prove ourselves in the sight of the future by continuing to exist.

To stay in existence, for us, means a constant process of fine tuning to find and to hold the middle ground between the two polarities of Responsibility and Freedom. These two opposites are the Scylla and Charybdis of democracy. To love one at the expense of the other is to fail, and to be doomed. In the seeking of orderliness in our society, we are constantly balancing between the extremes of usurpation and abdication by our governing agencies, be they public or private. Control, of ourselves or of our institutions, is, for us, a matter of extreme skill, and of unusual maturity.

However, in our dedication to the propositions of democracy, we are allowed certain predilections. We may not be able to love freedom *at the expense* of responsibility, but we can and do love it *more*. This means, in the concrete, that whenever occasions arise in which it is permissible to give the benefit of the doubt to one side or the other, our natural drift is always in favor of freedom. And because we have race memories, and are conscious of the tyrannies of the Past from which we sought escape, we are willing to bear the consequences of many insults to the body of society so long as the liberty to act is not impaired. Restraints, even in favor of order, are always suspect.

From this mentality, it is easy to rationalize self-indulgence. By a strange anomaly, we are in one sense a massively regulated people. On the other hand, we are steeped in self-gratifications almost beyond belief. For us, the maintenance of a middle ground is as difficult as trying to pick up a puddle of mercury between the tips of the fingers.

One thing is clear, however. In a climate of permissiveness, like the present, there is no body of respected opinion that forms a consensus on the side of controls. Instead, one hears slogans on all sides that are very popular with the electorate, but which are the fruit of a kind of anti-intellectualism that is against the hard think, and the honest think.

One is confronted, for instance, with the indignant demand, echoing Juvenal, as to "who is going to protect us from the protectors?" Built into the very marrow of our society is the answer to this shallow conundrum, and that is that our remedy lies in a system of checks and balances. As long as those in positions of power are subject to recall and are disenfranchisable, how can they turn into despots?

In like manner, it is said, "If it doesn't hurt *them,* it won't hurt me," meaning, of course, that what is sauce for the censors is sauce for the ganderers. There is some merit in this thought. However, I think that it is not the state of the question. The problem is not with this scene or that, or with whether any particular one is going to "hurt" anybody. An individual all that susceptible is probably going to be hurt anyway. No. The problem is with the accumulative process, in which a tyranny is set up of sordid competition for lowest common denominators, in which writer is set against writer, and creative mind against creative mind in a contest first for the bold, then the shocking, then the sickly fringe, and then, lastly, the corrupt. It is degrading to society to be party to a race into the lurid. This is what happened in the case of the late Roman theater, and it was symbolic of what was happening to the culture. The stage was, at one and the same time, both the victim and the stimulator of a malaise that denatured a whole people, and made them easy prey of outside forces.

So also with the old whiz that it is against the American grain for anyone to try to tell adults what they can see and read. Aside from the fact that there is an improper amalgam here, since reading and seeing are not always the same thing, the plaint is, more importantly, a prime example of poor thinking, in that it attempts to confound self-regulation with a dictatorial desire to regulate others. Even a child could see that if the editor of the New York *Times* deletes certain news that he judges not fit to print, he is not thereby "telling adults what they can read and what they can't." There is a certain fitness in what he does that is so obvious that it almost takes a deliberate act of naïveté to twist it out of shape.

More aptly, some will argue that the techniques employed by the movie industry are *fatuously* called "self-regulation." The argument goes, "If Antonioni did not voluntarily make alterations in his own film, how can the editing of *Blow-Up* be described as 'self'-control?" There is only one flaw to the question. The film is not Antonioni's. Surely it bears his signature. But that is what he has sold. He is, to put it plainly, not anything else but a contractee. Had he, in a spurt of altruism, put up his own money, as well as his time and his talents, then he would be completely at liberty to gamble with his very own product. But when he is only surrogate for the resources of others, then it is pompous to attribute to him the prerogatives of ownership. The Executive, which is the proxy for the investor, has every right to exercise quality controls either directly or through designees, and this is properly called "self-regulation."

Management, at the present time, is using violent evasive measures to avoid this function, and is putting discretion back into the laps of the patrons. In place of the defunct Code, the Motion Picture Association has initiated a system of classification, whereby the Industry claims it has discharged its obligations toward the public, by "informing" it. "We will no longer be your baby sitters," it says.

The whole argument sounds very much like the protestations of the smugglers of the early West who brought whiskey and guns to the Indians and then said, "What do you mean I'm responsible for those people in the covered wagons? Indians are grown up. They know what they're doing. What do you want me to do? Run their lives?"

A new legal concept has been broached that may someday be applicable to this situation, and that is the idea of "obtrusiveness." According to this theory, to disseminate publicly material that is near pornographic, and to make it both notorious and available, may be the equivalent of morally forcing it on the society.

Lastly, some say that too much of a fuss is made about sex, and not enough attention is given to violence, which is what threatens to destroy us. Those who argue this way will point to our Puritan background and claim that the suppression of sex produced a psychological gap that had to be filled with something else, and that something was brutality. We are turning into barbarians. A little more pleasure in each other would make us more sentimentally disposed and would melt away the urge to violence.

Aside from the fact that this would only stop fighting between men and women (which is not the problem), it would appear that, for the rest, the whole notion is merely wishful thinking. Perhaps that is why it was taken up, as a last resort, by the Flower Children. But the contradiction of the whole idea lies in the fact that today, when we have more freedom in the area of sex than ever, not only in books, magazines, the theater and the screen, but in our private lives as well, and even in our attitudes toward homosexuality and other forms of "non-normal" sex, we are at the same time more violent than ever before, with riots on the campuses and in the streets, assassinations, and wars. The malignancy is global and afflicts countries that can never be accused of having been puritanical. Had not the psychiatrists been trying to warn us and to tell us that violence *is* sex, only extended; and that sadism and masochism are only sicknesses in the order of sexuality? The common denominator between sex and violence may very well be self-indulgence. This is what they both seem to share. A habit of self-gratification leads inexorably to bacchanal, jade, and finally to infantile rage.

The new classification system, which rates all films "G," "M," "R," or "X" in terms of suitability of the material for various levels of audiences, has created a scheme in which just about everything is now possible in motion pictures. Judging from the first crop of films that introduced this system, and surmising from those that are waiting in the wings still unreleased, the term "possible" is very quickly being turned into "actual." Jack Valenti, who introduced the system, is a realist, and knows that the system is imperfect, "but you cannot get perfection in this world, my friend." Its main drawback may be that it is nothing else than an exercise in an American brand of the old black magic, in that it seeks to find a niche for everything that comes along, and then presumes that by "naming" it, it is brought under control of the conjurers.

Maybe it is just as well, because we seem to be heading into a whole new complex of mores, especially sex mores, anyway. Romain Gary, the popular French novelist who spent a good deal of time in Hollywood, had a peculiar and mystifyingly apt adjective for what seems to be coming up. He said that our sex practice was likely to become more free and "vestal." He may be right. All the value systems based on the fact that, through the centuries, man was a "landed" creature are beginning to dissolve in proportion to his release from dependence on the earth. And with the Nietzschean dogma that "God Is Dead" becoming more true, in various senses, every day, we may have to go back to some kind of Garden of Eden, and become innocent, and begin pretty much all over again.

In celebrating our new-found freedom, however, it behooves us not to confuse mature material with the effluvia of adolescence. Geoff Shurlock, who finally retired, summed it up very nicely one day for a stunned producer. "Hooray!" he said. "We've achieved the ultimate. At last we can say 'shit'!"

And if the Executive may be answerable for some dereliction in the field of self-regulation, it has to be remembered, in compassion, that no men can be better than their environment. In the long run, in our kind of culture, the public gets what it wants. No, worse. It gets what it deserves.

As for the Industry, it cannot be forgotten that all literatures, and all art forms, eventually peak out and begin to decay. This starts when the original élan that animated the form and stung it into blossom loses its upward thrust, and begins to become self-conscious and aware of its own details and techniques. A prime example of this phenomenon is the rococo school of architecture and painting. The style became so engrossed in acanthus leaves as to ultimately get lost in a jungle of scrolls, whorls, and nonentities.

The Movie Industry was an original form, sometimes resembling Art, sometimes the Carnival. But it was filled with dynamisms, the likes of which the world has seldom seen. Now, however, it is beginning to become turned in on itself, and is displaying a morbid tendency to experiment in bizarre techniques and bizarre material. It is not peaking out so much as freaking out.

If the public is going to accept what is appearing on the screen with a certain dumb insolence concerning its own fate, then it will be the victim of certain exactions. In a process of moral decay, we create our own monsters. We make the tyrants with which we will have to live tomorrow. The character of the tyrants is preprogrammed. One extreme generates the other.

If we do not learn from history, we will be condemned to relive it. What history teaches us is (as Arnold Toynbee points out) that of twenty-one civilizations that died, only two were brought to an end by conquest from without. All the others crumbled and fell apart from within. The dying begins when the *populus* no longer cares.

And, as Lawrence Gould has admonished, when the end comes, there will be no flags flying, no bands playing. The end will come quietly, in the silence of the night—like the knock of police-state knuckles on the door.

End Notes

END NOTE A
THE BAD SEED

THE REASON for the rejection of *The Bad Seed* is interesting, if for no other reason than that it dispels the notion that the only subject of concern for the Code staff was sex.

Technically, the script was rejected as being in violation of the "Special Regulations on Crime," Section 12:

> Pictures dealing with criminal activities, in which minors participate, or to which minors are related, shall not be approved if they incite demoralizing imitation on the part of youth.

The central character of the story was an eight-year-old girl, with no apparent conception of the difference between right and wrong, who successfully drowns one of her schoolmates and later burns a mature man to death. What kind of punishment could be devised that would counteract the obnoxious influence of this kind of story on susceptible children?

But the main concern was a philosophical one: namely, that the script presented a little creature with an inherited, perverted will, a disposition of soul that was transmitted through the seed, which would make her immune from moral judgment.

It was a foreshadowing of the idea of incarnate evil, later intimated in *Rosemary's Baby*.

END NOTE B
THE SUGGESTIVE AND THE
QUESTIONABLE

1964

TAMAHINE (MGM) Nude shot of female lead. Eliminated and approved.

WHAT A WAY TO GO! (20th Century-Fox) Nude bathing scene, scene of male lead starting to milk a bull. Bathing scene superimposed with a sign saying "Censored," and approved. Bull scene allowed.

YOUNG CASSIDY (MGM) Two questionable sex scenes. Both scenes re-edited and approved.

LILITH (Columbia) Questionable sex scene. Shortened and darkened in printing. Approved.

SHOT IN THE DARK (UA) Questionable scene in nudist camp. Deletions made in scenes of nude couple riding in car. Approved.

OUTRAGE (MGM) Questionable line of dialogue, Allowed and approved.

THE ROUNDERS (MGM) Shot of bare female posteriors. Eliminated and approved.

1965

MOLL FLANDERS (Paramount) Considerable re-editing of sex scenes and scenes of scantily clothed female lead. Approved.

ZORBA THE GREEK (20th Century-Fox) Nude love-making, long shot of nude male lead from rear. Allowed and approved.

In Harm's Way. (Paramount) Questionable line, "Screw the captain." Allowed and approved.

Synanon (Columbia) Scene of actual injection of heroin. Allowed and approved.

The Hill (MGM) Pervading flavor of sadistic brutality, some suggestive dialogue. Two cuts made in dialogue, approved.

Young Dillinger (Allied Artists) Overall flavor of gangster violence. Deletions made in some of the more excessively violent scenes. Approved.

The Sandpiper (MGM) Scene of semi-exposure of female lead's breasts. Re-edited and approved.

The Money Trap (MGM) Sex-suggestive bedroom sequence. Some deletions made and approved.

The Knack (UA) Suggestive sex dialogue. Allowed and approved.

Fog (Columbia) Somewhat vulgar hand gesture. Allowed and approved.

The Pawnbroker (Landau) Nudity. Basic position of the P.C.A. upheld, but an exception granted.

1966

The Chase (Columbia) Excessive brutality in one scene, use of expression "son of a bitch." Some deletions in brutality; expression allowed and approved.

The Silencers (Columbia) Excessive sex suggestiveness. Considerable shortening of bathing and undressing scenes. Approved.

Modesty Blaise (20th Century-Fox) Phallic symbol. Eliminated.

Who's Afraid of Virginia Woolf? (WB) Language outside of usual bounds of Code requirements. Two cuts in dialogue; picture taken before Appeals Board. Approved with the understanding that nobody under eighteen would be admitted unless accompanied by an adult.

ALFIE (Paramount) Abortion scene. Taken to Appeals Board; approved with agreement that film would be advertised for adult audiences.

GEORGY GIRL (Columbia) Sex scenes. Approved provided picture carried newly established S.M.A. label.

WHAT DID YOU DO IN THE WAR DADDY? (UA) Vulgar arm gesture. Approved.

1967
BLOW-UP (MGM) Two sex scenes. Antonioni refused to make cuts; company released film through subsidiary, Regal Films, without Code Seal.

HURRY SUNDOWN (Paramount) Several sex-suggestive scenes. Company refused to make cuts; picture eventually approved with S.M.A. label.

FOR A FEW DOLLARS MORE (UA) Violent and sadistic Western made in Italy. Approved. No S.M.A.

BEDAZZLED (20th Century-Fox) Shot of naked breasts. Approved. S.M.A.

1968
BARBARELLA (Paramount) Montage of nude shots of Jane Fonda behind main title. Approved with S.M.A. New classification system initiated subsequently.

Of this entire list, only three pictures ever reached the level of a formal Appeal, namely, were presented to the Board of Directors of the Motion Picture Association (together with their satellites) for a decision as to their acceptability. These three pictures were *Virginia Woolf, Alfie,* and *The Pawnbroker.* What happened to the first two is obvious from narrations elsewhere in this text. What happened to *The Pawnbroker* is a tidbit that may be of interest to scholars and cynics alike.

The elements of this picture that came into question were several scenes showing the exposed breasts of two different women, one, the wife of the pawnbroker in a Nazi extermination camp, and secondly, a Negro whore. Without attempting to comment on the human values at stake, suffice it to say that the resolution to the issue was that the Board of Directors felt there should be at least a token cut made. They directed Geoff Shurlock to negotiate with the film maker, Ely Landau, for some deletions. Landau asked Geoff for suggestions. Geoff shrugged his shoulders. In desperation, he remembered that the British system is to be more tolerant toward nudity that is motionless, and less liberal toward nudity that is active and mobile. Grasping for a straw, he pointed out to Landau that he might inspect one scene in which the Negro woman moved. Perhaps that could be deleted.

Landau came back with the word that he had examined the scene most carefully, and that he could not do without it. The very most he could sacrifice would be a few frames off the end of the scene. Geoff seized on the offer. "That's cuts" he declared, "and what they asked for is cuts. Technically that should suffice. I'll be able to tell them you made cuts as requested."

It is to be presumed that the film maker made the corrections as promised. But it is doubtful whether anybody went back to check.

END NOTE C
ERIC JOHNSTON

In Eric Johnston's time, there was a period when a system of barter had to be created that was reminiscent of the old Hanseatic League. These seems to have been such dealings as using frozen dollars to buy Spanish olive oil, which in turn was traded for Argentine beef, and eventually into some commodity wanted by an American buyer who would pay dollars for it. Some of the reasons for the problem of "runaway production" lay in the availability of dollars abroad. In a manner of speaking, Hollywood's profits were turned into tools to subsidize the creation of rival film industries. The drainage threatened to obliterate Hollywood. The threat was not lessened by the steep demands of the Hollywood labor unions, which seemed to have a proclivity to toy with the goose that laid the golden egg.

It is obvious that favorable connections with the White House were more than valuable in conducting business in these areas. Even in domestic issues it was a source of prestige and charisma, and allowed for a more facile settlement of such problems as the threat of strikes, tax legislation, public relations, and the like. To heighten this connection, President Eisenhower sent Eric Johnston as his special envoy in the Arab-Israeli water dispute, involving riparian rights on the Jordan River; and as a personal representative to the Crimea to negotiate with Premier Khrushchev regarding a cultural-exchange program between the Soviet Union and the U.S.A. This acquired status had its benefits in that it allowed Johnston to deal directly, person to person, with General Franco and the Premier of Italy in eliciting from these countries favorable contractual terms for the conduct of the movie business. As a matter of poignant fact, the whole process ended in a minor tragedy.

When J.F.K. unseated the Republicans for the Presidential chair, Eric Johnston, no Democrat, lost his favored-nation status in a twinkling. Those of us who had some remote acquaintance with the facts of the matter often wondered whether Arthur Houghton had anything to do with it. Arthur outlived everybody. Furthermore, his memory of having been fired from his job on the Code by Johnston remained green and bright. It was a question, and a reasonable surmise, that Arthur, no shrinking violet, had done his bit in jaundicing the mind of Joe Kennedy, the father, about Eric Johnston. Naturally, when the son became President, this evaluation carried over into the White House, and the President of the Motion Picture Association was suddenly on the outside looking in.

So great a personal blow was this to Eric Johnston that the office personnel in Washington reported that he took refuge in a sad ruse. He would leave word with the switchboard operator that he was going over to Pennsylvania Avenue for personal business, as in the old days. He would then disappear and skulk some place in hiding, confident that nobody could call the Presidential office to verify his presence. The next day he would come into the M.P.A.A. headquarters, a plush old mansion on "I" Street, all smiles and optimism, creating the illusion of having strolled once again through the corridors of power. It is a second fair surmise that the pressure of tactics like these contributed to his rather untimely death not long afterward.

PREAMBLE

The Motion Picture Production Code was formulated and formally adopted by The Association of Motion Picture Producers Inc., (California) and The Motion Picture Association of America, Inc., (New York) in March, 1930.

Motion picture producers recognize the high trust and confidence which have been placed in them by the people of the world and which have made motion pictures a universal form of entertainment.

They recognize their responsibility to the public because of this trust and because entertainment and art are important influences in the life of a nation.

Hence, though regarding motion pictures primarily as entertainment without any explicit purpose of teaching or propaganda, they know that the motion picture within its own field of entertainment may be directly responsible for spiritual or moral progress, for higher types of social life, and for much correct thinking.

During the rapid transition from silent to talking pictures they realized the necessity and the opportunity of subscribing to a Code to govern the production of talking pictures and of reacknowledging this responsibility.

On their part, they ask from the public and from public leaders a sympathetic understanding of their purposes and problems and a spirit of cooperation that will allow them the freedom and opportunity necessary to bring the motion picture to a still higher level of wholesome entertainment for all the people.

367

The Production Code

GENERAL PRINCIPLES

1. No picture shall be produced which will lower the moral standards of those who see it. Hence the sympathy of the audience shall never be thrown to the side of crime, wrong-doing, evil or sin.

2. Correct standards of life, subject only to the requirements of drama and entertainment, shall be presented.

3. Law, natural or human, shall not be ridiculed, nor shall sympathy be created for its violation.

PARTICULAR APPLICATIONS

I. CRIMES AGAINST THE LAW*

These shall never be presented in such a way as to throw sympathy with the crime as against law and justice or to inspire others with a desire for imitation.

1. **Murder**
   a. The technique of murder must be presented in a way that will not inspire imitation.
   b. Brutal killings are not to be presented in detail.
   c. Revenge in modern times shall not be justified.

2. **Methods of Crime** should not be explicitly presented.
   a. Theft, robbery, safe-cracking, and dynamiting of trains, mines, buildings, etc., should not be detailed in method.
   b. Arson must be subject to the same safeguards.
   c. The use of firearms should be restricted to essentials.
   d. Methods of smuggling should not be presented.

3. **The illegal drug traffic** must not be portrayed in such a way as to stimulate curiosity concerning the use of, or traffic in, such drugs; nor shall scenes be approved which show the use of illegal drugs, or their effects, in detail.**

4. **The use of liquor** in American life, when not required by the plot or for proper characterization, will not be shown.

II. SEX

The sanctity of the institution of marriage and the home shall be upheld. Pictures shall not infer that low forms of sex relationship are the accepted or common thing.

*See Special Regulations on Treatment of Crime

**As amended by resolution of the Board of Directors, September 11, 1946.

368

1. **Adultery and Illicit Sex,** sometimes necessary plot material, must not be explicitly treated or justified, or presented attractively.

2. **Scenes of Passion**
    a. These should not be introduced except where they are definitely essential to the plot.
    b. Excessive and lustful kissing, lustful embraces, suggestive postures and gestures are not to be shown.
    c. In general, passion should be treated in such manner as not to stimulate the lower and baser emotions.

3. **Seduction or Rape**
    a. These should never be more than suggested, and then only when essential for the plot. They must never be shown by explicit method.
    b. They are never the proper subject for comedy.

4. **Sex perversion** or any inference of it is forbidden.*

5. **White slavery** shall not be treated.**

6. **Miscegenation** (sex relationship between the white and black races) is forbidden.

7. **Sex hygiene** and venereal diseases are not proper subjects for theatrical motion pictures.***

8. Scenes of **actual child birth,** in fact or in silhouette, are never to be presented.

9. **Children's sex organs** are never to be exposed.

---

*Amended in Oct. 1961 to permit "sex aberration" when treated with "care, discretion, and restraint." Note the switch from the word "perversion" and the latent fear of legal consequences in its employment.

**Subsequently changed to read: "The methods and techniques of prostitution and white slavery shall never be presented in detail, nor shall the subjects be presented unless shown in contrast to right standards of behavior. Brothels in any clear identification as such may not be shown."

***Abortion was considered to come under the heading of "sex hygiene." In the amended Code of Dec. 1956, the subject was brought up specifically as follows: "The subject of abortion shall be discouraged, shall never be more than suggested, and when referred to shall be condemned. It must never be treated lightly, or made the subject of comedy. Abortion shall never be shown explicitly or by inference, and a story must not indicate that an abortion has been performed. The word 'abortion' shall not be used."

369

III. VULGARITY

The treatment of low, disgusting, unpleasant, though not necessarily evil, subjects should be guided always by the dictates of good taste and a proper regard for the sensibilities of the audience.

IV. OBSCENITY

Obscenity in word, gesture, reference, song, joke, or by suggestion (even when likely to be understood only by part of the audience) is forbidden.

V. PROFANITY*

Pointed profanity and every other profane or vulgar expression, however used, are forbidden.

No approval by the Production Code Administration shall be given to the use of words and phrases in motion pictures including, but not limited to, the following:

Alley cat (applied to a woman); bat (applied to a woman); broad (applied to a woman); Bronx cheer (the sound); chippie; cocotte; God, Lord, Jesus, Christ (unless used reverently); cripes; fanny; fairy (in a vulgar sense); finger (the); fire, cries of; Gawd; goose (in a vulgar sense); "hold your hat" or "hats"; hot (applied to a woman); "in your hat"; Madam (relating to prostitution); nance; nerts; nuts (except when meaning crazy); pansy; razzberry (the sound); slut (applied to a woman); S.O.B.; son-of-a; tart; toilet gags; tom cat (applied to a man); traveling salesman and farmer's daughter jokes; whore; damn, hell (excepting when the use of said last two words shall be essential and required for portrayal, in proper historical context, of any scene or dialogue based upon historical fact or folklore, or for the presentation in proper literary context of a Biblical, or other religious quotation, or a quotation from a literary work provided that no such use shall be permitted which is intrinsically objectionable or offends good taste).

In the administration of Section V of the Production Code, the Production Code Administration may take cognizance of the fact that the following words and phrases are obviously offensive to the patrons of motion pictures in the United States and more particularly to the patrons of motion pictures in foreign countries:

Chink, Dago, Frog, Greaser, Hunkie, Kike, Nigger, Spig, Wop, Yid.

*As amended by resolution of the Board of Directors, November 1, 1939, and September 12, 1945.

VI. COSTUME*

1. **Complete nudity** is never permitted. This includes nudity in fact or in silhouette, or any licentious notice thereof by other characters in the pictures.

2. **Undressing scenes** should be avoided, and never used save where essential to the plot.

3. **Indecent or undue exposure** is forbidden.

4. **Dancing costumes** intended to permit undue exposure or indecent movements in the dance are forbidden.

VII. DANCES

1. Dances suggesting or representing sexual actions or indecent passion are forbidden.

2. Dances which emphasize indecent movements are to be regarded as obscene.

VIII. RELIGION

1. No film or episode may throw **ridicule** on any religious faith.

2. **Ministers of religion** in their character as ministers of religion should not be used as comic characters or as villains.

3. **Ceremonies** of any definite religion should be carefully and respectfully handled.

IX. LOCATIONS

The treatment of bedrooms must be governed by good taste and delicacy.

X. NATIONAL FEELINGS

1. **The use of the Flag** shall be consistently respectful.

2. **The history,** institutions, prominent people and citizenry of all nations shall be represented fairly.

XI. TITLES

The following titles shall not be used:

1. Titles which are salacious, indecent, obscene, profane or vulgar.

2. Titles which suggest or are currently associated in the public mind with material, characters or occupations unsuitable for the screen.

3. Titles which are otherwise objectionable.**

---

* See Special Resolution on Costumes.

**As amended by resolution of the Board of Directors, December 3, 1947.

XII. REPELLENT SUBJECTS

The following subjects must be treated within the careful limits of good taste:

1. **Actual hangings** or electrocutions as legal punishments for crime.
2. **Third Degree** methods.
3. **Brutality** and possible gruesomeness.
4. **Branding** of people or animals.
5. **Apparent cruelty** to children or animals.
6. **The sale of women,** or a woman selling her virtue.
7. **Surgical operations.**

SPECIAL REGULATIONS ON CRIME IN MOTION PICTURES*

RESOLVED, that the Board of Directors of the Motion Picture Association of America, Incorporated, hereby ratifies, approves, and confirms the interpretations of the Production Code, the practices thereunder, and the resolutions indicating and confirming such interpretations heretofore adopted by the Association of Motion Picture Producers, Incorporated, all effectuating regulations relative to the treatment of crime in motion pictures, as follows:

1. Details of crime must never be shown and care should be exercised at all times in discussing such details.

2. Action suggestive of wholesale slaughter of human beings, either by criminals, in conflict with police, or as between warring factions of criminals, or in public disorder of any kind, will not be allowed.

3. There must be no suggestion, at any time, of excessive brutality.

4. Because of the increase in the number of films in which murder is frequently committed, action showing the taking of human life, even in the mystery stories, is to be cut to the minimum. These frequent presentations of murder tend to lessen regard for the sacredness of life.

5. Suicide, as a solution of problems occurring in the development of screen drama, is to be discouraged as morally questionable and as bad theatre—unless absolutely necessary for the development of the plot.

*As adopted by the Board of Directors, December 20, 1938.

6. There must be no display, at any time, of machine guns, sub-machine guns or other weapons generally classified as illegal weapons in the hands of gangsters, or other criminals, and there are to be no off-stage sounds of the repercussions of these guns.

7. There must be no new, unique or trick methods shown for concealing guns.

8. The flaunting of weapons by gangsters, or other criminals, will not be allowed.

9. All discussions and dialogue on the part of gangsters regarding guns should be cut to the minimum.

10. There must be no scenes, at any time, showing law-enforcing officers dying at the hands of criminals. This includes private detectives and guards for banks, motor trucks, etc.

11. With special reference to the crime of kidnapping — or illegal abduction—such stories are acceptable under the Code only when the kidnapping or abduction is (a) not the main theme of the story; (b) the person kidnapped is not a child; (c) there are no details of the crime of kidnapping; (d) no profit accrues to the abductors or kidnappers; and (e) where the kidnappers are punished.

It is understood, and agreed, that the word kidnapping, as used in paragraph 11 of these Regulations, is intended to mean abduction, or illegal detention, in modern times, by criminals for ransom.

12. Pictures dealing with criminal activities, in which minors participate, or to which minors are related, shall not be approved if they incite demoralizing imitation on the part of youth.

13. No picture shall be approved dealing with the life of a notorious criminal of current or recent times which uses the name, nickname or alias of such notorious criminal in the film, nor shall a picture be approved if based upon the life of such a notorious criminal unless the character shown in the film be punished for crimes shown in the film as committed by him.*

*As amended by resolution of the Board of Directors, December 3, 1947.

373

SPECIAL RESOLUTION ON COSTUMES

On October 25, 1939, the Board of Directors of the Motion Picture Association of America, Inc., adopted the following resolution:

> RESOLVED, that the provisions of Paragraphs 1, 3 and 4 of sub-division VI of the Production Code, in their application to costumes, nudity, indecent or undue exposure and dancing costumes, shall not be interpreted to exclude authentically photographed scenes photographed in a foreign land, of natives of such foreign land, showing native life, if such scenes are a necessary and integral part of a motion picture depicting exclusively such land and native life, provided that no such scenes shall be intrinsically objectionable nor made a part of any motion picture produced in any studio; and provided further that no emphasis shall be made in any scenes of the customs or garb of such natives or in the exploitation thereof.

SPECIAL REGULATIONS ON CRUELTY TO ANIMALS

On December 27, 1940, the Board of Directors of the Motion Picture Association of America, Inc., approved a resolution adopted by the Association of Motion Picture Producers, Inc., reaffirming previous resolutions of the California Association concerning brutality and possible gruesomeness, branding of people and animals, and apparent cruelty to children and animals:

> RESOLVED, by the Board of Directors of the Association of Motion Picture Producers, Inc., that
>
> (1) Hereafter, in the production of motion pictures there shall be no use by the members of the Association of the contrivance or apparatus in connection with animals which is known as the "running W", nor shall any picture submitted to the Production Code Administration be approved if reasonable grounds exist for believing that use of any similar device by the producer of such picture resulted in apparent cruelty to animals; and
>
> (2) Hereafter, in the production of motion pictures by the members of the Association, such members shall, as to any picture involving the use of animals, invite on the lot during such shooting and consult with the authorized representative of the American Humane Association; and
>
> (3) Steps shall be taken immediately by the members of the Association and by the Production Code Administration to require compliance with these resolutions, which shall

bear the same relationship to the sections of the Production Code quoted herein as the Association's special regulations re: Crime in Motion Pictures bear to the sections of the Production Code dealing therewith; and it is

FURTHER RESOLVED, that the resolutions of February 19, 1925 and all other resolutions of this Board establishing its policy to prevent all cruelty to animals in the production of motion pictures and reflecting its determination to prevent any such cruelty, be and the same hereby are in all respects reaffirmed.

Reasons Supporting Preamble of Code

I. Theatrical motion pictures, that is, pictures intended for the theatre as distinct from pictures intended for churches, schools, lecture halls, educational movements, social reform movements, etc., are primarily to be regarded as **ENTERTAINMENT.**

Mankind has always recognized the importance of entertainment and its value in rebuilding the bodies and souls of human beings.

But it has always recognized that entertainment can be of a character either **HELPFUL** or **HARMFUL** to the human race, and in consequence has clearly distinguished between:

a. Entertainment which tends to improve the race, or at least to re-create and rebuild human beings exhausted with the realities of life; and

b. Entertainment which tends to degrade human beings, or to lower their standards of life and living.

Hence the **MORAL IMPORTANCE** of entertainment is something which has been universally recognized. It enters intimately into the lives of men and women and affects them closely; it occupies their minds and affections during leisure hours; and ultimately touches the whole of their lives. A man may be judged by his standard of entertainment as easily as by the standard of his work.

So correct entertainment raises the whole standard of a nation.

Wrong entertainment lowers the whole living conditions and moral ideals of a race.

Note, for example, the healthy reactions to healthful sports, like baseball, golf; the unhealthy reactions to sports like cockfighting, bullfighting, bear baiting, etc.

Note, too, the effect on ancient nations of gladiatorial combats, the obscene plays of Roman times, etc.

II. Motion pictures are very important as **ART.**

Though a new art, possibly a combination art, it has the same object as the other arts, the presentation of human thought, emotion, and experience, in terms of an appeal to the soul through the senses.

Here, as in entertainment,

Art enters intimately into the lives of human beings.

Art can be **morally good,** lifting men to higher levels. This has been done through good music, great painting, authentic fiction, poetry, drama.

Art can be **morally evil** in its effects. This is the case clearly enough with unclean art, indecent books, suggestive drama. The effect on the lives of men and women is obvious.

Note: It has often been argued that art in itself is unmoral, neither good nor bad. This is perhaps true of the THING which is music, painting, poetry, etc. But the thing is the PRODUCT of some person's mind, and the intention of that mind was either good or bad morally when it produced the thing. Besides, the thing has its EFFECT upon those who come into contact with it. In both these ways, that is, as a product of a mind and as the cause of definite effects, it has a deep moral significance and an unmistakable moral **quality.**

Hence: The motion pictures, which are the most popular of modern arts for the masses, have their moral quality from the intention of the minds which produce them and from their effects on the moral lives and reactions of their audiences. This gives them a most important morality.

1. They **reproduce** the morality of the men who use the pictures as a medium for the expression of their ideas and ideals.

2. They **affect** the moral standards of those who, through the screen, take in these ideas and ideals.

In the case of the motion pictures, this effect may be particularly emphasized because no art has so quick and so widespread an appeal to the masses. It has become in an incredibly short period **the art of the multitudes.**

III. The motion picture, because of its importance as entertainment and because of the trust placed in it by the peoples of the world, has special **MORAL OBLIGATIONS:**

A. Most arts appeal to the mature. This art appeals at once **to every class,** mature, immature, developed, undeveloped, law abiding, criminal. Music has its grades for different classes; so has literature and drama. This art of the motion picture, combining as it does the two fundamental appeals of looking at a **picture** and **listening to a story,** at once reaches every class of society.

B. By reason of the mobility of a film and the ease of picture distribution, and because of the possibility of duplicating positives in large quantities, this art **reaches places** unpenetrated by other forms of art.

C. Because of these two facts, it is difficult to produce films intended for only certain classes of people. The exhibitors' theatres are built for the masses, for the cultivated and the rude, the mature and the immature, the self-respecting and the criminal. Films, unlike books and music, can with difficulty be confined to certain selected groups.

D. The latitude given to film material cannot, in consequence, be as wide as the latitude given to **book material.** In addition:
   a. A book describes; a film vividly presents. One presents on a cold page; the other by apparently living people.
   b. A book reaches the mind through words merely; a film reaches the eyes and ears through the reproduction of actual events.
   c. The reaction of a reader to a book depends largely on the keenness of the reader's imagination; the reaction to a film depends on the vividness of presentation.
   Hence many things which might be described or suggested in a book could not possibly be presented in a film.

E. This is also true when comparing the film with the newspaper.

a. Newspapers present by description, films by actual presentation.

b. Newspapers are after the fact and present things as having taken place; the film gives the events in the process of enactment and with apparent reality of life.

F. Everything possible in a **play** is not possible in a film:

a. Because of the **larger audience of the film**, and its consequential mixed character. Psychologically, the larger the audience, the lower the moral mass resistance to suggestion.

b. Because through light, enlargement of character, presentation, scenic emphasis, etc., the screen story is **brought closer** to the audience than **the play.**

c. The enthusiasm for and interest in the film **actors** and **actresses,** developed beyond anything of the sort in history, makes the audience largely sympathetic toward the characters they portray and the stories in which they figure. Hence the audience is more ready to confuse actor and actress and the characters they portray, and it is most receptive of the emotions and ideals presented by their favorite stars.

G. **Small communities,** remote from sophistication and from the hardening process which often takes place in the ethical and moral standards of groups in larger cities, are easily and readily reached by any sort of film.

H. The grandeur of mass settings, large action, spectacular features, etc., affects and arouses more intensely the emotional side of the audience.

In general, the mobility, popularity, accessibility, emotional appeal, vividness, straightforward presentation of fact in the film make for more intimate contact with a larger audience and for greater emotional appeal.

Hence the larger moral responsibilities of the motion pictures.

Reasons Underlying The General Principles

I. No picture shall be produced which will lower the moral standards of those who see it. Hence the sympathy of the audience should never be thrown to the side of crime, wrong-doing, evil or sin.

This is done:

1. When **evil** is made to appear **attractive** or **alluring,** and good is made to appear **unattractive.**

2. When the **sympathy** of the audience is thrown on the side of crime, wrong-doing, evil, sin. The same thing is true of a film that would throw sympathy against goodness, honor, innocence, purity or honesty.

Note: Sympathy with a person who sins is not the same as sympathy with the sin or crime of which he is guilty. We may feel sorry for the plight of the murderer or even understand the circumstances which led him to his crime. We may not feel sympathy with the wrong which he has done.
The **presentation of evil** is often essential for art or fiction or drama. This in itself is not wrong provided:

a. That evil is **not presented alluringly.** Even if later in the film the evil is condemned or punished, it must not be allowed to appear so attractive that the audience's emotions are drawn to desire or approve so strongly that later the condemnation is forgotten and only the apparent joy of the sin remembered.

b. That throughout, the audience feels sure that **evil is wrong** and **good is right.**

II. Correct standards of life shall, as far as possible, be presented.

A wide knowledge of life and of living is made possible through the film. When right standards are consistently presented, the motion picture exercises the most powerful influences. It builds character, develops right ideals, inculcates correct principles, and all this in attractive story form.

If motion pictures consistently hold up for admiration high types of characters and present stories that will affect lives for the better, they can become the most powerful natural force for the improvement of mankind.

III. Law, natural or human, shall not be ridiculed, nor shall sympathy be created for its violation.

By natural law is understood the law which is written in the hearts of all mankind, the great underlying principles of right and justice dictated by conscience.

By human law is understood the law written by civilized nations.

1. The presentation of crimes against the law is often necessary for the carrying out of the plot. But the presentation must not throw sympathy with the crime as against the law nor with the criminal as against those who punish him.
2. The courts of the land should not be presented as unjust. This does not mean that a single court may not be represented as unjust, much less that a single court official must not be presented this way. But the court system of the country must not suffer as a result of this presentation.

Reasons Underlying Particular Applications

I. Sin and evil enter into the story of human beings and hence in themselves are valid dramatic material.

II. In the use of this material, it must be distinguished between sin which repels by its very nature, and sins whch often attract.

a. In the first class come murder, most theft, many legal crimes, lying, hypocrisy, cruelty, etc.
b. In the second class come sex sins, sins and crimes of apparent heroism, such as banditry, daring thefts, leadership in evil, organized crime, revenge, etc.

The first class needs less care in treatment, as sins and crimes of this class are naturally unattractive. The audience instinctively condemns all such and is repelled.

Hence the important objective must be to avoid the hardening of the audience, especially of those who are young and impressionable, to the thought and fact of crime. People can become accustomed even to murder, cruelty, brutality, and repellent crimes, if these are too frequently repeated.

The second class needs great care in handling, as the response of human nature to their appeal is obvious. This is treated more fully below.

III. A careful distinction can be made between films intended for general distribution, and films intended for use in theatres restricted to a limited audience. Themes and plots quite appropriate for the latter would be altogether out of place and dangerous in the former.

Note: The practice of using a general theatre and limiting it patronage during the showing of a certain film to "Adults Only" is not completely satisfactory and is only partially effective.

However, maturer minds may easily understand and accept without harm subject matter in plots which do younger people positive harm.

Hence: If there should be created a special type of theatre, catering exclusively to an adult audience, for plays of this character (plays with problem themes, difficult discussions and maturer treatment) it would seem to afford an outlet, which does not now exist, for pictures unsuitable for general distribution but permissible for exhibitions to a restricted audience.

I. CRIMES AGAINST THE LAW

The treatment of crimes against the law must not:

1. Teach methods of crime.
2. Inspire potential criminals with a desire for imitation.
3. Make criminals seem heroic and justified.

Revenge in modern times shall not be justified. In lands and ages of less developed civilization and moral principles, revenge may sometimes be presented. This would be the case especially in places where no law exists to cover the crime because of which revenge is committed.

NOTE: When Section I, 3 of The Production Code was amended by resolution of the Board of Directors (September 11, 1946), the following sentence became inapplicable:

Because of its evil consequences, the drug traffic should not be presented in any form. The existence of the trade should not be brought to the attention of audiences.

The use of liquor should never be excessively presented. In scenes from American life, the necessities of plot and proper characterization alone justify its use. And in this case, it should be shown with moderation.

•II. SEX

Out of regard for the sanctity of marriage and the home, the triangle, that is, the love of a third party for one already married, needs careful handling. The treatment should not throw sympathy against marriage as an institution.

Scenes of passion must be treated with an honest acknowledgment of human nature and its normal reactions. Many scenes cannot be presented without arousing dangerous emotions on the part of the immature, the young or the criminal classes.

Even within the limits of pure love, certain facts have been universally regarded by lawmakers as outside the limits of safe presentation.

In the case of impure love, the love which society has always regarded as wrong and which has been banned by divine law, the following are important:

1. Impure love must not be presented as attractive and beautiful.
2. It must not be the subject of comedy or farce, or treated as material for laughter.
3. It must not be presented in such a way as to arouse passion or morbid curiosity on the part of the audience.
4. It must not be made to seem right and permissible.
5. In general, it must not be detailed in method and manner.

379

III. Vulgarity; IV. Obscenity; V. Profanity; hardly need further explanation than is contained in the Code.

VI. COSTUME

General principles:

1. **The effect of nudity or semi-nudity** upon the normal man or woman, and much more upon the young and upon immature persons, has been honestly recognized by all lawmakers and moralists.

2. Hence the fact that the nude or semi-nude body may be beautiful does not make its use in the films moral. For, in addition to its beauty, the effect of the nude or semi-nude body on the normal individual must be taken into consideration.

3. Nudity or semi-nudity used simply to put a **"punch"** into a picture comes under the head of immoral actions. It is immoral in its effect on the average audience.

4. Nudity can never be permitted as being **necessary for the plot.** Semi-nudity must not result in undue or indecent exposures.

5. **Transparent** or **translucent materials** and silhouette are frequently more suggestive than actual exposure.

VII. DANCES

Dancing in general is recognized as an **art** and as a **beautiful** form of expressing human emotions.

But dances which suggest or represent sexual actions, whether performed solo or with two or more; dances intended to excite the emotional reaction of an audience; dances with movement of the breasts, excessive body movements while the feet are stationary, violate decency and are wrong.

VIII. RELIGION

The reason why ministers of religion may not be comic characters or villains is simply because the attitude taken toward them may easily become the attitude taken toward religion in general. Religion is lowered in the minds of the audience because of the lowering of the audience's respect for a minister.

IX. LOCATIONS

Certain places are so closely and thoroughly associated with sexual life or with sexual sin that their use must be carefully limited.

X. NATIONAL FEELINGS

The just rights, history, and feelings of any nation are entitled to most careful consideration and respectful treatment.

XI. TITLES

As the title of a picture is the brand on that particular type of goods, it must conform to the ethical practices of all such honest business.

XII. REPELLENT SUBJECTS

Such subjects are occasionally necessary for the plot. Their treatment must never offend good taste nor injure the sensibilities of an audience.

Resolution for Uniform Interpretation

as amended
June 13, 1934.

1. When requested by production managers, the Motion Picture Association of America, Incorporated, shall secure any facts, information or suggestions concerning the probable reception of stories or the manner in which in its opinion they may best be treated.

2. That each production manager shall submit in confidence a copy of each or any script to the Production Code Administration of the Motion Picture Association of America, Incorporated (and of the Association of Motion Picture Producers, Inc., California). The Production Code Administration will give the production manager for his guidance such confidential advice and suggestions as experience, research, and information indicate, designating wherein in its judgment the script departs from the provisions of the Code, or wherein from experience or knowledge it is believed that exception will be taken to the story or treatment.

3. Each production manager of a company belonging to the Motion Picture Association of America, Incorporated, and any producer proposing to distribute and/or distributing his picture through the facilities of any member of the Motion Picture Association of America, Incorporated, shall submit to such Production Code Administration every picture he produces before the negative goes to the laboratory for printing. Said Production Code Administration, having seen the picture, shall inform the production manager in writing whether in its opinion the picture conforms or does not conform to the Code, stating specifically wherein either by theme, treatment or incident, the picture violates the provisions of the Code. In such latter event, the picture shall not be released until the changes indicated by the Production Code Administration have been made; provided, however, that the production manager may appeal from such opinion of said Production Code Administraton, so indicated in writing, to the Board of Directors of the Motion Picture Association of America, Incorporated, whose finding shall be final, and such production manager and company shall be governed accordingly.